OFF SCREEN

OFF SCREEN: A MEMOIR

SHEAMUS SMITH

Gill & Macmillan

Published by Gill & Macmillan Ltd
Hume Avenue, Park West, Dublin 12
with associated companies throughout the world
www.gillmacmillan.ie

© Sheamus Smith 2007
978 07171 4061 9
Index compiled by Cover to Cover
Typography design by Make Communication
Print origination by Carrigboy Typesetting Services
Printed by MPG Books Ltd, Bodmin, Cornwall

This book is typeset in Minion 12pt/15pt

The paper used in this book comes from the wood pulp
of managed forests. For every tree felled, at least one tree
is planted, thereby renewing natural resources.

The author and publishers have made every effort to trace all
copyright holders, but if any has been inadvertently overlooked,
we will be pleased to make the necessary arrangement
at the first opportunity.

A CIP catalogue record for this book
is available from the British Library.

5 4 3 2 1

CONTENTS

This book is dedicated to all those who contributed to an exciting and enjoyable life. Many feature in the text. Others, by accident or design, do not.

It is especially for my daughter, Teri, and grandchildren, Jessie and Richy—a record.

PREFACE

When Michael Gill invited me to lunch in Dobbins, my favourite Dublin restaurant, he initially suggested that I might write a book that would deal with the seventeen years of my career as Film Censor. Although it happened by accident, this was the longest job I ever held. It was one in which there was an opportunity to make the radical changes that started the Office on the road that would take it from its traditional role, as a restrictive force, to its proper place as responsible purveyor of consumer advice and guidance on film and video material. For me, however, it was not the most interesting or fulfilling facet in a long career. After a brief discussion, Michael agreed and encouraged me to write about other aspects of my life. Although on the cusp of retiring as Managing Director of his publishing house, he offered to perform the first edit of the material. His guidance and encouragement were a fundamental part of the exercise.

Now in the autumn of my days, it is a good time to reflect on what many would consider a charmed life. In fact, I have lived a number of lives as my career rotated on its constant axis of camera, cinema and television screen. It has been my good fortune to experience aspects of living denied to many of my contemporaries. Over the years I have been lucky enough to meet royalty in varying degrees, including one king, to meet presidents, prime ministers, politicians, movie stars, film directors, distinguished actors and actresses, celebrated writers, international sporting personalities and many ordinary people of different nationality and race with a variety of religions and some with none. I always found other people more interesting than me and at a young age became a good listener and observer. As an adult, I have had eight homes while living in three countries. I had one wife, one long-term partner and a number of liaisons, some more memorable than others. I have endeavoured to present some of these experiences in an interesting and forthright manner.

It is difficult to believe that I have lived seventy-one years, but on the evidence in this book, it is a fact. It seems like a short time ago that I used to be the youngest in any group. Now I am frequently the oldest!

At the age of seventy-three, film director John Huston, whom I knew, wrote in his autobiography:

> I envy a man who leads one life, with one job, and one wife, in one country, under one God. It may not be a very exciting existence but at least by the time he's seventy-three he knows how old he is.

I now know exactly what he meant!

In his eighties, the painter Seán Keating told me that one of the advantages of old age was that it allowed people total honesty. For much of my life, I have been a public servant in one form or another. The obligatory circumspection was often frustrating. Now, all can be revealed!

ACKNOWLEDGMENTS

Reflecting on my life and recalling those who have helped me along the way, it is remarkable how frequently the same characters appear and reappear in different roles—like stars in different movies. There are many, some sadly departed, who deserve special thanks, but it would be invidious to name them. My heartfelt thanks to all who have assisted me with this book or who feature in it.

I should also like to extend my gratitude to each of the following: Cathal O'Shannon, Paul Gleeson, Pat Hughes, Kathleen Hunt, Grainne Barron, Godfrey Graham, Pat Heneghan, Muiris MacConghail, Niall Munroe, Owen Dawson, Barbara Statham, Sarah Bannan, Colm O'Byrne, Louise Clarke, Michael McNulty, Tara Murphy, Joe Gavin, Brendan McCaul, Michael Collins, Jo Wheatley, Kevin Moriarty, Noel Barron, Paddy Kelly, Barbara Murphy, Sharon McGarry, Terry Molloy, Niamh McCaul, Yseult Thornley, Kevin O'Connor, Suzanne Macdougald, Micheal and Pat Johnston, John Kelleher, Hugh Leonard, Bill Harpur, Seamus Corcoran, Bill O'Herlihy, Anne Shannon, Enda Marren, Vivian Kenny, Linda Moor, Niamh White, Pauline Bracken, Joanne Smith, Lena King, Steve Brennan, Muriel Moxon, Catherine Hughes, Mike Burns, Sean Corcoran, Kathleen Arton, Charles Byrne, Maura Quinn, Greg Smith, Seamus Deasy, Diana Shapiro, Rita Culkeen, Pierre Joannon, Stuart Hetherington, Rosaleen Rogers, Joe Malone, Dana Wynter, Jim King, Sheila Pratschke, Addie Ryan, Arthur McGuinness, Liam Healy, John Donovan, James Barry, Tony Murphy, Sue Mitchel, Colman Doyle, Mary Gallagher, Tom Lawlor, Deirdre O'Neill, Michael and Pat York, Liam Neeson, Olivia Tracey, Maeve Binchy, John Boorman, Mary Crotty, Carrie Crowley, Christine Allanson-Bailey, Fiona Mullally, Ger Connolly, Brendan Neilan, Valerie Milton, Conor Brady and Sheila Hampson, who has lived with me for nearly forty years.

Most of my close friends throughout my life were women. Many had a profound influence on me. Some have been among the group of production assistants with whom I worked in RTÉ. From Pauline Kelly, who guided me through my initial studio programme, to Joan Caffrey, my first regular PA, to Janet Couchman, who was the last. The names of Anne Logue, Maura Lee, Marita Lawlor, Ina Hosey, Colette Kavanagh, Nuala Malone, Esther Byrne, Aine O'Connor, Jane Robinson, Felicity Connolly, Carmel Duignan, Drusilla Wynne, Anna Boylan and Irene Carroll evoke countless memories. There were also special secretaries, such as Marie Travers in RTÉ, Gemma Fallon and Hilary Staves in National Film Studios of Ireland and Rita Culkeen and Thérèse Hogan in the Film Censor's Office.

There are many press photographers who, presumably realising that I come from their own gene pool, have been inordinately generous over the years in maintaining my presence in the public eye.

In Gill & Macmillan I would like to thank: Michael Gill, whose editing skilfully reduced my original copy by more than 50 per cent; Managing Editor, Emma Farrell; Copy Editor, Rachel Pierce; Anita Ruane, who supervised the cover design; and Liz Raleigh and Lisa Buckley, who are responsible for publicity. Working with all has been a great experience.

Sheamus Smith
October 2007

Chapter 1

SNAPSHOTS FROM MEMORY

It was May 1936 when my mother gave birth to her second child in Ballaghaderreen, a son this time, whom they called Seamus. This story starts nine months earlier, however, in Dún Laoghaire, County Dublin. That is an area that has always been special to me because as a child I spent holidays in nearby Glenageary with my favourite auntie, my mother's sister, May, or sometimes in Dalkey with her other sister, Kay. Auntie May and Auntie Kay were married, but as they didn't have any children of their own, I provided a welcome distraction during the summer months. But I think my instinctive liking of this place goes back much further. In August 1935, my parents and their only child, my sister Muriel, spent a holiday at the Hotel Sandycove in Dún Laoghaire, which was owned and run by a Mrs Chilton. The total account for twelve days' full board for the family was the equivalent of €13. I know this anecdotal fact because when I was going through my mother's papers after she died, I found the receipt, neatly inscribed by Mrs Chilton. I believe my mother kept that seemingly unimportant piece of paper for all those years because she knew that it was during that holiday that I was conceived.

* * *

My birthplace, Ballaghaderreen in Co. Roscommon, or 'Ballagh' as it was affectionately known by the natives, was a sleepy backwater in 1936, like so many towns in the west of Ireland at that time. In the 1800s it had been addressed as Ballaghaderreen, Co. Mayo, but at the end of the nineteenth century had been relocated to Co. Roscommon, where it has resided ever since. Liam Healy, former Chief Executive and now Deputy Chairman of Independent News & Media PLC, who was educated in the town at St Nathy's College, told me that this reordering was due to the fact that taxes were lower in Roscommon. Liam's uncle was the Bishop of Achonry, so he seems a responsible source. Even 100 years on, many of those who come from or live in Ballaghaderreen give their allegiance to Co. Mayo, particularly in their support of the Mayo Gaelic football team. The people of Ballagh have long memories!

In my youth it was a 'market town', the market being held in the town square every Friday. There was also a monthly fair day when cattle were bought and sold. On those days, the cattle took over the town, milling about everywhere—on the footpaths, in the roadway and down all the back lanes, or 'backways' as they were called. Although there was an overabundance of pubs in Ballagh, drunkenness was never apparent—except on fair days. A young boy could earn a shilling by minding the cattle while their owner went for a drink or a meal before or after a sale. There was much spitting on hands before the handshake to seal each deal. Frequently, after completing a successful sale and imbibing a generous amount of drink the farmer would fall asleep in his donkey-cart. The donkey would then, without any supervision, take him home safely.

Then there were the tinkers, who lived in great hardship in primitive, makeshift tents on the sides of the roads; few had caravans. On fair days they came into town in great numbers. Back then, the tinkers made a living as tinsmiths, making and selling tin cans that were used to carry milk, mugs and various other utensils. Others came to sing ballads, the words of which were printed on pamphlets that they sold for one penny. The prominent tinker families were the McDonaghs and the Wards. Nan Ward, a fine-looking woman who lived in a caravan with her husband and large family, was a favourite of my mother, who always gave her the clothes we had outgrown for her own children.

The town had the usual array of business premises, with virtually all the owners living over the shop or in the attached house. The number of public houses was disproportionate to the population: seventy-six bars served the town, which had a total population of less than 1,000 souls. All were described as 'Select Bars'. It should be said that not all of these licensed premises were active—some might only sell bottles of stout and had no spirits or draught beer, others might only open on the monthly fair day.

Tinkers were not welcome in every bar in the town. They mostly gathered at Towey's, which was across the street from our house. Inevitably, at the end of the day a fight would break out. The word would go out that 'The tinkers are fighting', and we youngsters would rush to the scene. Mostly the fighting was just posturing or shouting—only occasionally was a serious blow struck. The protagonists, with fists closed and arms flailing, were usually held back from each other by their supporters. They would roar at the top of their voices, 'Let me at him', while murmuring under their breath to those restraining them, 'Hold me back'.

❉ ❉ ❉

The cathedral town for the Diocese of Achonry, Ballagh was dominated by St Nathy's Cathedral and the nearby St Nathy's College, a second-level day and boarding school for boys. Girls and boys were initially educated by the Sisters of Charity at the convent school. After their primary education the boys went on to the Brothers' School where three de la Salle Brothers taught, while the girls remained at the convent school to take the Leaving Certificate examination.

The Catholic bishop lived in a splendid palace some miles north of the town. Bishop Morrisroe, whose funeral we schoolchildren lined the streets to watch, and his successor, Dr Fergus, were kindly, saintly men. Unlike the present incumbent, who warned every Catholic of the woeful consequences of voting 'Yes' in the Divorce Referendum in 1995, neither man had a high profile outside his own diocese nor showed an interest in becoming involved in national politics. The community was staunchly, and indeed enthusiastically, Catholic. In the late 1930s young men indicated a willingness to fight for General Franco in the Spanish Civil War, but I am not aware of any who actually did so. On reflection, I suspect this profession of valour may have been a ploy used by some to persuade their girlfriends to surrender their virginity before the hero sailed away to almost certain death and glory in the service of the Fascist dictator.

The annual mission, or retreat, during the Lenten season was conducted by visiting missionaries of various religious orders. They were different from the ordinary priests: they wore long habits, like monks, and were usually three in number. This was the once-a-year opportunity to cleanse one's immortal soul. Everyone in the town and the surrounding areas attended, with the exception of my friend, Mr Johnston. Devotions, as the evening service was known, was held in the cathedral every evening for a week. Temporary canvas-covered stands, lit with hanging Tilley lamps, were set up on the street outside the church grounds and they sold statues, rosaries, scapulars and all kinds of religious objects. They were so positioned as it was considered inappropriate to allow trading within the actual precincts of the cathedral.

Each night at Devotions a different missionary would deliver the sermon. The climax of the week was the last night—the grand finale. On that night, the leader of the group delivered a real 'fire and brimstone' sermon, usually on the dangers of promiscuity and illicit sex. This was the kind of material that the film censor would never allow, so naturally the place was packed. It was an 'adults only' show, but altar-boys were required to be in attendance for other parts of the ceremony, such as the final Benediction, which meant they were allowed to witness the spectacle. Despite my scepticism towards religion, like most others of my age I was an altar-boy. There was no great joy to be derived from serving the early morning Mass, but there were some compensations. Wedding ceremonies and baptisms, in particular, and sometimes funeral ceremonies, too, provided generous gratuities for the acolytes. However, the real benefit was to be present on the altar for the final night of the annual mission.

I achieved that coveted position only once, but I was not disappointed. That year the Redemptorist order was conducting the mission. The missioners wore long, black habits, like the Passionist Fathers, but unlike the Franciscans or Dominicans, who dressed in brown. The leading priest in this instance was an outstanding orator. He terrified his congregation with the promise of eternal damnation, which could be visited upon a poor soul even for *entertaining* impure thoughts. Sitting on the altar, the altar-boys could see the frightened faces of the gathered penitents. My own personal theory was that the information garnered in the confessional over the course of the week contributed to the script for the final performance. We passed the time trying to match an individual in the sea of faces to a particular sin of the most grievous sexual nature! The peculiar thing was that many of those who attended the mission would afterwards visit my parents' bar, or one of the other pubs in town, before going home. Alcohol appeared to be a satisfactory antidote for sex!

* * *

We were told there was the ruin of a Protestant church near the Catholic cathedral, but no member of that faith lived in the town. There was Mr Johnston, however. Mr Johnston was an extremely well-dressed, tall, slim gentleman who owned a bar in the main street. In common with all the business premises in town, the sign over the bar carried the owner's name. He wore a bow-tie and occasionally sported a straw boater hat. He spoke with a loud voice and as a 'returned Yank' had the appropriate accent. He never seemed to leave his home, and appeared to do any business in his bar only on the monthly fair day.

We children were told that Mr Johnston was a Protestant and that this was the reason he had no friends in the town. He was nothing of the sort! I discovered that he had lived in America and either while there or at home had chosen to leave the Catholic Church. He was separated from his wife; he may even have been divorced. They had three very beautiful daughters. His wife, or ex-wife, lived abroad and came to stay for a few days every year, bringing expensive presents for her daughters. Thanks to the rumour mill, Mr Johnston was an object of terror to most young children, but I liked him. He often called me in from the street and asked me to do an errand for him, such as fetching groceries from a nearby shop. The threepenny bit he offered in return was a handsome reward for the effort.

* * *

The Roxy Cinema, later renamed The Ariel, was located in St Mary's Hall. Like the hall, the picture-house was owned by the Church and supervised by the parish priest. There had been a cinema in the town since the late 1920s. My Auntie Kay, who was an accomplished pianist, sometimes accompanied the silent films when she was a young girl. My mother often spoke fondly of seeing one of the first 'talking pictures' in a makeshift outdoor cinema near the railway station in the early 1930s. It was *The Singing Fool*, and in it Al Jolson sang 'Sonny Boy'.

As a child, my first cinema experiences were remarkably similar to those of the young boy in the wonderful Italian film, *Cinema Paradiso*. I too collected the bits of film discarded by the projectionist in the local cinema and kept them in an old biscuit tin. One Christmas I received a present of a small, toy film-projector. It ran loops of film that I projected onto the bedroom wall, or any other white surface around the house. Later, I acquired a more sophisticated projector that could use real 35 mm cinema film.

As well as going to the town 'cinema', I also had the opportunity to attend the larger cinemas in Dublin. The once-daily steam train, which carried passengers and goods, met the Sligo–Dublin train at Kilfree Junction, some 10 miles north-east of Ballaghaderreen. There was an intermediate station at Edmondstown, close to the Bishop's Palace. I can remember the excitement of travelling on the train to Dublin with my mother, enthralled by the black smoke belching from the engine. Twice, sometimes three times a year we went to the city to visit my Auntie Kay, who then had a chemist shop in Harold's Cross. For me, the highlight of these trips was our visits to the Dublin cinemas. Frequently we would go to see a film in the Savoy and immediately afterwards cross O'Connell Street to attend another in the Carlton. Another great adventure when in Dublin was to visit Glencairn, an extraordinary house owned by Michael O'Neill, who founded the well-known Dublin pub, O'Neill's of Suffolk Street and later married Auntie Kay. It was previously the home of Richard 'Boss' Croker, a leading Tammany Hall politician. Boss Croker's greatest ambition was achieved when his horse, *Orby*, won the English Derby in 1907 (at odds of 100–6). The horse was laid to rest under a tall headstone in the garden. This was intriguing to me. The house was sold to the British government in 1953 and is now the home of the British Ambassador.

In those pre-television days most people went to 'the pictures' at least once a week. There were four changes of programme each week, with a children's matinée on Saturday afternoon. My first memory of a 'grown-ups' movie was *How Green Was My Valley*. It was made in 1941, directed by John Ford and starred Walter Pidgeon, Maureen O'Hara, Roddy McDowell, Sara Allgood and Barry Fitzgerald. It was so good, I went to see it twice. I was not aware then that it had received eight Academy Award nominations and wound up winning four Oscars. The films I saw in that cramped little hall were to influence and shape my life more than I could possibly have foreseen.

When I think of that hall and its magical cinema moments I am reminded that Ballaghaderreen had a town-crier named Murty Foley. A man of small stature, whatever the weather he wore an oversized raincoat tied with string around the waist and a soft hat. Attached to his back would be a poster announcing a forthcoming event, such as the cinema programme for the coming week or a play, an auction or concert. He marched up and down the centre of the streets, ringing a handbell vigorously. He would choose appropriate places to stop and announce the event through a simple home-made megaphone. In a place like Ballagh, where everyone knew everyone else's business and all about upcoming events, the town-crier's function was to remind rather than to inform.

※　　※　　※

The two major business outlets in Ballagh were John Flannery & Sons, which was owned by the Doyle family, and Monica Duff & Co. Ltd, which was owned by James Dillon, the TD representing Monaghan. They were always simply referred to as 'Flannery's and 'Duff's'. During his long lifetime, James Dillon was the most important resident of Ballaghaderreen. His family home is now named Dillon House and is the headquarters of the Western Development Commission and the town's public library.

The Dillon family business was founded in 1812 by James Dillon's great-uncle, Luke Dillon. It was later passed on to his aunt, Monica Duff. Under her name, she made the shop started by her father the dominant commercial enterprise in the area. Indeed, our family owed a lot to Duff's as it was my father's employer for a number of years.

Flannery's and Duff's were large wholesale and retail outlets that supplied most of the smaller businesses in the surrounding towns and villages. Each had a hardware, grocery, haberdashery, millinery, ladies' and gents' clothing and footwear departments, along with a bottling plant for Guinness and the inevitable 'select' bar, complete with private 'snugs' for ladies or those who wished to imbibe in private. Duff's also had a mineral water factory, a builders' providers' yard and a very fine bakery, which supplied bread to the town and surrounding district. I have never in my life come across any to equal the quality of Duff's barm brack, truly one of the great memories of my youth. It was said that the head baker took the recipe to his grave!

The Doyle family and James Dillon, then a bachelor, did not live on the business premises but in substantial detached houses. The Doyle family home stood in large grounds just outside the town, while James Dillon's house, a family home for generations, had an imposing position on the town square. It was the first building one saw on entering Ballaghaderreen from the Dublin direction. Both families had extensive farms.

In 1937 James Dillon was elected Fine Gael TD for Monaghan, a constituency far removed from Ballagh. He later became leader of Fine Gael. He was a tall, broad-shouldered man and he wore heavy black-rimmed spectacles and a distinctive homburg hat. He used a long black cigarette-holder and smoked a brand of cigarettes called Passing Cloud. These were oval-shaped, rather than round, with a pink-coloured cigarette paper. He dressed impeccably, sometimes wearing his light-coloured tweed overcoat on his shoulders in cape-like fashion.

In terms of political allegiances, Ballaghaderreen was divided equally. Those who supported Fianna Fáil did their shopping in Flannery's, while Duff's had a reliable clientele comprising the supporters of Fine Gael and other parties. (Our family were all Fine Gaelers.) Both the Doyles and the Dillons prospered. While James Dillon would never have approved of Civil War politics, and I am sure the Doyle family would have felt likewise, both businesses benefited in their own way from the political division resulting from it.

Another major enterprise in the town was Cunniff's Bacon Factory, which was located behind the Cunniffs' family home, butcher-shop and, of course, select bar. On killing days when pigs were slaughtered, particularly in summer, the malodorous pong from the bacon factory permeated the town. There was also a local co-operative creamery. The farmers would line up their donkeys and carts outside to deliver the full milk churns. These were returned to them with skimmed milk, which was brought back to be fed to the pigs on the farms.

* * *

I well remember my first day at school. My mother waved goodbye at the door as my sister Muriel took me by the hand and led me up the street. I was wearing a teddy-bear overcoat (a present from an aunt in America), which Muriel had outgrown. I enjoyed school from the beginning, and invariably fell in love with one of the female teachers. I would fervently wish that I would grow up fast while the object of my affection remained the same age, so that we could marry. The names are long forgotten, but I recently came across a photograph of a most attractive 'Miss Roe', for that was how we knew her.

It was in preparatory school that the seeds of my atheism were sown. I simply could not comprehend that there was a place called 'Limbo' where the souls of children who died before baptism languished for a time. They could never go to Heaven nor 'see the face of God'. After the last day, when the world was ended, only Heaven and Hell would remain; Limbo would no longer exist. It seemed grossly unfair to commit these innocent souls to Hell for all eternity! I also pondered on the belief that if baptism removed the stain of all sins from our souls, why baptise babies? To me it seemed more logical to wait until people were dying, thereby ensuring salvation and eternal happiness. I also had difficulty in understanding why a god who knew all things and who could see into the future created babies who would turn out badly and eventually be condemned to the fire of Hell forever. It was not reasonable, in my childish opinion. When my family later went to live in Dublin, I finally met some Protestants and quickly realised that had I been born into a Protestant family, my faith might have been more secure. They seemed to have a more practical attitude towards God!

* * *

My best friends were Michael Murphy, whose father was a Garda, and Paddy Regan, eldest son of the butcher whose shop was close to ours. Together we played Cowboys and Indians, raided orchards, went to the pictures, competed in school sports and played football along with our other friends. Because it was wartime there were few cars, so we frequently played our football in the street. During the Second World War double summertime applied, which meant the clock was advanced two hours beyond GMT during the summer period. I remember often being called home from the street by our mothers shortly before 11.00 at night, which was long before daylight had faded.

Orchards worth raiding were divided on a territorial basis. The orchard in the Sisters of Charity convent near the top of the town was the preserve of the boys who lived there. The mastermind behind the raids on that target was another friend of mine, Vivian Kenny. Brilliant manager of human resources that he was, Vivian supervised the operation while keeping watch as he lay on the top of the high wall surrounding the orchard. Little wonder that he turned out to be an outstandingly successful businessman in later life.

Vivian tells an amusing story of going to confession as a child. When invited by the local curate, Fr McVann, to confess his sins, Vivian stated that he was guilty of 'bad actions'. The priest asked if he were alone or with others at the time. 'With others,' Vivian replied. 'Were they boys or girls?' asked the priest. 'Boys,' said Vivian. 'And were you standing up or lying down?' was the priest's next question. 'Lying down,' confessed Vivian, puzzled as to why the priest was so interested in his exact body position on the top of the high wall as he kept watch while his friends raided the nuns' orchard! Vivian's firm resolve never again to offend God and to amend his life resulted in a light penance of one 'Our Father' and six 'Hail Marys'!

The most attractive garden to raid for those of us living in the centre of the town was that of the manager of the Hibernian Bank. As well as the usual apples and pears, there were also exotic fruits to be had, such as strawberries, raspberries and plums. The garden in question was just three doors away from our house and next to that of my friend, Paddy Regan. It presented quite a challenge: it was protected by a stone wall about 15 feet high and its thick, solid wooden gates were impregnable.

As luck would have it, however, every year the Regans built a rick of turf against their side of the garden wall, and it reached almost to the top. Scaling sods of turf was no challenge for our young bodies. But climbing the inside wall of the orchard to get back out again was another matter. We were assisted, to some extent, by the wire trusses and their anchors in the wall, which supported growing trees and plants. The difficulty posed to a safe exit meant the coveted haul had to be limited to what was consumed in the garden or carried in bulging trouser pockets. We all knew that in the event of discovery, no escape was possible. Our small, but determined raiding party often included one of the Hanrahans, whose father was the Garda sergeant in the town. There was a double risk for that chap!

Another exciting activity of our childhood was helping to save the turf on the bogland near the town in summer. During the War, turf was the principal fuel used in the home. Every family had its own stretch of bog, from which the heavy, water-soaked sods of turf were cut. These were then dried in the sun before being taken home by donkey and cart and stored for the following winter.

We also helped my uncles to save the hay, a laborious activity that always seemed to take place on long sunny days. Our 'helping' with cutting the turf or saving the hay involved bringing large tin cans of sweet tea and sandwiches to the bog or the meadow at lunchtime. The cans had tight-fitting lids and the milk and sugar had already been added to the tea. I can still remember the taste of that light brown, hot, sweet liquid.

As youngsters we attended every wake in the town. Wakes were held in the home of the deceased person. The corpse, whether male or female, was dressed in a dark brown habit, similar to those worn by monks. It was laid out on the bed in the best bedroom in the house, with candles lit on a bedside table. Members of the family would keep vigil in the room while friends and neighbours arrived to sympathise, pay their last respects and kneel by the bed to say a prayer for the immortal soul of the deceased. Downstairs, tea would be offered to the women, sometimes with a glass of port wine from the better-off families. Whiskey and porter were always available for the men, as were white clay pipes already filled with tobacco. For each child there would be twopence, or sometimes threepence, to buy sweets. This incentive was sufficient to encourage most of us to become inveterate wake-goers. We even attended the wakes of people we had never laid eyes on because they had been housebound by infirmity. We would kneel piously by the bed, but rarely say the prayer, being much too intrigued by the strange yellowish pallor on the face and hands of the lifeless body.

Another of our favourite pastimes was watching the blacksmith at work in his forge. There were two forges in the town and the black-smiths were always busy. They shoed horses (there were few tractors then) and made or repaired farm implements and iron gates of all sizes. The heat of the forge fire was comforting, and the rhythm of the hammer on the anvil made a weird kind of music. Watching the blacksmith shoe a horse was fascinating. Clad in a heavy, black leather apron, his bare muscular arms glistening with sweat and with his back to the animal, the blacksmith gently lifted the horse's large hoof and held it between his thighs. Then, using both hands, he removed the old worn shoe. Next, the hoof was trimmed with a short, sharp knife. Bringing the seemingly dormant fire to life with a giant bellows, the blacksmith heated the iron shoe until it glowed red. When it had cooled slightly it was placed onto the horse's hoof, burning itself in and ensuring a perfect fit. Finally, the special horse-shoe nails—which might well have been bought in my father's shop—were hammered home and trimmed where they came through the side of the hoof. In my olfactory memory is embedded the distinct smell of the burning hoof when touched by the hot iron shoe, and the sizzling, acrid odour from the forge's water trough when the red hot metal was plunged into it.

Naturally boys and girls played together at these various pastimes, but as I got older I began to realise that not all young females were created equal. There were many beautiful girls in Ballaghaderreen, with the Shannon girls and the Keanes leading the field. Dr Shannon had one son, who was a few years older than me, and seven daughters, while the Keanes, whose father was a bank official, boasted six daughters in their family. Each girl was as lovely as the next and I had been in love with more than one girl in both families, even those who were much older, at some time in my young life. Paddy Shannon was my first love. She was ten years older than me—a considerable age gap considering that I was only eight years of age. I fell in love with her when she played Prince Charming in the Christmas pantomime, 'Cinderella', in St Mary's Hall. I attended every performance that was staged and can still hear her lovely rendition of the songs 'Beautiful Dreamer' and 'Let the Rest of the World go by'. Given half a chance, I would have run away and spent the rest of my life with her! Nonetheless, my true love in those childhood days, my very first sweetheart, was Mary Keane, the third daughter of that family. As a nine-year-old I took her photograph, but I was too shy to tell her of my feelings.

* * *

For the first few years of my life our family lived in a two-storey house opposite the railway station. My father, who was a skilled craftsman, had helped to build it and had done all of the interior carpentry work. It was in that house that I was born in the early hours of Wednesday 13 May 1936. Our family doctor was the father of all the Shannon beauties, Dr Shannon, and he was a gentle, elegant and cultured gentleman. Upon examining the newborn infant, he informed my mother that as my head had two crowns, I would grow up to be a wealthy man. It did not take a lifetime to determine that, good doctor as he was, Dr Shannon was an unreliable prophet!

My father, Joseph Christopher (Joe) Smith, was a native of Kells, Co. Meath. He came to Ballaghaderreen as a young man. He served a three-year apprenticeship in Duff's shop and eventually became manager of the hardware department. My mother, Margaret 'Dotie' Deery, came from a family of six girls and four boys. She was born in December 1901 and was two years younger than my father. She was proud of her education at Loreto College in St Stephen's Green, Dublin. My parents were married in Rathmines Catholic Church in Dublin on 21 April 1930.

I got on well with my sister, Muriel, who was born in November 1931. She looked after me. As a child I thought she was so much older. Muriel was an accomplished pianist, as was her close friend, Kathleen O'Donnell, daughter of the hackney driver 'Rambler' O'Donnell. We also owned a gramophone. It was the old-fashioned type with a wind-up handle. The individual little needle was changed frequently. There were a few semi-classical records, such as John McCormack singing operatic arias, but most were music for Irish dancing, usually referred to by my father as 'rigs and jeels'. My sister and Kathleen O'Donnell were excellent dancers, but my own attempts, despite the efforts of a fine dancing master who charged sixpence a lesson, fell short of any satisfactory standard.

Ours was a reasonably well-off household. My parents bought quality books from a British-based mail order outlet. As a result, there was always a good supply of reading material, which I very much enjoyed as a child. In fact, my reading was so voracious that my grandmother became concerned, as she felt I should be outside playing, not 'stuck with my head in a book by the fire'. My sister Muriel and I also received private piano lessons from a quiet and gentle man named Willie Feely. Muriel became quite a proficient pianist. I hated learning scales and wanted to play tunes instantly! Practice was a bore. I used to watch from behind a curtain and when I saw the piano teacher approaching the house, I would run away and hide.

The family business was relatively successful. During the summer holidays we went to nearby Strandhill or Rosses' Point in Co. Sligo, or to Enniscrone in Co. Mayo. The journey was made by hackney car, a number of which were available for hire in the town. My favourite driver was a lovely man called 'Rambler' O'Donnell, who had presumably acquired his colourful nickname from extensive travel abroad. Another of our regular drivers was Bill Butler. He would let me sit on his lap and help with the steering, which was always a treat. He would spend the day on the strand with us before returning home.

My father was an enthusiastic fly fisherman. During the summer he spent most evenings and Sunday afternoons fishing for trout on the nearby Lung River. He attached a small saddle to the crossbar of his bicycle and foot-rests so that I could accompany him on these outings. It was he who taught me how to cast a line, and I will never forget the thrill of catching my first trout. When I was still very young, my father also taught me about woodwork and electricity. Before I was nine years old I knew how to use a fret saw, change an electric plug, wire a lamp or generally fix things. I still get great satisfaction from what we now call DIY.

I was about three years old when my father left his job in Duff's to start his own business: a hardware shop and public bar on the main street. The shop stocked everything from needles to horse-drawn ploughs, and carried the most comprehensive array of rods and fishing tackle in town—it was truly a place of wonder for a young boy to grow up. The kitchen was on the ground floor, with bedrooms and the drawing-room upstairs. The premises adjoined that of my grand-parents, which also had a bar. Next-door to them was a newsagent with a confectionery shop and yet another bar.

During the day my father ran the hardware shop while my mother looked after whatever little business there might be in the bar, located at the back of the building. Like almost every other family in town, we had a live-in maid, or 'servant-girl' as some referred to such staff. There was also a male apprentice who worked in the hardware shop.

In the evening the bar would get very busy. It was divided into three sections, with the counter running along all three. The first section was a private 'snug' that was the exclusive domain of the bank manager, teachers from the college, the local solicitors and other valued customers. The entrance door was controlled from inside—only those with their own special knock were admitted. The most popular drink was a 'half-one' (a small whiskey), followed by a bottle of stout (Guinness). Draught porter was also available, but the bottles were usually preferred. Most publicans, however small their premises, bottled their own Guinness. The brewery in Dublin, at St James's Gate, supplied labels on which the individual bottler's name was printed.

Every morning, at precisely 11 a.m., one of the local butchers came into our kitchen, where he drank his half-one and bottle of stout rapidly and left. Few, if any, words were ever spoken. My parents knew the preferences of their regulars, so the only order ever given was for 'the usual'! As a child, I thought 'the usual' was a type of drink and could never understand when different versions of it were presented to customers.

One afternoon, when I was about six years old, a guest came into our kitchen. He was the tallest man I had ever seen. A member of the Palestine Police Force home on leave, he was travelling to his birthplace in Kiltimagh, Co. Mayo. I will always remember looking up at this giant. Little did I know that we would meet again in later life. That imposing man was Liam O'Hora, Ireland's Film Censor from 1956 to 1964.

* * *

Late one Sunday night, or early one Monday morning, in the dark of winter, as my family slept, a neighbour saw the dramatic sight of the long curtains on the upstairs windows in our house going up in flames. Our parents were alerted, but by the time Muriel and I were taken safely downstairs, everything seemed to be on fire. My mother stumbled against the blistering paint on the handrail of the stairs, and carried the resulting scar on her arm to the grave. Otherwise there were no other injuries. It was freezing outside that night. We children were put into ice-cold and rarely used beds in our grandparents' house next-door. I will never forget shivering spasmodically on the freezing damp bed in which I lay, in terror. There was no fire engine in the town at that time, so neighbours rose from their beds to help and fought the fire as best they could. Buckets were filled with water in their homes and carried to the conflagration. As one uncle filled his bucket with steaming hot water someone was heard to say, 'Don't use that. It will only make the fire worse!'

The next day was like a traditional wake. My parents stayed in the burnt-out shell of their home while people came from near and far to express their sympathy. It was established that the fire had probably been caused by a faulty electrical connection in the wireless, which had been destroyed. (The last thing I recall listening to on that trusty old Murphy wireless was de Valera's reply to Churchill after the War. Our kitchen was full that evening, and not a word was spoken as the Taoiseach droned on in what seemed to me a boring voice. It was only in later life that I appreciated the importance of that riposte.) Most of our collection of beautifully bound books did not survive the flames. In the event, we all stayed on in my grandparents' house while our home was being rebuilt. This took some time as building material was in short supply after the War, but eventually it was completed and we returned home.

I do remember a wonderful thing that happened after that. The 'wireless and electrical' department in Flannery's placed in its window a brand new Philips radio—the first new radio to be seen in the town since pre-War days. It was priced at over £20, which was a small fortune in those days. However, others had little time to admire it before, at my mother's instigation, my father made the purchase. Now our home was complete once more. In fact, the days of the wireless were over. Radio had arrived.

My mother was by far the more dominant of my parents. She was ambitious for her children. She felt that there would be a better life for us living in Dublin, where three of her sisters were already successfully established. In 1946 Muriel was sent to boarding school, the Dominican College on Eccles Street in Dublin. Eventually, my parents decided that the whole family should relocate. The shop and bar, which was our home, was sold and in February 1948 we moved to a rented house in Glenageary, Co. Dublin, for a new chapter in our family's story.

Chapter 2 ～

FROM BALLAGH
TO GLENAGEARY

When I was about eight years old I discovered my father's camera. It was an Eastman Kodak model made in Rochester, New York. A folding camera, it was finished in a leather covering. There were four different shutter speeds and an adjustable lens aperture; for the time, it was a sophisticated piece of equipment. (In recent years I have come across similar models on sale as antiques for exorbitant prices in places as far apart as Prague, Cairo and Cyprus.) My father was a good photographer and had taken many pictures of the family when Muriel and I were small children. I quickly learned to use the camera and became totally hooked on photography.

While I loved that Eastman Kodak, I badly wanted to have a camera of my very own. There was a new Kodak model, a Baby Brownie, on display in the window of Carney's chemist shop, just down the street from our house. The price, as far as I can remember, was one pound and ten shillings. My parents weren't entirely willing to part with this sum and they were not convinced that I would not tire of this, as I did with most other toys. Instead, my father used his collection of cigarette coupons—there were two coupons on a pack of twenty and he smoked at least twenty Sweet Afton cigarettes every day—to acquire a Kodak Box camera for me. It was not as smart-looking as the Baby Brownie and had none of the sophisticated features of the Eastman Kodak. So after a few weeks I did indeed become bored with it, and returned to my father's folding camera. I took photos of everyone, including Mr de Valera on one of his visits to Ballagh. The first time I saw Dev, he was walking to Mass in Ballaghaderreen: a very tall, thin man in a long, black coat and black hat with a sombre expression. I could well understand why he was called 'The Long Fellow'.

My passion for photography grew and I was now using all my pocket money, and any other available financial resources, to fund photo=processing through the chemist shop. It was only after we moved to Dublin that I learned from books how to develop and print my own photographs, and I set up a temporary darkroom in the corner of our garage.

*   *   *

Leaving my beloved Ballagh to live in Dublin was not all bad. The main attraction for me was, of course, the many cinemas to choose from for my favourite pastime. There was a positive glut of them: the old Astoria, later called the Forum, in Glasthule; the Pavilion at the bottom of Marine Road; the Picture House in George's Street, Dún Laoghaire; the Adelphi, a brand new cinema that opened in Dún Laoghaire soon after we moved into the area; and the Regent in nearby Blackrock. The forty-minute train journey into Dublin city centre opened up another world of cinemas and cine-variety theatres. Europe's largest theatre, the Theatre Royal, was located on Hawkins Street, with the Regal Rooms cinema next-door to it. North of the Liffey, beside the GPO, was the Capitol. O'Connell Street had the Savoy and the Carlton. The Corinthian was located on Eden Quay. Grafton Street boasted its own cinema, the Grafton, and later another small venue, the Cameo, which was a small café-cinema with 16 mm projection equipment. In order to comply with some strange licensing law, the Cameo had no admission charge. Patrons were offered a cup of coffee and a biscuit, for which they paid one shilling, before entering the tiny cinema. Two movies, *Bitter Rice*, the Italian film that made a star of the well-endowed Silvana Mangano, and *The Glass Mountain*, a British film starring Dulcie Gray and the great Italian tenor Tito Gobbi, seemed to play there incessantly. Beyond the city centre, Rathmines had the Stella cinema, Harold's Cross had the Classic and Ringsend had the Regal. All of these were within my reach by train, tram or bus. It was certainly a long way from the old Roxy of my early childhood in Ballaghaderreen.

The house, which we rented for £4 a week, was brand new. It was on the corner of a wide residential road, beside the railway. It was all very exciting. Now we were living in Dublin, not just visiting. My uncle Jimmy came from Ballagh to stay for a few days to help us settle into this new and different environment. My father was now a commercial traveller. On Saturdays he would empty his brown leather attaché case and we would take the train from nearby Glenageary station into the city. There we visited Moore Street, where the street traders filled up his case with different fruits. My father knew them all by their first names. Rosie, 'the Queen of Moore Street', was a particular favourite of his. Then it was off to Haffner's to join the queue for their famous sausages, which were sold only in the Henry Street shop, before returning home in time for lunch. My mother dedicated herself to housework.

Once ensconced in our new family home on St Catherine's Road in Glenageary, my great wish was to attend Blackrock College for my second-level schooling. When travelling on the Dalkey tram to or from Dublin, I passed and gazed upon the majestic building with its large expanse of grounds in front. Then, as now, the grounds were surrounded by tall railings and impressive iron gates set in granite pillars. Invariably, students in blue-and-white striped jerseys were engaged in a vigorous game of football on the playing fields. The whole picture was reminiscent of stories I had read of English boarding schools. Unfortunately, it was not to be as the fees in Blackrock College were too expensive.

Instead I was sent to the Christian Brothers College in Dún Laoghaire. The Principal, Brother Buckley, a scholarly and kind man, decided that I should start in the second-year class. This caused me some concern because I had not even a rudimentary knowledge of geometry or algebra, in which subjects my fellow pupils seemed well versed. The school was a rugby-playing one, but that didn't interest me. It was a sport I had never even seen played before, although my Dublin cousins, educated at Belvedere College and Clongowes Wood, were proficient at the game. In fact, one first cousin, Mick Dargan, was capped for Ireland in both rugby and cricket. Aptitude in sports was a quick route to acceptance, but that route was not open to me. I wasn't all that interested in sport, particularly rugby. At school I was regarded as a 'culchie', which made me inferior and I lacked self-confidence as a result. On my first day I was befriended by a boy named Noel Barron. A competent rugby player, but not a great student, he nevertheless had time for me when others were indifferent, or even appeared hostile.

There are few outstanding memories of my time at school. I got on well with the other boys, but never developed any interest in rugby. Apart from Noel Barron, my other close friend was Bob Dowling, a real charmer who rejoiced in his proper name of Robert Rochfort Dowling. Bob left school even earlier than me. He maintained that as no one had ever doubted his intelligence, he saw no point in doing exams!

There is one undisputed highlight from my early years in Dublin: the day Mayo won the All-Ireland Football Final in 1950. The county team was captained by Séan Flanagan, a young solicitor who had set up practice in Ballaghaderreen. My father took me to the match. There was great excitement as we took our places on the terrace under the Hogan Stand. In those days, after the presentation the winning captain carried the trophy from Croke Park to Barry's Hotel in Gardiner Place, then the social headquarters of the GAA. When we met Séan Flanagan after the match, he asked me to take the other handle of the Sam Maguire Cup. We carried it together on the twenty-minute walk to the hotel. It was a proud and memorable moment in my young life. Séan Flanagan later became a Fianna Fáil TD for East Mayo and eventually held two ministries under Taoiseach Jack Lynch.

Shortly after I started in the Christian Brothers, the college moved from the centre of Dún Laoghaire to its present site in Monkstown Park. At about the same time our family left St Catherine's Road and moved to Trimleston Gardens, a new housing estate nearer the city, in Booterstown. There was still sufficient money left from the sale of our house in Ballaghaderreen to provide a substantial deposit on the new house, which cost just under £2,000.

I enjoyed life in Dublin and the variety of people with which it brought me into contact. There was one visitor I was not pleased to see, though. Back in Ballaghaderreen, I had been taught by three senior De La Salle Brothers, who were all good men. There was one young novice, however, Brother Gregory, who had a sadistic streak. As punishment, he would lift young boys up by their ears, holding them some inches above the floor. It was a painful and cruel act, and one for which a teacher

would, quite rightly, be prosecuted today. Of course, in my day we never told our parents of this unacceptable treatment. In those days if one admitted to being punished at school, parents were likely to repeat the dose on the basis that it must have been well deserved. What really infuriated me was that when Brother Gregory was sent to study in University College Dublin, he had the nerve to contact my parents. My mother frequently invited him to our home for tea, a practice of which I thoroughly disapproved. As the young man sat sipping his pre-prandial sherry, I would glare at him, remembering the pain he had so casually inflicted on me and my schoolfriends. I have met many good men of the cloth in my time, but the brutality of that 'Christian' Brother had a profound effect on my attitude towards the clergy.

*   *   *

Outside school hours I became captivated by an exciting new sport that had just arrived in Ireland. Motorcycle speedway was introduced into Shelbourne Park Greyhound Stadium, near Ringsend, where a special track was built for the purpose. Speedway is a thrilling race involving four riders who compete in four laps around an oval track. The 'home' team, Shelbourne Tigers, selected entirely from the London-based Wimbledon Dons, competed against other visiting British speedway teams. My father also developed an interest in the sport and together we went to see the events every Sunday afternoon. The team members were mostly from Australia, where the sport had originated, from New Zealand or the United States, with a few British men thrown into the mix. Shelbourne Tigers was captained by an eighteen-year-old Australian dare-devil named Ronnie Moore. His boyish good looks and high earning power were sufficient to put him into the David Beckham category of international sporting personalities. Speedway racing became so popular that a second track was built at Chapelizod Greyhound Stadium, on Dublin's west side. There racing took place under lights on Wednesday evenings.

I became an active member of the Shelbourne Tigers Supporters' Club, and was seduced by the high-octane races. Shelbourne had a cycle speedway team. We raced pedal cycles, of similar design to the

motorbikes, around small cinder tracks. I built my own bike from
various old parts. Custom-built models were available, of course, but
few of us had parents rich enough to buy such a coveted item. We raced
on summer evenings or at the weekends on the old Ringsend dump.
The refuse from the city of Dublin was being used to reclaim that part
of Dublin Bay, which is now the site of Shelbourne Football Stadium.
Like all such dumps, the pungent smell of decaying material was ever-
present. Usually the prevailing south-west wind carried it out over the
bay, but there were times when it became overpowering. This might
have explained the lack of spectators enjoying our activities!

I used to ride my brightly painted speedway bicycle from our home
in Booterstown along Sandymount Strand Road and up to the
Ringsend dump, with my crash helmet—decorated in the same colours
as the bicycle—swinging from the handlebars. These helmets, used by
all speedsters, were US Army surplus worn in the Second World War by
tank operators. To me, the journey to the smelly dump was as exciting
as if I was a young footballer in transit to the hallowed turf of Croke
Park to participate in an All-Ireland Final. Another boy, John Ferguson,
who lived near me in Booterstown, was also a speedway fan. He took up
cycle speedway and joined our club. Perhaps like me, he too was
escaping from rugby, which was a fundamental part of education at his
school, Blackrock College.

* * *

I joined the Dún Laoghaire troop of Boy Scouts. To be honest, the main
attraction was the uniform, which my parents bought for me.
Unfortunately, there was a shortage of hats at the time, so I did not have
the complete rig-out. In fact, at the open-air investiture ceremony held
in the grounds of the Dominican Girls' School in Dún Laoghaire, I was
the only bare-headed boy in the line-up; the other new recruits had
borrowed hats from older brothers or friends for the occasion. My
enthusiasm for scouting was short-lived. Shortly after our investiture,
the troop embarked on a summer camp in Co. Wicklow. Rucksacks
bulging with all our requirements for the two-week holiday, we set off
by train for Rathdrum. From there we marched for about 3 miles along

country roads until we reached the open field that had been chosen as our campsite. The tents and other necessary equipment had arrived before us by lorry. The day was dull, and very shortly after our arrival it began to rain. Under the supervision of the Assistant Scoutmaster and other officers, we set about erecting the tents and preparing the site for our sojourn. One of the more unpleasant, and back-breaking, tasks was digging the latrines. It certainly did not resemble my idea of a holiday! As the rain continued and we ate our badly cooked meal under the dripping canvas of the rain-sodden tents, I began to feel like the boy in the popular song, 'Hello Muddah! Hello Faddah!' sung by the American comic, Allan Sherman.

This being the scouts, we did of course learn some valuable new skills, for example how to use one's finger to channel the drops of water slithering steadily through the porous tent canvas in an unremitting small stream to prevent them dropping on our upturned faces. Unlike the song's happy ending, in our case the sun did not appear. After two sleepless nights, watching the earwigs and other insects seeking shelter in our tent, I packed my rucksack, took leave of my hardier fellow scouts and departed on the long trek to Rathdrum Station and, ultimately, the comfort of home. It was my one, and only, experience of back-packing.

*   *   *

For my fourteenth birthday my parents gave me a road-racing bicycle. It was a Hercules Kestrel model, with a gold-coloured frame and white mudguards, and it was my pride and joy. I rode this bicycle to school every day, cycling the 7 miles home and back for lunch. During the holidays or at weekends it would take me to cinemas around the city or in the suburbs. Frequently I cycled from Booterstown to the Fairview Grand or to the Drumcondra Grand to see any movie in which Ann Blyth appeared. I often went five or six times to see her films, so great was my love for and loyalty to the lady!

Ronnie Drew—another who did not serve the full-term at Monkstown Park but went on to become a huge success in life—was in my class. Ronnie was also interested in cycling and had a racing bicycle. We used to mitch from school and cycle up to the top of the Featherbed, in the

Dublin Mountains, where a film was shooting on location. The film was *The Gentle Gunman*, a black-and-white movie starring John Mills, Dirk Bogarde, Elizabeth Sellars, Eddie Byrne, Belfast actor Joseph Tomelty and BBC personality, Gilbert Harding. The Director of Photography was Gordon Dines, assisted by a camera operator by the name of Chick Waterson. He was my target. I approached Chick during a lunch-break and told him of my dreams and ambitions of becoming a photographer and cameraman. He was helpful, but explained the obstacles I would face if I attempted to become involved in the film industry.

Ronnie was a great man for the horses, and we sometimes went to the Leopardstown races together. I was very impressed that he seemed to know most of the jockeys. As they rode out of the paddock towards the start of the race, Ronnie's greeting of 'Howya, head?' was always acknowledged with a nod and a wave. We were usually outside the enclosure, at the rails, on the free side of the racecourse. I have no recollection of Ronnie gambling; he just loved to watch the horses run. He was also a keen trout fisherman and would take me to a favourite fishing place: a small lake close to the old lead mine at Ballycorus in the foothills of the Dublin Mountains.

* * *

I quickly realised the world of academia was not on the cards for me. I was eager to move on and, like my friend Bob Dowling, continue my education in the University of the World. Although my mother did not totally approve of my leaving school after achieving Honours in the Intermediate Certificate examination, she accepted my ambition to get on with my chosen career. My easy-going father, who was dominated by my mother, did not express an opinion. He was not earning much money as a commercial traveller, so the money with which my mother managed the household was scarce, which no doubt meant it would be a relief not to have to pay school fees for a further two years. I was happy to leave school for the last time in the summer of 1952. With the Intermediate Certificate examination behind me, I was confident that, for the present, I had acquired sufficient education to make my way in the world. I was absolutely determined to break into the glamorous realms of professional photography.

Chapter 3 ∾

A FOOT IN
THE DOOR

The decision to embark on an exciting new career is one thing; actually making strides in your chosen profession is quite another. As on previous occasions of need, I started by seeking out the help of my reliable Auntie May. She immediately had a good idea: she offered to seek the advice of Tony O'Malley, a photographer who worked for the *Sunday Independent* and was regarded as something of a celebrity. Unfortunately, his response was that it was highly unlikely that I would get a placement as a trainee in any newspaper's photographic department. However, he mentioned a neighbour of his who ran a photographic studio. Richard C. Gavin owned the Grafton Studio, which was located at 1 St Stephen's Green, just around the corner from Grafton Street—the nexus of Dublin social life. My dear aunt followed the lead and in no time had arranged an interview for me with Mr Gavin. Togged out in my best clothes, I went to meet the man. He was extremely encouraging, and agreed to take me on as a trainee immediately. So here I was, a few weeks out of school and I had taken the all-important first step in what I was certain would be an agreeable career.

The Grafton Studio had three photographers: Dick Gavin, his younger brother Frank and a TCD graduate named David Jackson. Dick was a great boss and I prospered under his tutelage. Frank was also a brilliant photographer and he was particularly helpful with my training. He eventually left the Grafton Studio and set up business in Dorset Street, on the north side of the city. Frank married the love of his life, Noreen Hooper from Dalkey. They had eight children—five sons and three daughters. After Noreen's death, Frank, who was aged fifty-eight, entered a seminary in Rome. In 1992 he was ordained a priest in Dublin.

The main activity of the Grafton Studio was wedding photography and most of the fashionable weddings came our way. One I remember well was that of the singer, Veronica Dunne. Her lavish wedding reception was held in the Shelbourne Hotel. Veronica was very particular and insisted that only the boss could take her pictures.

The studio used large Speed Graphic cameras. These were manufactured in the USA and were the accepted newspaper photographer's camera the world over. It was bulky and heavy and used large glass plates, rather than film, to produce the photographic negative. The plate was changed after each exposure. By today's standards the process was slow and cumbersome. A heavy, battery-operated flash-gun was attached to the side of the camera, which used one flash bulb at a time; changing a hot flash bulb after an exposure often led to burnt fingers.

On days when we had no firm bookings the photographers would 'church-hop' from 8.30 a.m. in the hope of finding a wedding for which no photographer had been engaged. Such weddings were not uncommon, but of course there were many other photographers on the same circuit and on a similar quest. We all knew one another and treated each other well. Whoever got to the wedding first was acknowledged to have staked his claim, and the others would not interfere.

Sometimes when one arrived at the church a wedding would already be in progress. A quick scan of the church confirmed whether a photographer was present—if none was, it meant the happy couple had not engaged one. When this was the case, we would just starting shooting pictures and hope to be approved post-nuptials. The interior of the church, with the couple at the altar, would be photographed during the ceremony. To do this, the heavy camera was placed on the front rail of the choir loft and a time exposure was employed of anything from one to five seconds, depending on the available light. Light meters were not available then, so exposures were determined by experience. (Flash photography was strictly forbidden inside the church during the ceremony.)

There was a standard set of wedding photographs that were presented in a wedding album. The first of these was usually the bridegroom and best man standing outside the church—invariably smoking a nerve-calming cigarette. This was followed by the arrival of the bridesmaids at the church door. Then there were photos of the bride arriving with her father, stepping out of the bridal car and walking up the aisle. After the church ceremony there was a posed picture of the newly-weds signing the register in the sacristy. Some priests frowned on this as, quite correctly, they considered it to be a civil act and therefore not part of the religious sacrament. Among the stock photographs, the great money-spinner was the 'large group'. This was usually taken on the church steps, with the entire congregation arranged in staggered lines. The steps were surely designed for this purpose—they provided platforms of different levels for the lines of guests. The main bridal party was assembled on ground level, at the front. For the photographer, it was essential that every face in the crowd was clearly visible, otherwise a potential sale could be lost. Assembling these large groups, particularly on a cold winter's morning, was not easy. And, of course, once they were successfully assembled, one had to ensure that nobody had their eyes closed. In order to safeguard against this, two photographs were taken. This was the only shot that was duplicated because the cost, and indeed the weight, of the glass plates used for producing the negatives meant duplication was not a viable option.

If a photographer was covering the wedding on spec, he would approach the couple either in the sacristy, as they signed the register, or afterwards at the church door and get their agreement to pose for further photographs. There was no fee involved. Once he had taken the various group shots at the church, the photographer would accompany the bridal couple to the wedding reception. There, a posed photo cutting the—usually three-tier—wedding cake would complete the series of photographs. The photographer then returned to the darkroom and developed the photographic plates. Enlargements were made from the wet-glass negatives and a set of twelve to fifteen large prints was assembled. Then either the photographer or a special salesman went back to the wedding reception and showed the hastily printed photographic proofs to the bridal party and their guests. The standard wedding album contained twelve photographs. The price varied according to the cover finish, which could be anything from plastic to expensive genuine soft leather, and the quality of the paper used, but was generally between 8 and 20 guineas. This would be about €10 to €26, which sounds cheap but certainly wasn't a measly sum back then. (You will have noticed that photographers, like doctors, surgeons—as consultants were then known—architects, better-class tailors and horse-dealers, always dealt in guineas rather than the pounds of common trade!) By the time the photographer or salesman returned to the wedding reception with the proofs of the photographs, all the guests were usually in good form after being wined and dined. The photos were shown, orders were taken, names and addresses were noted and the money was collected.

I thoroughly enjoyed the work and progressed quickly—thanks to Richard and Frank—in the skills of photography. The training they provided, and my own enthusiasm, ensured that I advanced rapidly from being an assistant salesman/photographer to being a fully-fledged member of the photographic team. Within three months I replaced Dave Jackson, who left Grafton Studio to pursue a career in other aspects of photography.

Now that I was an experienced wedding photographer, I knew the tricks of the trade. There were a number of ways to obtain potential business. One was to peruse the Social and Personal columns of the newspapers for announcements of engagements. Another was to contact the sacristan in the various churches and obtain a list of upcoming marriages. One evening I cycled to the local Catholic church in Booterstown for this very purpose. As I returned down the steep hill that leads back to Merrion Road, a child riding an adult's bicycle far too large for him to handle came from a side laneway, crossing suddenly onto my path. I swerved to avoid the boy and was thrown over the handlebars of my bicycle, landing heavily on the tarmacadam roadway. My spectacles shattered and small shards of broken glass entered my left cheek; there seemed to be blood everywhere. As I was being picked up and dusted down by some pedestrians who had witnessed the accident, one old lady remarked that she had seen me coming out from the church—presuming I had gone there to pray. An even older man, who had also come to my aid, immediately replied, 'Yes, and if he hadn't gone there, he wouldn't be in this state now.' Luckily, there was a doctor's surgery just a few doors away, and I was taken there for treatment. Afterwards, elaborately bandaged, I walked home and went to my bed. My parents were out at the Regent cinema in nearby Blackrock. When they returned, I shouted to them not to come upstairs until I had told them the story of my accident—the blood-soaked bandage gave the impression that I was much more seriously injured than was really the case.

* * *

My first motorbike, which I got soon after my cycling mishap, was a BSA Bantam with a 125cc, two-stroke engine. I well remember riding it home to Booterstown from the shop on Bachelor's Walk, near O'Connell Bridge, where I bought it. After a very brief lesson on the use of the controls, I was released into the city traffic. Riding south along Leeson Street towards Donnybrook that sunny Saturday morning, I really felt the world was my oyster: a good job, nice friends and colleagues and my own motorbike—what more could anyone want? Like Leonardo DiCaprio standing on the prow of the ship in *Titanic*, I was on top of the world!

Independent transport meant I could now cover the north and south city church circuits alone, which greatly increased my earning potential. An old commission book I discovered recently shows that I was earning approximately £6 a week in 1953—more than my father earned at that time. However, there were two barren periods in the wedding photography business. Roman Catholics did not marry during the six weeks of Lent or Advent, which meant our earnings dropped dramatically. The normally reliable supplementary income provided by dress dances was not available because such dances were banned during the holy seasons.

During these times there might be a few Jewish or Protestant weddings, or some limited work in the studio. Decent man that he was, Richard Gavin always made sure I was never short of money during the lean weeks. One memory I have of one such fallow period is of photographing the flamboyant actor, Mícheál Mac Liammóir. It was for an advertising picture, which showed Mícheál buying a shirt in

Kingston's menswear shop in O'Connell Street. Their motto was 'A Kingston shirt makes all the difference'. I had never seen a man wearing a wig or make-up on the street before, but Mícheál carried it off with great aplomb. Aware of his talent and great reputation as an actor, writer and artist, I felt sad that he had been reduced to posing for advertising photographs in order to earn a crust.

* * *

While working at the Grafton Studio I acquired a small cine-camera. In those pre-television days home movies were popular. I saw an advertisement in the *Evening Mail* announcing the formation of a new cine-club in Terenure, and I signed up. A small group of enthusiasts met each week in the home of Pat and Stella Whelan, where we discussed and watched demonstrations of different aspects of film-making and screened films made by members.

It was at the Stella Cine-Club (named after Stella, who was the honorary treasurer) that I met Norman Cohen. He was the same age as me, but to me he was unique. Norman was Jewish, but he was not rich, in spite of the general perception of Dublin Jews at that time. His family was supported by his mother, who was a dignified lady. I got to know her better some years later, when she managed the Old Dublin restaurant in Francis Street. When we first met, Norman was still at school, was hugely enthusiastic about film-making, but had no money for film or equipment. I, on the other hand, had a good income to match my enthusiasm. Norman often borrowed my camera, and I could afford to let him have some film, too. He made good use of his opportunities and went on to become a well-known film director in London. In partnership with producer Greg Smith, who is now one of my oldest friends, Norman directed films such as *Brendan Behan's Dublin*, *The London Nobody Knows* and *Adolf Hitler, My Part in his Downfall*, which starred Spike Milligan. Tragically, Norman died suddenly in Los Angeles when only in his forties and while he was preparing to direct his first major Hollywood movie.

* * *

Although he represented a number of well-known Irish manufacturers and importers, my father's career as a commercial traveller did not seem to be prospering. Money was short and our lifestyle at home was slowly deteriorating. My sister was working happily in Lee's department store in Dún Laoghaire, and I was making a fair contribution to household expenses. In the midst of his gathering misfortune, my father apparently found a new enthusiasm for religion: he would walk from home to early Mass in the nearby church on Merrion Road every morning.

In fact, his real motivation for leaving the house early was to intercept the post man and collect the mail. This mostly comprised bills and final-notice demands for payment, which he wished to conceal from my mother. Unfortunately, he had reverted to his old habit of gambling. While supposedly at work, he was actually spending an inordinate amount of his time in city bookmakers' shops. Finally, he was forced to admit all this to my distraught mother. To compound the problem, he had not only lost all of his own money on the horses but a considerable amount of other people's, too, which he had collected on behalf of his employers. It was a bad situation.

A decision was made that my father would seek work in London and pay off his debts from there. Within a few days of his disclosure to my mother, he was on his way. On the evening of his departure, my sister Muriel and I accompanied him to the mail-boat in Dún Laoghaire harbour. He was not alone; there were hundreds of returning or first-time emigrants boarding the ship with him. Our father was in his mid-fifties. He left wearing his raincoat and hat—a sad figure carrying a small suitcase with all his personal effects. He had never been to England or London before. We loved our Dada. Muriel and I were heartbroken. We did not speak a word to each other as we returned home on the bus.

After my father's departure for England, I went around on my motorcycle visiting the various customers whose money he had misappropriated. I explained the situation and promised that their money would be repaid as soon as possible. As my father was a popular person, and possibly because of my youth, each one agreed to take no action and await repayment. My father was fortunate to secure a reasonable job as barman in a pub near Piccadilly Circus in London. He was happy working there and each week sent money home. Within a few months, thanks to my mother's prudence and our own contributions, all of his outstanding debts had been settled. My mother and Muriel would later join him in London.

* * *

After little more than a year with the Grafton Studio I decided the time had come to branch out on my own. I rented a small basement in Lower Mount Street, near the Grand Canal, in a building that has long since been demolished. I converted the area into a studio and office. The only heating available was a smelly oil heater; it was cold and damp. But I survived and made a living photographing weddings, graduations and other social events. Just as I was becoming established, I was approached by Hallie O'Callaghan, a chemist who lived near our home and was a friend of my parents. He was bored with his pharmacy job, so he suggested we set up a laboratory to develop and print black-and-white films. (Colour photography was unknown to the amateur photographer in the early 1950s.) Our clientele would be chemist shops, which in those times had a complete monopoly in the business of 'photo-finishing', as it was known. With my connections of four chemist shops in the family and Hallie's own contacts, our prospects were excellent.

The laboratory was set up in Hallie's garage and the business proved to be an immediate success. We each had a motorcycle, and every morning we rode around and collected the exposed films from the chemist shops. These were processed and the photographs printed that day, or frequently into the night. The finished work was returned the following morning. This twenty-four-hour turn-around was a unique new express service. The only cloud on the horizon was that my partner had no experience of, and little flair for, our work, which meant I was responsible for much more than my fair share. After a few months of up to twenty-hour days with little or no sleep, I inevitably became ill. The first sign of this was a serious and painful swelling of my ankle. I tried to carry on working with my foot in a bucket of ice water that was replenished constantly, but eventually had to give up. My partner made an effort to keep the business going, but his lack of experience and stamina were difficult obstacles to overcome. Sadly, our promising enterprise failed.

*   *   *

After my recovery I was offered a job by David Ross of Ross's Studio in St Stephen's Green. The studio was operated by two brothers, Joe and David Ross, who were highly esteemed members of Dublin's vibrant Jewish community. Their business was long established and well respected, concentrating mainly on portraiture, First Communion and graduation commemorative photographs.

Ross's Studio was the official photographer for Dublin's Metropole Ballroom. The era of the ballroom is now long gone, but I remember vividly the early 1950s and the big bands, with the dance programme numbered and tied with ribbon, the unwritten law of dancing around the perimeter (it was bad manners to hog the middle of the floor) and the obligatory National Anthem to bring an end to the proceedings each night. The Metropole was a large cinema, restaurant and ballroom complex situated near the General Post Office in O'Connell Street, on the site now occupied by Penney's department store. From Monday to Friday staff dances of various organisations, or past-pupils' unions, were held in the Metropole's large upstairs ballroom. These were black-tie affairs, serenaded by a full orchestra under the baton of Phil Murtagh. At midnight a three-course supper was served. Afterwards, dancing resumed and continued until 3.00 or 4.00 in the morning. Across the road, Clery's Ballroom ran a similar operation for a slightly lower end of the market. This also had a full orchestra and formal dress was the norm.

Further up O'Connell Street was the Gresham Hotel, then under the management of the elegant and sophisticated Toddy O'Sullivan. It ran the most expensive and exclusive dress dances of all. The clientele were usually the professional associations, high-powered charities, past-pupils' unions of the more exclusive male and female second-level colleges and various hunts. The hotel orchestra was conducted by Neil

Cairns and at many of these events the gentlemen wore white tie and tails, no less.

My work with Ross's Studio involved photographing the couples or groups attending the dances at the Metropole. This was easy because the clients needed no encouragement—what young man, or even not-so-young man, could take his beautifully gowned and coiffured lady to a dress dance and not want to have a souvenir photograph? So great was the demand that our cameras were set up in a lounge below the ballroom, and the enthusiastic customers came to us. Couples or groups were lined up, a quick flash, cash exchanged for a receipt and the job was done. Our pockets bulged with banknotes; we often took in over £100 in an evening. My employer, Dave Ross, was a kind, gentle and good-humoured man, and he was also generous. I was paid 25 per cent commission, which meant I was well-off by the standards of the day. We photographers also wore evening dress and each night had our three-course supper with the band. In the early hours of the morning, with the trousers of the dress-suit tucked into my socks and still wearing my fashionable patent leather shoes, I went home on my motorcycle, my pockets filled with my share of the night's takings.

I felt things couldn't really get any better, but then, there were some things still lacking in my life: a girlfriend, for one, and also the kind of progression I wanted to be making towards fulfilling my dream of becoming a professional cameraman. It turned out that 1954 was to be an interesting year on both counts.

Chapter 4 ～

PRESS
GANG

In the summer of 1954, Irish Press Group announced the launch of a new paper, the *Evening Press*. The Group already published the daily *Irish Press* and the phenomenally successful *Sunday Press*. Now it wished to stake a bid against the existing evening newspapers: the *Evening Herald*, with wide circulation in Dublin and Leinster, and the *Evening Mail*, which, like *The Irish Times*, was regarded as a 'Protestant' paper but had a solid Dublin-based circulation. The publication of the first edition of the *Evening Press* was scheduled for September, a date described by the paper's editor designate, Douglas Gageby, as 'the traditional date for starting newspapers and for starting wars'.

My friend and neighbour in Booterstown, Tom Hennigan, a senior journalist with the *Sunday Press*, arranged for me to meet with Bob Dillon, Art Editor of the Irish Press Group. Mr Dillon was pleasant, but explained that he had sufficient photographers to cope with the demands of the new publication. Nevertheless I was persistent, and eventually Bob Dillon looked at my portfolio of photographs. I continued to telephone him every other day in the hopes of getting some freelance work. After some weeks of my pestering, Bob finally relented and offered me a three-day trial. As the Rolleiflex camera I owned at the time was not suitable for newspaper work, it was necessary to buy a large press camera. Although money was still scarce at home and I had not saved any, my mother managed to find enough to help buy a brand new German Linhof camera, which cost £120. Armed with this fine piece of equipment, I started my three-day trial with the *Irish Press*. Tom Hennigan was encouraging of my prospects. Always a good-humoured man, his theory was that anyone who was fortunate enough to get inside the Burgh Quay offices could stay forever—he said that if your hat blew into the front office and you followed to retrieve it, you would get a permanent job!

Like any fledgling enterprise, working for the *Evening Press* was an exciting experience. I started on Monday 23 August 1954. The first edition of the new paper was published nine days later, on Wednesday 1 September. The staff of the *Evening Press* were young and enthusiastic and there was a great buzz of enjoyment and expectation around the offices. Those who had spent years with the Group's established newspapers were also splendid people with whom to work, such as reporters like the legendary John Healy or Ted Nealon, who would later fill the roles of newspaper editor, outstanding political television pundit, a politician and junior government minister; Dominick Coyle, later an editor of the London *Financial Times*; a young sub-editor named Tim Pat Coogan, whom I had last seen when he was a lifeguard, sitting atop an observation tower on Killiney strand. There was James Downey, who subsequently played a leading role in the revitalisation of *The Irish Times* under the editorship of Douglas Gageby, and a young copy-boy named Jim King, who would later enjoy a prominent career as a newspaperman, public servant and an executive in the international airline industry. Conor O'Brien—usually referred to as Conor 'News' O'Brien to distinguish him from an up-and-coming young diplomat, Conor Cruise O'Brien, who was making his name on the world stage—was also a member of the editorial team. Another young journalist was Peter Lennon, who later was for many years Paris correspondent of the *Guardian* newspaper and in the late 1960s made the controversial film, *The Rocky Road to Dublin*.

I already knew many of the photographers who were my new colleagues. The doyen of the Art Department was a lovely man, Tommy Lavery. A native of Belfast, he mostly covered horse-racing. Another member of the older brigade was Mick Loftus, a fine photographer and an artist as well, who painted landscapes in oils. There was also the eccentric, dry-witted Douglas Duggan. Paddy Barron, a handsome, charming and talented young man from Drumcondra, was another staff photographer. As it turned out, Paddy's presence would be writ large in my later life.

The younger group was led by Colman Doyle, a distinguished photographer even at that early stage. His talent for any aspect of photography was acknowledged as being unparalleled in this country. He rightly went on to achieve international acclaim, working not just in Ireland but around the world for the French news-magazine, *Paris Match*.

Our first edition had the right impact. The three-column photograph on the front page of the *Evening Press* published on 1 September 1954 captivated everyone. Taken by Basil King, it was a splendid picture of the model Betty Whelan leaving for the church on the morning of her wedding. (In later editions the resident artist adjusted slightly upwards her revealing neckline; it was also something of a scoop!) Thanks to his natural initiative and news sense, unlike the other press photographers Basil didn't go to the church, but instead went to the Whelan home to get his picture. As luck would have it, the bridal car was late. The bride and her father accepted Basil's invitation to travel to the church in the *Evening Press* car, thereby creating an additional story under the headline: 'Betty's taxi late—came in *Press* car.' The pretender newspaper had begun as it planned to continue. Incredibly, the lead story in that very first edition was that the RUC had banned a march in Newry! It certainly took a long time for things to change.

The newspaper was an instant success. It came onto the streets in Dublin much earlier in the day than its competitors and was distributed to every street vendor and newsagent by young men riding specially adapted Vespa motor-scooters. The country edition, which went to the most remote parts of Ireland, to areas where evening newspapers were unknown, always left a section of the front-page blank. This section was then printed with local, national or international news at specially equipped stations in different regions.

In my first months with *Irish Press* newspapers I covered all sorts of assignments in news, social events and sports. My photographs were published in all three of the Group's newspapers. Most of my work was located in Dublin and the surrounding area; travel to the country, or to exotic places abroad, such as Liverpool for the Grand National, was a privilege reserved for the senior photographers. Colman Doyle usually covered the Grand National. One of his specialities was high-speed sequence photography. For this he used a special spring-driven camera capable of capturing up to ten single pictures in rapid succession. His photographs of the horses falling at Beecher's Brook were spectacular. He went to Liverpool on the morning of the races and, to ensure their publication the following morning, returned with his undeveloped photographs immediately afterwards. This was the extent of foreign travel for a photographer in those days.

My own first front-page scoop came on 31 March 1955. It concerned the custody case of a nine-year-old girl, Evelyn Doyle. A year earlier Evelyn had been put in the care of the Monastery of Our Lady of Charity of Refuge in Whitehall, Dublin. The previous Christmas her mother had deserted her father, an unemployed house painter, and run away with another man. The girl's father, Desmond Doyle, was devastated when his young children were taken away from him by the authorities. Eventually, having found work and a new home, he wanted to be reunited with his children, but as he had originally, albeit reluctantly, consented to the little girl being sent to the orphanage, when he sought her return he was faced with a legal battle involving the Minister for Education and the Attorney-General. He was fortunate to receive the support of some generous lawyers, who represented him at no cost.

At this stage the High Court had decreed that Evelyn should be returned to her father's care pending a final decision by the Supreme Court. Dominick Coyle, then a bright, determined young reporter working in the *Evening Press*, had used his sources to get information on the Court's decision ahead of any other journalist. Together we travelled to the north city convent with the child's overjoyed father. My camera was ready when Evelyn was released by the nuns and ran through the iron gates and straight into the outstretched arms of her waiting father. In the cold, clear sunlight of a March morning, it made a great photograph. (Forty-eight years later I attended the Dublin premiere of *Evelyn*, the film based on this true story, in the company of Pierce Brosnan who produced and starred in it. Outside the cinema a large group of fathers who had been separated from their children through marital breakdown demonstrated their recognition of the support the film had brought to their cause. They carried placards with the words: 'Thank you, Pierce'.)

That photograph of nine-year-old Evelyn Doyle and her jubilant father was published over three columns on the front page of the *Evening Press* under the headline, 'Together Again'. I received my first by-line: *Exclusive* Evening Press *Photo by Seamus Smith*. (The spelling of my name had not yet changed to Sheamus, of that more anon.) The excitement of seeing my name in print on the front page of a national newspaper for the first time was short-lived, however. My colleague, Mick Loftus, deflated my ecstasy with the cynical remark that 'It takes a lot of by-lines to fill a pint'. Perhaps that is why I never developed a taste for Guinness.

In the 1960s everyone worked a five-and-a-half- or six-day week. As a freelancer paid on a daily rate, I was always prepared to work the full seven days if necessary. I was eighteen years old when starting work in the *Evening Press*; I had in fact lied about my age and claimed to be twenty-one. In those days, to qualify for a full senior journalist's salary one had to be twenty-four years of age. However, because of the generosity of Bob Dillon, I received the full senior salary from the start; he told me it was because of the high standard of my work. Whatever the reason, I was very grateful and worked hard to prove him right.

*   *   *

A few months after the *Evening Press* was launched, Terry O'Sullivan was taken on to write a nightly column under the title 'Dubliners' Diary'. Terry, whose real name was Thomás O'Faolain, was a close friend of Douglas Gageby: they had worked together previously on the *Sunday Press* and had served in the Irish Army with Major Vivion de Valera, who was now Managing Editor of the Irish Press Group. Another army colleague and close friend of Terry's was Seamus Kelly, who wrote 'An Irishman's Diary', under the pseudonym Quidnunc, in *The Irish Times*. Terry had previously written a 'Roving Reporter' column called 'On the Road' for the *Sunday Press*. For that column he had traversed the thirty-two counties with photographer Joe Shakespeare or Colman Doyle, covering all sorts of stories—and sometimes creating their own. It was one of the elements that had contributed to the phenomenal success of the Sunday newspaper.

In much the same way, 'Dubliners' Diary' was designed to sell the new paper. The more functions we attended each evening and the more names Terry mentioned in his column, the greater were the sales the following day. Reminiscing on the twenty-fifth anniversary of the *Evening Press* in 1979, Terry O'Sullivan wrote:

> With a very young photographer named Sheamus Smith, the then editor gave us our head and we simply waded into the social life of Dublin with a reckless disregard for our own welfare. Every night we came back to the office with a catch which always included pictures of the most elegant and sometimes beautiful people.
>
> We brought the name of the young and, to a large extent, unknown newspaper into all walks of life, and we called to innumerable twenty-first birthday parties in private homes and of course to the now long-gone ballrooms. At these twenty-first birthday parties, I was usually invited into the kitchen and given a huge ball of malt.
>
> But it was on the big ballrooms that the brand new "Dubliners' Diary" really concentrated and of course, twenty-five years ago, the Metropole, Clery's, the Gresham and the Shelbourne had their own house bands, and every business had an "Annual Dance".
>
> It was quite normal for the "Diary" team to go to three or four dances in one night and to stand for the National Anthem in, say, the Gresham at 2 a.m. and again for the Anthem in the Shelbourne at 3 a.m. And then come back to the office here to develop and print and write. The real tests of stamina were the very big annual dances which went on till 4 a.m.
>
> Since we kept turning up, Sheamus Smith and I gradually began to be taken for granted and we had entrée everywhere and we went to everything from horse-meat butchers to the Galway Blazers Hunt Ball.
>
> I think that we both loathed the Horse Show Week Hunt Balls with their patronising and insufferable bad manners.

Terry was a gregarious man and he loved women. The great pride and joy of his life was his second daughter, Nuala, now the celebrated writer, Nuala O'Faolain. Even when she was just a schoolgirl, he was proud of her academic achievements. He never paid the same attention to his eldest daughter, Grainne, whom I liked very much, nor to his other children. Terry was always more interested in the welfare and happiness of his daughters than that of the boys in the family. But Nuala was special; he really cherished her. Nuala, and to a much lesser extent his younger daughter, Deirdre, were the only members of the family he ever spoke much about.

Our friendship was destined to be long and eventful, but it all started the first time I met Terry O, on a Sunday evening when I was assigned to go with him to a function in Balbriggan Golf Club. Terry always travelled in a large, chauffeur-driven American car. Like the limousine of today, this was the VIP transport of the time. That evening, his wife Katherine accompanied him. Terry and I had an instant rapport. I admired his obvious sophistication, style and talent for writing. I also suspected that, behind his self-confidence, he was a naturally shy person. He, I think, recognised this and also felt that I was easy to get along with. He admired my enthusiasm and liked the style and quality of my work. I was not aware then that this chance meeting of minds would have such a profound influence on my future life.

*   *   *

Working for 'Dubliners' Diary', our 'day' started at about 7 p.m. when Terry and the driver would pick me up at the office. We finished anytime between 1.30 a.m. and 3 a.m. the following morning. We attended eight to ten functions each night and as several were formal events, evening dress was required. I was given a daily allowance of 30 shillings to pay for the hire of the dress-suit. Terry O, who had a much larger salary than me, was expected to provide his own evening-wear. Having neither a desire to make frequent visits to rental outlets or an inclination to wear second-hand clothes, I made the obvious choice and bought a new dress-suit. This was a good business decision, as it happened. The weekly dry-cleaning and laundry bills were more than paid for by my expense-account allowance. In fact, I was showing a handsome profit; my dress-suit was earning as much as I was!

The other member of our happy little crew was the driver, and among them there were some unusual characters. Ryan's Car Hire, based in Hawkins Street, beside the Theatre Royal and just around the corner from the *Irish Press* building, provided our nightly transport. This car-hire company was a brave new enterprise founded by Dermot Ryan, a young entrepreneur just out of college. He had started the business with one rental car and expanded rapidly. When we were on the client list, it boasted the largest fleet of self-drive cars in the country plus a thriving chauffeured limousine section, mainly catering for wealthy American tourists. The general manager was a young Mayo man, Joe Malone, who would eventually become the Director General of the Irish Tourist Board.

Driving the night reporter team of 'Dubliners' Diary' was considered a real perk—one of the *recherché* jobs on offer. For this reason many of the regular drivers were bypassed and the assignment taken by junior executives of the company. Con Murphy, an impressive young man who later rose to become the Irish boss of Avis Car Hire, was one of these, as was Joe O'Reilly, a Cavan man with a tremendous sense of humour. Joe went on to found a large and very successful travel business in Cork City. During the summer periods, when the chauffeur business was at a premium, our driver was sometimes a university student working to pay or supplement his college fees. One of our medical student drivers was Maurice Neligan, who went on to enjoy an illustrious career as the country's most eminent cardiac surgeon, leading the team that performed the very first heart transplant operation in Ireland, in 1985.

*   *   *

It was a time of characters in Dublin. 'Bang-bang', whose fantasy was that he was a cowboy in a western movie, hopped on and off the rear platforms of the double-deck buses in the city centre, gunning down all and sundry with his imaginary six-shooter.

Terry O and I often went to the pubs around Grafton Street, such as Larry Tobin's in Duke Street, which was a favourite of Terry O's, the Bailey and Davy Byrne's in the same street or Neary's in Chatham Street. We frequently met the poet Patrick Kavanagh in those establishments. He sometimes drank with Brendan Behan—if they were on speaking terms and not banned from their favourite pubs at the same time. Few people took his work seriously then. He was dismissed as cantankerous and eccentric. As a person, Patrick Kavanagh was dishevelled, unkempt and dirty. He drank heavily and shouted at people in his raucous voice. He was always short of money. Observing the adulation heaped upon Kavanagh's memory during the celebrations of the centenary of his birth, I remembered with amusement the man I had met in the 1950s. Few of those attending the ceremony in his homeplace would have sought his company when he was alive. In fact, I doubt if any would have allowed him inside the front door of their house! The fine statue of Patrick Kavanagh, seated on a bench on the banks of the Grand Canal, is affectionately and aptly named by Dubliners, 'The Crank on the Bank'.

* * *

Shortly after I joined the *Evening Press* I met my first serious girlfriend, June Elmes. June was a secretary in the offices of the Dublin Gas Company on D'Olier Street. Every evening we would meet after she had finished work. Hand in hand we walked down Pearse Street and through Ringsend to her home in Sandymount. I would then return by bus to meet Terry O and set out on our night's adventures. I would pass June's house on my way home in the early hours of the morning. Sometimes there would be a letter left for me beside the empty milk bottles on the doorstep. Invariably it was addressed to 'Sheamus', a spelling that I adopted for the rest of my life.

Along with a group of friends, on Saturday nights June and I usually went to a dance in one of the local tennis or cricket clubs. The dancing lasted from 8 p.m. until midnight, and of course there was no bar. An independent young lady, June insisted on paying her way if we went on a day trip to visit somewhere like Butlin's Holiday Camp in Mosney,

Co. Meath, which was hugely popular back then. We went to our first dress dance with my friend Noel Barron and his girlfriend, Maureen Mulvihill. It was the Monkstown Park past-pupils' dance and it was held in the Top Hat Ballroom, Dún Laoghaire. Located on a corner of the main road near the Purty Kitchen pub and owned by a Scottish family of Italian extraction named Di Felice, the Top Hat was the newest dancing venue in Dublin. It featured a revolving stage that allowed the orchestra to disappear from the dancers while still playing. The incoming side of the stage would then reveal the supporting band. I remember that June wore a gorgeous, pink, net-covered, long dress that she had made herself. Elegant long white gloves completed her outfit. I had the dress-suit that was still earning its way thanks to the *Evening Press* expense account!

Those were wonderful days and nights. I was never happier than when I had June by my side and the band was playing. We had great fun together, and I dared to think that she might be the woman who was meant for me.

*   *   *

About this time, my mother decided to sell our house in Booterstown and move to London. My father's ability to run a bar successfully had been recognised by his employers, who owned a chain of pubs. They offered him a position as Manager of a fine premises in South Kensington, with good living accommodation over the bar. My mother would assist him in managing the business. My sister decided to move to London also. She found a good job in Harrods of Knightsbridge.

Once my family had left and the house had been sold, I was really on my own in the world for the first time. My initial problem of where to live was, thankfully, solved quite quickly. I was lucky enough to find exceptional living accommodation at the home of Miriam Woodbyrne, owner of one of Dublin's fashion modelling agencies. She rented a large redbrick Edwardian house on Morehampton Road, near the Grand Canal, and to subsidise her own elegant lifestyle she took in carefully selected boarders. I shared a large bedroom with her brother, Len, and a Cork-born civil servant in the Tax Department, Noel Lynch. Noel later became an actor and joined the Radio Éireann Players, while his older brother was the fine all-round actor and singer Joe Lynch, whose career in films and television was just about to take off. Another lodger was Ted Curtin, who came from Limerick. He was a close friend of the actor Richard Harris and was a remarkably good-looking young man who had great success with women.

I was now living near my workplace and frequently walked home in the early hours of the morning along Nassau Street, Merrion Square and Lower Mount Street. Along my route was Bernardo's, an Italian restaurant in Lincoln Place. It was owned by a great chef, Mario Gentile, who had left his homeland to take up a position in the Italian Ambassador's residence in Leixlip, Co. Kildare. Bernardo's, or Mario's as it was known by the regular customers, was one of the restaurants that remained open until the small hours of the morning, so I often stopped in for a meal after a hard night's work.

An advantage of working as a freelance and being on permanent night duty was that I was free to undertake other work during the day. I rented the top floor of No. 23 South Anne Street. There I set up a studio in the fairly large front room, using the two smaller rooms at the back as an office and dark-room. Miss Patterson, who owned the building, had a children's clothes shop on the ground floor. Rosemary Smith, a full-time fashion designer, occupied the first floor. Rosemary later left the fashion world and in a rather lateral career move became a professional rally driver.

My studio business was quite successful. I concentrated on general commercial and some wedding photography. The beauty of it was that having a regular salary from the *Evening Press* meant I could be selective about the work I undertook. I wasn't relying on the studio business to pay the bills, so I could take on the most enjoyable assignments and use them to perfect my photographing techniques.

Joe Malone used close friends like me to 'run-in' the new cars which were replaced in his company's fleet each year. One was encouraged to drive as much as possible. So now I was not only working hard, playing hard and earning decent money, I was also travelling in style!

*   *   *

As a freelance photographer, I also worked part-time for two British newspapers, the *Sunday People* and the *London Evening News*. Jim King, my former colleague in the Irish Press Group, became Irish correspondent of the *Sunday People*. Brendan Behan was contracted to write a weekly column in that paper, but his actual contributions were much less frequent. To help him out, Jim King would recycle material Brendan had written for the *Irish Press* some years previously. Every few weeks we did a photo session with Brendan on the banks of the Grand Canal near his home. This provided pictorial material for future editions of the paper. When the material was submitted on a weekly basis to the editorial offices in London, no one was any the wiser that the writing was not hot off Brendan's typewriter nor that the photographs had not been taken the day before.

One of my early assignments for the *London Evening News* was to photograph an up-and-coming young Irish rugby player, who had just been selected to play for his country. This was in January 1955 and Tony O'Reilly was a solicitor's apprentice working in the offices of Dublin solicitor Gerry Quinn, who, like himself, was a past pupil of Belvedere College. The match against France was scheduled for later that month, at Dublin's Lansdowne Road stadium. This was the first of many caps Tony O'Reilly would receive as one of Ireland's star players. We had never met before I went to his office in Clare Street that day. Tony was already well-known and respected as a rugby player with a promising future. Some weeks earlier I had photographed his father, Jack O'Reilly, a senior official in the Customs and Excise service, at a dress dance in the Gresham Hotel. Terry O'Sullivan suggested taking that picture because the man was Tony O'Reilly's father. Not having a particular interest in rugby, it was the first time I had heard the name.

Tony was a bright, friendly, very good-looking young man with a ready smile, infectious laugh and pleasant manner. His face was freckled and he had a fine mop of red hair. He was tall and well-built. It was obvious that he would be very attractive to women. After a few minutes our conversation revealed that we were almost exactly the same age: we were both nineteen at that time. In fact, Tony was six days older than me.

We spoke of our long-term ambitions. Tony said confidently that in time he would become a millionaire—a highly unlikely prospect, even for a successful lawyer, in a country where a respectable lifetime's earnings would amount to no more than £20,000. I was a bit surprised at his naïvety, but at the same time impressed by his dream. I had no such grand ambition. Mine was simply to lead an interesting life and get to know some rich people, even millionaires. I did not ever want to own a yacht or a mansion. An open-top sports car and invitations from well-heeled friends would do me nicely.

Whenever I visit Castlemartin, Tony's extensive estate in Co. Kildare, and see the O'Reillys' splendid collection of paintings, featuring works such as Claude Monet's magnificent picture of Rouen Cathedral, I reflect that by an ironic little twist, the beginnings of this collection lay in my home town of Ballaghaderreen. It was there that Tony O'Reilly bought his first original painting for £10. 'The Potato Digger' is an interpretation by local artist Michael Gara of Paul Henry's original work. When Tony called to the impoverished artist's studio shop to view his work, all was in darkness. He shone his car headlights through the window in order to see the painting. As he now enjoys his fine collection, Tony sometimes recalls that dark night in the west of Ireland when he acquired what he describes as 'a charming little picture'. As a child I knew Mikey Gara and his paintings well. He lived just down the street from us and designed sets for the infrequent plays in St Mary's Hall. In better times his father's grocery shop had specialised in selling bacon, as well as doubling up as one of the town's seventy-six bars.

Tony and I remained friends and we meet often. When, more than thirty years later, I reminded him of our youthful conversation, he was by then a millionaire many times over and living in the luxury of his Georgian mansion. I had led an interesting and exciting life in my own way. Tony's shrewd observation that we had indeed both achieved our ambitions was not quite true in my case. I had to wait until a year before retirement to get the open-top car—my first Saab convertible.

*   *   *

On the romantic front, my hitherto serene and innocent love life had taken a turn for the worse. June met a much better-looking young man, who lived in the fashionable suburb of Mount Merrion. After he invited her to lunch, they started going out together. I was devastated. Friends tried to console me, but without success. However, June's romance with the other young man was short-lived and we were reunited. But now other factors threatened our relationship. Young, beautiful and attractive to all the young men around, June was understandably becoming discontented with someone who worked unsocial hours. More ominously, her father had learned of Terry O'Sullivan's 'immorality' from a workmate and was concerned that such a bad influence on me might affect his daughter's future happiness. June's parents were good-living, God-fearing people and they wanted the same kind of life for their daughter. The final straw was her mother's view of my living situation: she decided that someone who was sharing with a group of young, unmarried people of opposite sexes in an unsupervised situation was definitely unsuitable for her only daughter. Reluctantly, June and I accepted the inevitable and went our separate ways.

June's mother was right, as it turned out. It was not long after our relationship ended that I lost my virginity. My collaborator was another lodger, an attractive lady some years older than myself. The incident did not take place in our 'house of immorality', however, but on the Merrion Strand, on the back seat of a Morris Cowley car, the property of Ryan's Car Hire. Joe Malone's generosity has a lot to answer for!

Chapter 5 ∿

LIFE WITH
TERRY O

'Dubliners' Diary' was thriving and Terry O and I were partnered indefinitely, which suited me perfectly. Apart from important social engagements, we were welcomed at sports fixtures, theatres or receptions to meet the many celebrities visiting Dublin. We also covered some out-of-town assignments, such as the Oyster Festival and the Galway Races. Terry and I had our own personal, complimentary passes from the Irish Turf Club—an accreditation normally reserved for specialist racing correspondents. It allowed us access to all areas on every racecourse in Ireland, including the owners' and trainers' enclosure. The Wexford Opera Festival, then under the direction of its founder, Dr Tom Walsh, was another of our annual jaunts. We always travelled there on the special 'opera train', dining in style on the way.

Another of our annual visits was to the Irish Kennel Club's Dog Show, which took place in the RDS, in Dublin, on St Patrick's Day. This event attracted an attendance out of all proportion to a love of or interest in the canine species. The reason was simple: the Dog Show was the only place in Ireland where you could legally get a drink on St Patrick's Day. Strange as it may seem today, all other licensed premises were closed on that day, so the opportunity to 'wet the shamrock' was limited in the saint's country of adoption. As a result, all sorts of people turned up at the Dog Show and the bars did a steady trade until closing time at 6 p.m. More than once an inebriated customer in the bar, who had incurred the wrath of the innocent show entrant he had just stepped on, was heard to exclaim, 'What a place to bring a bloody dog!'

One out-of-town trip took us to the legendary Ashford Castle in Cong, Co. Mayo, which at the time was owned and managed by Noel Huggard of the well-known hotel family. We spent the weekend with the American writer Paul Gallico, who was holed up there writing his new book. A tall, powerfully built man, Gallico was in his early sixties and an author of international repute. Before becoming a best-selling writer with the publication of *The Snow Goose* in 1941, he had been the film critic for the *New York Daily News*, later joining that newspaper's Sports Department. Gallico was a natural storyteller and he kept us entertained with reminiscences of his many adventures. As a sports reporter, he had been assigned to cover the training camp of the world heavyweight boxing champion Jack Dempsey before a title fight. He decided to ask Dempsey if he could spar with him, to get an idea of what it was like to be hit by the world champion. The result was spectacular: Paul was knocked out inside two minutes. But he had his story, and from there on his sports-writing career flourished.

No matter where we went or who we met, Terry O was unphased. He was a wonderful companion and his presence always ensured a lively time. Although we got on extremely well, we were very different. For someone from my background, Terry O's lifestyle was somewhat bohemian. He lived with his wife and family in Clontarf. He had an interest in sailing and was a member of the local yacht club, where he drank at the weekends. He rarely went sailing, although I do remember a splendid day we spent on a 21-foot yacht. The weather was sunny, with a strong wind, and we sailed from Dún Laoghaire into Dublin Bay. We were strictly guests, not part of the crew. I got some good pictures.

It was obvious from our first meeting that Terry's wife, Katherine, had a problem with alcohol. Their home was very badly kept because Katherine spent a great deal of time in the pub. On the few occasions I was invited inside the house, I politely declined any offer of hospitality; in any case, I was a strict teetotaller until well after my twenty-first birthday. While Terry drank a bottle of Power's Gold Label (his favourite whiskey) in the course of our evening's work, only twice in the four years we spent together did I see him even slightly intoxicated. On both occasions it was long after he had finished writing and put his column to bed. Terry was careful about the quality of his whiskey. At any event, if the whiskey was not up to his standard, he would manoeuvre himself into a position beside the nearest chrysanthemum or aspidistra plant and surreptitiously empty his glass into the pot. Although he was well-paid, being on the same salary as the paper's editor, Terry was always short of money, which was due to his generosity and his many responsibilities.

On our second meeting Terry O introduced me to his girlfriend. She had just left school and was about my own age, which made her about twenty-five years Terry O's junior. A very attractive and pleasant young lady, we got on well together. She lived in her home county of Meath, but most nights she accompanied us on our rounds. Whenever he mentioned his wife, Katherine, Terry always referred to her as 'a certain person'; he called his mistress 'Chickabiddy'. On the rare nights when we finished early, there would be time for a drink before the pubs closed. We usually went to The Silver Swan or The White Horse on Burgh Quay, or Mulligan's in Poolbeg Street, just behind the office. Terry would have a pint, while the lady drank a glass of Guinness, which was unusual at the time. I had my usual: pineapple juice. Afterwards, Terry returned to his desk to write his column and I would go to the dark-room to develop and print the photographs. The driver would take Terry's lady home to Co. Meath, although Terry sometimes accompanied her, returning quite late to finish his work.

*   *   *

One of the lasting friendships Terry O and I made was with Lord Killanin, or, to give him his full title, The Right Honourable Michael Morris MBE, 3rd Baron Killanin. He later became a global figure as President of the International Olympic Committee. Lord Killanin lived in Lansdowne Road, near the international rugby stadium, with his attractive wife, Sheila, and their family. His sons all became well-known: 'Mouse' Morris as a jockey and racehorse trainer; Redmond as a feature-film producer; and Johnny as a photographer. A distinctive-looking, tall, well-built man with a streak of grey in the centre of his dark hair, Lord Killanin had previously been a journalist and had worked as a political correspondent for the *Daily Mail* in London

My parents, Joseph C. (Joe) Smith and Margaret 'Dotie' Deery, on their wedding day in Dublin, 21 April 1930. *Photo: Stanley Studio*

Strandhill, Co. Sligo, in 1944. The start of a two-week holiday. *L to R*: Hackney driver, Bill Butler, grandmother, me, Auntie May, grandfather, mother, my sister Muriel and her friend, Kathleen Butler.

Just three months old with my mother and five-year-old sister, Muriel.

As a nine-year-old, I photographed my first sweetheart, Mary Keane.
Photo: Sheamus Smith

O'Connell Street, Dublin, in 1950. On my new racing bike with school friends Eric O'Toole and Paddy Freeney.

Aged seventeen, I went back to Ballaghaderreen on my newly acquired motor bike to see Mary Keane. *Photo: Sheamus Smith*

One of my first
'professional'
photographs.
American 'Rosary'
priest Fr Patrick
Peyton leads a rally
in Ballaghaderreen
in 1954.
Photo: Sheamus Smith

In Dublin's Gresham Hotel with world-
famous singer Frankie Laine, in 1953.

With my brand new Linhof press camera when I started working in the *Evening Press* in August 1954. *Photo: Colman Doyle*

This photograph of my first serious girlfriend, June Elmes, received a 'red star of merit'—the highest award in the 1955 Irish Professional Photographers' Exhibition. As a nineteen-year-old, I was by far the youngest entrant.
Photo: Sheamus Smith

My first dress dance with June, in the Top Hat Ballroom, Dún Laoghaire. *Photo:* Evening Press

In Kilkee with my first car, a Volkswagen Beetle, in 1956. *Photo: Colman Doyle*

The abortionist, Nurse Mamie Cadden, who shortly afterwards was convicted of murder.
Photo: Sheamus Smith

This exclusive picture was a front-page scoop in the *Evening Press* under the heading 'Together Again' on 31 March 1955. I received my first by-line. Nine-year-old Evelyn Doyle is reunited with her father after a spell in care. Forty-eight years later the movie, *Evelyn*, starring Pierce Brosnan, told their story.
Photo: Sheamus Smith

My favourite model and special friend, Kay Toal.
Photo: Sheamus Smith

Maureen O'Hara at her aunt's home in Blackrock, Co. Dublin, in 1955. She is wearing a silver-blue mink coat. When signing this picture at her eightieth birthday in 2000, Maureen told me that she remembered that day well.
Photo: Sheamus Smith

Teri's first St Patrick's Day! In Canada with our French–Canadian neighbours, Claude and Hélène Fournier. *Photo: Eamon Murphy*

In 1959 on a film course at the University of British Columbia in Vancouver. *Photo: Sheamus Smith*

Just after my first assignment, a football game in Vancouver's Empire Stadium, a few days after our arrival in Canada. *Photo: Basil King*

The school photograph of Teri that I carried with me during our ten-year separation.

With Angela and one-year-old Teri, 1960. Our first Christmas in Hollywood. *Photo: Sheamus Smith*

At San Francisco's Golden Gate Bridge while driving from Vancouver to Los Angeles. *Photo: Angela Smith*

before the war. Approachable and friendly, when we encountered him he was a writer and a director of many prestigious companies. Along with Hollywood film director John Ford, the architect Michael Scott and others, he formed an Irish film production company. He had earlier collaborated with John Ford when he directed *The Quiet Man*, which was filmed in Cong, Co. Mayo. Terry O called Lord Killanin by his first name, Michael, as did a rather self-assured young *Irish Times* reporter named Cathal O'Shannon, who knew him well from his days as a journalist. Although we met frequently over the years, I always addressed Lord Killanin by his title.

*   *   *

The stage door of the Theatre Royal was opposite the photographic department of the *Irish Press*. This theatre was a constant source of photographs. On an otherwise quiet night, it was easy to pop across the street and find one or more visiting stars whose picture would decorate the next day's column. People I met in the star dressing room included Nat King Cole, a gentle and charming man who smoked constantly; Johnnie Ray; Petula Clarke, then a very beautiful young woman who was accompanied by her mother; and Bill Haley, the rock and roll singer whose song 'Rock Around the Clock', originally recorded in 1954, is credited as introducing rock and roll music to white America. Incidentally, in 1955 the song was used as the title music on *The Blackboard Jungle*, a movie about juvenile delinquency.

Some of the other major stars I met during those years included Danny Kaye, who was one of the world's most beloved entertainers— his staccato delivery of tongue-twisting lyrics was his trademark. Another visitor was Cary Grant. At the time he was aged fifty-two and was a simple, tall man with an appealing smile. While all around him were enjoying the traditional hospitality of a star's reception, he ordered black tea and, sustained by this, made his rounds and signed autographs. I met James Cagney, an actor I had always admired, when he was attending a performance in the Gaiety Theatre. He was starring in *Shake Hands with the Devil*, then in production at Ardmore Studios with female lead Dana Wynter. In the film, which is set in Dublin in

1921, he plays a surgeon who is the secret leader of the IRA and who comes to take pleasure in violence as an end, rather than as a means.

Judy Garland played in the Theatre Royal for a week. The waif-like actress filled the large theatre every night. It was magical to photograph this talented artist during her stage performance. She had been making movies before I was born, and she was a true star. Her early films, with her frequent screen partner, Mickey Rooney, had been part of my introduction to cinema. She had entertained me during my schooldays when I saw her in the great MGM musicals, such as *Easter Parade* with Fred Astaire, *In the Good Old Summertime* with Van Johnson and one of my favourite character actors, S.Z. Zakall, and in *Summer Stock* with Gene Kelly, all of which I saw in the Adelphi cinema in Dún Laoghaire. I also remembered her magnificent dramatic vignette in Stanley Kramer's *Judgement at Nuremberg*, which brought her an Oscar nomination for Best Supporting Actress.

*   *   *

'Dubliners' Diary' wasn't all glitz and glamour—we also covered some really daft stories. One of the most memorable of these concerned a man who had built a boat in an upstairs bedroom, over his shop. The building of boats in bedrooms can lead to some remarkable results, as we found out when we helped the Cullens to get their creation out through the bedroom window and into the street below.

Paddy Cullen owned a small grocery shop, which still exists at 95 Lower Mount Street, and was one of those men who could not stop making things. A few months earlier he had begun building a full-size rowing boat in his bedroom. It became increasingly difficult for him to get into bed as his contraption grew and grew. Finally, after screwing up the last of more than 700 nuts and bolts that held the timber in place (ordinary white deal, by the way) it became necessary to launch the boat … into the street. It would not fit down the stairs, so Paddy took out the window. After that the only problem was how to lower the strange-looking, armour-plated thing from the first-floor window into the street below. There was no complicated hydraulic lifting equipment available then. When Terry O and I arrived on the scene, the bedroom looked as if a tidal-wave had hit it. The sight of a large row-boat between the bed and the dressing-table was the kind of thing you would not come across very often. The problem was to get it out of there and away somewhere out of sight before the Gardaí and the men in white coats arrived!

Six strong men solved that problem. They were the four Cullen brothers and two friends. The Cullens backed their car, which had a sun-roof, in underneath the window, thereby blocking all access to the still-open shop. From then on the only thing that was missing was the Marx Brothers. The astonished passers-by in Mount Street saw the stern of a boat appear out of a first-floor window, while three men stood on a plank laid across the sun-roof. The men at the bedroom end tied a rope around the bow. The men on the straining roof of the car, which was destined to let in more sunshine than was ever intended, began to accept the boat gradually as it slid out through the window. Dreadful language filled the evening air as the men struggled with the ungainly object. It only needed one thing to really make the story: if only the hand-brake on the car had slipped! But gradually the boat was fed, upside-down, onto the roof of the motor vehicle, while each and every one of the six men working on the project shouted and cursed and bellowed instructions to the rest. As a conclusion to this bizarre happening, the chap who was in charge of the stern of the boat as it left the hands of the bedroom squad and became entirely car-borne was pushed onto the front of the car's bonnet. The last anguished roar we heard from him was a wild-eyed request to the street in general as to where he was supposed to go from there. With more nuts and bolts in the extraordinary craft than in an ocean-liner, our suggestion was that when it was eventually launched into the waters of the nearby Grand Canal, it should be christened *Nuts*.

* * *

Terry O'Sullivan always seemed loath to go home after our work was finished. I imagined it was an unwillingness to depart from the unreality of our glamorous lifestyle and face again the awfulness of returning to a wife he did not love and the disarray of their badly kept home. Frequently, we opted to head to the Gresham Hotel instead, sometimes as late as 3.00 in the morning, to join manager Toddy O'Sullivan for a drink in a comfortable little alcove off the main lobby. There I would relax, drink my customary pineapple juice and listen to tales of the earlier adventures of my worldly companions.

Toddy told of how he ran away to sea at the age of fourteen and travelled the world before settling down and becoming a lowly hotel worker in London. Now a close personal friend and confidant of international celebrities, visiting royalty and some of the world's top people in other spheres, this elegant, stylish man had even less formal education than me. When he was relaxing, Terry O always drank bottled Guinness. My theory was that he drank his Power's Gold Label as a stimulant when on duty, but afterwards it had to be Guinness to unwind. Toddy, who never took a drink when on duty, would sometimes have a small whiskey or a cognac with us after work.

It was on one such visit to the Gresham, after Toddy had retired to his suite, that Terry told me of an extraordinary incident from his earlier life. It happened before his newspaper career, when he was working for the Tourist Board and trying to break into radio broad-casting. He was friendly with Eamonn Andrews, who was then making the transition from Radio Éireann to BBC Radio in London. Through Eamonn, Terry met a beautiful lady. They fell in love instantly and saw each other regularly. At this stage Terry was, of course, a young married man with two children. A crisis arose when it was discovered that his new love was pregnant. He considered leaving Ireland and going to live with her in London. Eamonn Andrews arranged for him to meet the legendary Grace Wyndham Goldie, who was in charge of 'talk programmes' on BBC Radio. (She later went on to become the first Head of News and Current Affairs at BBC-TV and remained a formidable figure in British broadcasting until her death at the age of eighty-six in 1986.) Mrs Wyndham Goldie was impressed by the young Irishman and offered him a job as a reporter in her department. It was an incredible opportunity to start a new life, have a successful career and settle down in London with the woman he loved and their expected child. Terry returned to Dublin and spent a few days considering what to do. Eventually, he came to the conclusion that, great as the opportunity was and while he would welcome a new life without his wife, Katherine, he could not leave his two children. After a tearful final meeting, the lovers parted. Utterly heartbroken, Terry went home; the lady remained in London.

Four years later, Terry received a letter from her. She had married an airline pilot and was living in Kuala Lumpur, the capital of Malaysia. She informed him that two weeks hence, along with her husband and only child, she would visit Dublin for one night. They would stay at the Gresham Hotel. In the final sentence of the letter she suggested that if Terry would like to see their daughter, he should be in the lobby of the hotel at a certain time on the day of their visit. Overjoyed at the prospect, he arrived in good time and placed himself in a strategic position with a view of the lobby. At exactly the pre-arranged time the lady, as stunningly beautiful as ever, walked through the lobby. She did not linger. Looking neither to her left nor her right, she carried on up the wide staircase. She was holding a beautiful raven-haired child by the hand. As he finished the story, Terry leaned over towards me. He touched the arm of my chair and said, 'That's the chair I was sitting in.' There were tears in his eyes. We never discussed the subject again.

*   *   *

Although my parents enjoyed managing the bar in London, the work was hard and after a few years it became too much for my father. He was unable to carry on running the business and reverted to being a barman again. Shortly before my twenty-first birthday, in 1957, my mother and sister returned to Dublin and set up home in a large apartment over another aunt's chemist shop on Home Farm Road in Drumcondra. My father remained in London and got a job as a barman in the original Irish pub, Mooney's on the Strand. He was home on a visit for my birthday, which we celebrated with a family dinner in the downstairs restaurant of the Metropole, one of the city's top eating places. The hoarse-voiced Peggy Dell, who sang to her own piano accompaniment, was then the permanent cabaret act. My parents' gift was the proverbial gold watch.

About this time, Miriam Woodbyrne decided to move to a smaller house in Ballsbridge. She was keen to reduce the number of boarders and only invited her brother, Len, Ted Curtin and me to join her. The excitement of communal living diminished. Like it is said of the actress Julie Andrews, I had become a virgin again before my twenty-first birthday!

*   *   *

Frank Hall was Terry O's opposite number in the *Evening Herald*. He came from Newry, Co. Down. Looking old for his age with heavily oiled, combed-back, long, black hair, he had an engaging personality and a rather striking appearance. He wrote his nightly column under the pseudonym Frank Lee. He did not have a driver, so was forced to confine his activity to attending press receptions, theatrical openings or interviewing celebrities. Unlike us, he never went to birthday parties, annual dinners or dress dances. As his events were mostly based in the city centre, he usually walked to the various venues. He did not have an accompanying photographer—the few pictures illustrating his column were usually provided by the regular news photographer covering the event.

Frank cut quite an impressive figure, moving briskly along the street wearing his distinctive long dark overcoat and black homburg hat. His girlfriend, Frankie Byrne, was constantly by his side as he made his rounds. Frankie, who had previously had a high profile job as an assistant in the Brazilian Embassy, now worked as a public relations officer with McConnell's advertising agency. Good-humoured, with an infectious laugh and lovely husky voice, Frankie was tall with jet-black hair. She was an attractive lady, who had a combination of the best physical features of Ava Gardner and Lauren Bacall, two of the greatest movie stars of the time.

As a relatively innocent and unsophisticated eighteen-year-old, I was intrigued that these otherwise apparently respectable married men had mistresses. Perhaps it was something to do with being a newspaper columnist? Seamus Kelly, who was the *Irish Times'* Quidnunc, had an extra lady in his life, too. A cantankerous man, Seamus got on well with Terry O'Sullivan. They shared the common interest of having served together in the army during the Emergency. Seamus Kelly took his former army service seriously and returned for annual training each summer. He seemed to delight in swaggering into the Red Bank, a fashionable restaurant and bar on D'Olier Street, wearing his officer's uniform. He cultivated an air of superiority and rarely spoke to the lower orders, such as photographers, but for some reason he made an exception in my case. Seamus had played the ship's mate in John Huston's film *Moby Dick*, which was shot on location in Cobh, Co. Cork. He was undoubtedly cast because of his weatherbeaten face and rasping voice.

Frankie Byrne, elegant, charming and sophisticated, exuded self-confidence and was admired by all who crossed her path. She was obviously as much in love with Frank Hall as he appeared to be with her. Her client base, personal contacts and well-connected friends meant she was a tremendous help to Frank. She had been at the heart of Dublin's privileged and influential social set for years. As a social columnist, Frank was the new boy on the block. So Frankie introduced him to the right people and generally marked his card at the functions they attended. Many of these were functions arranged by Frankie on behalf of her agency. Apart from State-owned companies like the ESB, which had its own PR officer, a man named Michael Colley, Frankie Byrne was probably the first person to offer a professional public relations service in the private sector. Her organisational skills were exceptional. An invitation printed on McConnell's notepaper was enthusiastically received in the certain knowledge that, in addition to generous hospitality, an interesting story and photographs would result. I could not know then that Frank Hall and Frankie Byrne would play such an important part in my later life.

Shortly after our first meeting, Frankie became one of my close personal friends, as did her younger sister, Esther. My friendship with both Frankie and Esther lasted until they died. When we first met, I had no inkling that within six years I would be working with Frank Hall in the newly established Telefís Éireann, or that a quarter-of-a-century later I would succeed him as Ireland's Official Film Censor.

More than thirty years after their love affair started, Frank left Frankie for a young lady less than half her age. That relationship lasted until his death. It was years later that Frankie confirmed something I had always suspected: the father of her daughter, who was born in 1956, was Frank Hall. The event had been kept secret from all but her sister, Esther, and another close friend and colleague, Mildred O'Brien. As Frankie was a large, statuesque lady, concealing her pregnancy was not difficult. The baby, named Valerie, had been put up for adoption. Frankie never recovered from her loss. Valerie had a very happy childhood with her adoptive parents and later, after she herself was married, was reunited with her natural mother. Frankie was delighted and immensely proud of her daughter. At first she pretended to everyone, including Valerie, that the father was an American journalist with whom she had had a brief liaison before he returned to the US, where he died in a car crash. That story was an attempt to hide the truth—of love and of loss—from everyone. Outwardly, Frankie always appeared self-assured and self-confident, but she was in fact deeply insecure. Her wounding betrayal by Frank and his new affair with a much younger woman had a profound effect on her life.

In 1993 Frankie died of Alzheimer's disease at the age of seventy-two. Frank Hall was unable to attend her funeral in Donnybrook Church because he had a head cold. It was a tribute to a very special lady that the large church was crowded beyond its doors with loyal friends, journalists, press photographers, television personalities, theatre people, politicians, former clients and most of the residents of Donnybrook village, who had grown to know and love Frankie during the years she lived there. Frankie Byrne's last journey on this earth epitomised the style in which she had lived: the Garda Commissioner assigned a motorcycle escort to accompany her coffin to the cemetery. Preceded by police sirens, the hearse taking Frankie's body to its final resting place and the funeral cortège that followed drove at speed through her beloved Donnybrook. It was a scene that Frankie Byrne would have enjoyed. Her grieving friends knew her real worth.

*   *   *

Whenever Terry O was away, either on a short holiday or through illness, the column was written by a stand-in journalist. The most regular of these was Des Moore, a debonair, silver-haired, easy-going man. An expert in local history, Des normally wrote vignettes of Dublin or other places under the title 'Yesterday' for the paper. He had a delightful sense of humour and was a close friend of both Douglas Gageby and Terry O. Des and I got on well and liked working together. Another 'stand-in' was James Downey, who later became a respected political commentator with *The Irish Times* and *Irish Independent*. Jim was somewhat lacking in humour and took himself very seriously. He became unpopular with some of the other late-night photographers when he discontinued the practice, initiated by Terry, of the driver taking them home after work. The driver, who was normally on duty until Terry was ready to leave, was always happy to do this, but the procedure was not acceptable to his new temporary boss. Of course, his instructions were heard but not heeded. In their attempts to flout his law and avoid discovery, large men were obliged to climb through the small, high window of the photo department at the back of the building to reach the waiting car on the street below.

Although he did not realise it at the time, Jim Downey had a profound influence on my life. One evening we attended a reception together to launch a new agency for Bollinger champagne. It was held in a wine-merchant's cellar that ran under the Olympia Theatre in Dame Street. The host was Tom Noonan, a large, gracious man who was well-known to me and Terry O. When he offered us a glass of the vintage champagne, Jim Downey snapped, 'Sheamus doesn't drink'. Infuriated, I immediately made it clear that I did indeed drink and accepted the proffered glass. In that split-second I eschewed my signature drink of pineapple juice for evermore. It was a good decision. Since then my favourite drink has been champagne. I have been indebted to James Downey for the best part of my life!

Sometimes if Terry wanted to leave early, I would finish writing the column for him. By this stage I was familiar with his style and no one was ever the wiser. Once when Terry O was laid low with 'flu, the editor decided that instead of assigning a replacement to write the column, he would let me fill the page with pictures. I would have to write more comprehensive captions, which would describe the particular event attended. This new arrangement was an interesting challenge. It turned out to be successful, and I continued doing the job, with the assistance and support of the driver—usually Maurice Neligan—until Terry recovered. We had a great time. Thereafter, whenever Terry was indisposed or wanted a night off, the responsibility of filling the 'Dubliners' Diary' column was left to me.

*   *   *

After enjoying the benefits of Joe Malone's generosity for almost two years, I decided it was high time to get my own car. Through Leslie Somers, an executive in Ryan's Car Hire, I purchased a one-year-old Volkswagen Beetle. Dark green in colour with a registration number KRI 932, it was a delight to own. With a nearly-new car, Noel Barron and I cut a much greater dash on our trips to Dún Laoghaire than in our motorcycle days. Afterwards, as a result of some irregular accounting practices with his employer, to which he owned up in a gentlemanly manner, Leslie Somers spent a few months in Mountjoy Jail. I visited him there and collected him on his release. I told my mother that I had invited a friend home for dinner that evening. We were just seated at the table when, to my embarrassment, my mother asked Leslie if he too knew my friend who was in jail!

*   *   *

Terry O'Sullivan and I once called to the Catholic Archbishop of Dublin, John Charles McQuaid, at his palace in Drumcondra. He was a man who ran his diocese with an iron fist and was much feared by the members of his Church. He would not allow Catholics to attend the 'Protestant' university of Trinity College. Known as an austere, authoritarian figure, he was surprisingly friendly towards us in person. He chatted freely to Terry and showed a great interest in my German-made Linhof camera. He told me that his principal hobby was photography and that he used a 35 mm Leica camera. This would have been a professional, rather than an amateur, standard at that time. As always, he was dressed in a long colourful purple soutane and purple skull cap, which was never removed in public. His remarkably small feet were clad in black velvet shoes embroidered with an ornate design. To me they looked like bedroom slippers. A vain man, he seemed to enjoy posing for photographs.

One summer evening before the General Election of 1957, Terry O and I went to meet a young man in a semi-detached house in the northside Dublin suburb of Marino. His election office was in the small front room that would normally be used as the family's drawing room. He had previously been a member of Dublin City Council, but was now concentrating all his energy towards becoming a TD for the constituency of Dublin North-East. He had failed to achieve this in the General Election of 1954 and again in the by-election in 1956. Well-dressed, self-confident, friendly and personable, he showed no sign of arrogance. Terry was very impressed and assured me that this was a young man to watch as he was 'going places'. His name was Charles J. Haughey. Terry was a strong supporter of Fianna Fáil and accepted everything that de Valera and his party stood for. He continued to be an admirer and supporter of Charlie Haughey, in whose constituency he lived.

*　　*　　*

Sometimes when I required a night off, I would work a normal day duty as a news photographer. On one such day I was sent to get a picture of Nurse Cadden, who lived in Hume Street. A qualified nurse who had worked in England, she was an American citizen. She had acquired a criminal record after being convicted of carrying out an abortion. This was not the type of assignment I liked. Nurse Cadden was now the chief suspect in a murder case as a few days earlier the body of a woman who had died while undergoing an abortion had been found near her home by a milkman doing his early morning deliveries. When I called to the upstairs flat in Hume Street, to my surprise I was not only admitted but welcomed into her home by Nurse Cadden. It was a bizarre experience. She wore a grey fur coat. The kitchen and living room area of the apartment were cluttered and dirty. She had no objection to being photographed and moved around doing normal housekeeping chores in her fur coat. She had been visited by the Gardaí and knew that she was the prime suspect. I took several pictures while she discussed the police, for whom she had little respect, and protested her innocence. She was a strange individual. I declined the tea she offered. The last picture I took of Nurse Cadden was as she opened her large handbag, took out a small Baby Power whiskey and poured it into her tea-cup. She was later convicted of murder and died while serving a life sentence in prison.

*　　*　　*

Early one summer morning in 1956, Colman Doyle, Paddy Barron and I set off in my car for Co. Clare. There John Ford, the famous Hollywood director, was making his second Irish film, *Three Leaves of a Shamrock*. It was later released under the title *The Rising of the Moon*. Produced by Lord Killanin, the film was directed by Ford, who had made *The Quiet Man* four years earlier in Cong, Co. Mayo. The cast, mainly comprising Abbey Theatre players, was headed by Cyril Cusack and Eileen Crowe and included Donal Donnelly, Jimmy O'Dea, Maureen Potter and Noel Purcell. The film was a trilogy based on the works of Irish writers Frank O'Connor, Michael McHugh and Lady Gregory. The particular story they were shooting on the day of our visit was 'A Minute's Wait', an amusing account of a Dublin-bound train's delay at the local station. My photograph of John Ford, clad in a white bawneen jacket and wearing his distinctive black eye-patch, relaxing in the director's chair, was published widely.

*　　*　　*

In the mid-1950s, apart from cafés and chip-shops, there were a number of good late-night restaurants in Dublin. These included the Paradiso in Westmoreland Street, Bernardo's in Lincoln Place, both of which were well-established, and a newcomer, Alfredo's, hidden in the unfashionable back-street of Mary's Abbey, near Capel Street, on the north side of the Liffey. The Paradiso and Bernardo's always did good business with the professional classes, politicians and late workers, such as actors, actresses and theatre folk, who went after their shows. Two people I often met in these restaurants were the very well-known stage actress Maureen Toal, an older sister of the model Kay, whom I so much admired, and her husband, Milo O'Shea, who then worked primarily as a mime artist in cabaret or one-man shows. Then a young actor, Milo had not yet become the international star of stage and screen he would later be; he was frequently referred to as 'Maureen Toal's husband'.

Drinking alcohol after pub closing time was against the law, but that did not bother either the customers or the proprietors of Dublin's late-night restaurants. Apart from such restaurants, there were also opportunities to drink after the official closing times in places such as Groom's Hotel. This comfortable late-night rendezvous was located opposite the Gate Theatre and owned by Joe Groom and his wife, Patty. The liquor licensing law allowed hotel residents to drink without any restrictions. The Grooms were strong supporters of Fianna Fáil and most of their after-hours drinking clientele were made up of government ministers and senior politicians. In a way, Groom's Hotel was the most sought after and the most privileged club in town. It was a hotel and there were bedrooms, but if you were allowed in about midnight it was obvious that all the bedrooms were occupied—indeed by about four to each room! During a Fianna Fáil Árd Fheis the bedroom occupation rose to something like 1000 per cent. Here at night you might see young men like John Hume in earnest conversation with Brian Lenihan or Charlie Haughey.

Alfredo's restaurant was by far the most exclusive and the most expensive in town. The owner, a middle-aged, slightly eccentric and kind-hearted Italian, was more famous for the prices he charged than for his culinary expertise, although he was a capable chef all the same. It was the haunt of the really high-flyers, in much the same way as Sean Kinsella's Mirabeau Restaurant would be years later. Alfredo's was the restaurant favoured by visiting celebrities. The lighting was dim and the atmosphere discreet—perfect for those wishing to keep a low profile, for couples engaging in illicit love affairs and for members of the diplomatic corps. Alfredo had an assistant named Elizabeth, who hailed from one of Dublin's less fashionable suburbs. Elizabeth dressed in a chef's tall white hat, with a stiff, sparkling white chef's garment that almost touched the floor. Her feet were never visible nor did they make a sound, which gave the impression that she moved about on casters. Like Sean Kinsella, Alfredo was always keen to obtain publicity through the social columns of the newspapers. He would frequently telephone me or Terry to enlighten us of any special guests. I remember meeting and photographing there the movie star Tyrone Power, then at the height of his fame. A few years later, it was in Alfredo's that Tony O'Reilly introduced me to his Australian fiancée, Susan Cameron.

Terry O and I were always welcome to dine at Alfredo's. When one asked for the bill, Alfredo's reply was forever the same, 'Not bill tonight,' he would say and, pointing at the host of some larger table, would add, 'Him pay'. For Alfredo's regular guests, money was never a problem.

Possibly because his restaurant remained open and served wine later than his competitors or possibly because he was new in town, Alfredo was more careful about screening his patrons. No one was admitted without a prior reservation. Entrance to the restaurant was through a solid wooden door, bolted securely on the inside. At eye-level a sliding hatch in the door enabled Alfredo to inspect the customers before allowing them to enter. One night the famous British jockey Sir Gordon Richards arrived at the door with an equally vertically challenged friend. Opening the sliding hatch in response to their knock, Alfredo could not see anyone. That was one celebrity who returned to his hotel hungry!

I got to know Alfredo well and sometimes helped him to organise his accounts, which were in a permanent state of disarray. His prestigious clientele never knew of his enormous generosity. Alfredo gave a Christmas party for the poor children of the area every year. He also looked after and provided meals for the badly paid junior doctors in the nearby Jervis Street Hospital. When the restaurant failed in the mid-1960s and Alfredo's remaining money was seized by his only daughter, who had little regard for him, he developed cancer and was left destitute in his native Italy. Upon learning of his plight, the grateful men who had been the impoverished junior doctors of Jervis Street Hospital, and were now prosperous and well-established consultants, brought Alfredo back to Dublin. He was booked into the Shelbourne Hotel, where he lived in luxury and comfort, with the best medical attention, until his death.

*   *   *

Basil King, my colleague at the *Evening Press*, met and fell madly in love with a very beautiful young woman who came from Co. Galway. Her name was Lena Keavney and she was a receptionist in Dublin's most exclusive hotel, The Russell on St Stephen's Green. Basil was ambitious for himself and his beloved Lena. He cared deeply about Ireland, but was not content to face a future as a press photographer earning £500 a year. He decided to emigrate to Canada, where he was determined to make a fresh start and then ask Lena to marry him. At his farewell party, Basil said that if there were ever a prospect of earning an annual salary of £1,000 in Ireland, he would never leave.

Arriving in Canada by boat, Basil then travelled cross-country by train. He settled briefly in Uranium City, in north-western Saskatchewan, where he worked in a mine and in the local post office before moving on to Edmonton in Alberta. There he found work as a photographer with the *Edmonton Journal*. After a short time Basil moved further west and settled in British Columbia. A gifted writer, his wonderfully descriptive letters of his travels across the vast expanse of Canada were inspirational. Mostly these letters were hilarious as he recounted his adventures, but sometimes they had a certain poignancy about them. It was not easy at first for a well-educated young man who came from a comfortable home to suffer the hardship of life alone in a sometimes unfriendly atmosphere. But within a relatively short time of leaving Ireland, Basil had found his feet in the city of New Westminster, south-east of Vancouver. There he took over the photographic department of the only daily newspaper, *The British Columbian*. A short time afterwards Lena, who was now officially his fiancée, joined him. They were married and settled down to their new life in the New World. I had no idea then that their upheaval foreshadowed a new chapter in my own life.

Chapter 6 ~

MARRIAGE AND MIGRATION

I was twenty-two years old when I met Angela Whyte, who was destined to become my wife. She had qualified as a barrister, but did not practise. She worked for Ryan's Car Hire and managed the only car-hire desk at Dublin Airport. Our first date was on a Sunday evening. I went into Ryan's Car Hire head office that morning in the hopes of meeting another girl to whom I was attracted. I had two tickets for the Savoy cinema that night. Sunday-night cinema tickets were like gold-dust because they were unavailable to the ordinary person. All the seats were booked in advance by ticket-touts, who bought them in large quantities early in the week. They then sold their tickets at black-market prices outside the cinemas on the Sunday evening. But newspaper people had an inside track. We could always get the 'house-seats', which were the best in the cinema. These were held back by management and were usually complimentary. It was a surefire way to impress the girls!

That Sunday morning, Angela was the only person on duty; the airport desk did not operate at the weekends. We had met previously and I considered her something of a snob. But I had the tickets, so I took a chance on asking her out. To my surprise, she accepted. Most of the important events in my life are associated with a particular film I saw at the time, and this was no exception. On our first date it was a low-budget, black-and-white British picture, *The Smallest Show on Earth*. It was produced by Michael Relph and directed by Basil Dearden, both of whom Ronnie Drew and I had met when we mitched from school to visit the set of *The Gentle Gunman* in the Dublin Mountains.

Angela and I enjoyed our first evening together and our relationship blossomed thereafter. Soon we were seeing each other every day. Angela was the middle of three sisters. She was seven years older than me. Her parents lived on a farm in Co. Westmeath. Her father, a lovely man, had a *laissez-faire* attitude to life. He did not believe in over-extending himself on the land. Her mother was one of the Maguires, a well-off Dublin family who lived in Bullock Castle, overlooking the sea at Dalkey. She had snobbish tendencies. Her original attitude toward her daughter's new boyfriend was less than enthusiastic: a photographer was not looked upon as the greatest potential son-in-law. Angela's mother's attitude towards me changed dramatically, however, when Princess Margaret became engaged to the British society photographer, Anthony Armstrong-Jones. Photographers suddenly took a giant leap up the social scale … and in her estimation! After their marriage, Angela's parents had emmigrated to America and settled in Los Angeles, where Angela was born and therefore became a US citizen. Her father was a chauffeur for film director Sam Wood, who is best remembered for his films *Goodbye Mr. Chips*, *For Whom the Bell Tolls* and the Marx Brothers' *A Night at the Opera*.

Angela was attractive rather than beautiful. She had a good figure, dressed fashionably and had an elegant gait. Her family returned to Ireland when Angela was still a young child. She was educated at a boarding school in Monaghan and later studied for the Bar, a decision possibly influenced by the fact that her uncle (aunt's husband), Sir Gerard Howe, was Lord Chief Justice of Hong Kong.

She frequently joined Terry O'Sullivan and me on our social rounds, and sometimes she came away on our country trips. We spent a few days together in Ashford Castle as a guest of the owner, Noel Huggard, and also stayed in Kruger's guesthouse in Dunquin, on the Dingle Peninsula. Kruger was an old friend of Terry's and I had met him several times. His establishment had no telephone, so before we went there Terry sent him a telegram which read, 'Sheamus Smith arriving tomorrow with decoration'!

Kruger Kavanagh was a tall, muscular, handsome Kerryman. He had immense charm, a constant twinkle in his eye and a great way with women of all ages. He was much older than us. His diminutive wife, Cáit, only spoke Irish. Kruger's pub and guesthouse was perched near the cliffs in the tiny village of Dunquin. The breathtaking views included the nearby Blasket Islands. Before his marriage Kruger, who came from the area, had gone to America. There he had worked as an advance publicity agent for the orchestra of the well-known Irish-born composer, Victor Herbert, which toured America and Canada. Victor Herbert is credited as the first composer to write a fully original score for a film when, in 1916, he composed the music for the silent epic, *The Fall of a Nation*.

A long, single-storey building, Kruger's consisted of a pub at one end with guest rooms attached. These were like the carriages of a train. The best accommodation was the bedroom nearest the bar, which was assigned to the most important guest, who retained possession until someone more worthy arrived. The new guest then moved in while the previous occupant was shifted towards the back of the 'train'. I was once evicted in favour of a visiting American and found myself in a room with giant mushrooms flourishing on the damp, badly plastered walls. The pub had done a roaring trade for many years without the benefit of a publican's licence. An ingenious system of signalling was in place to alert Kruger of an imminent raid by the Gardaí, who had to travel from Dingle. Invariably, when the forces of the law arrived to raid Kruger's, the barrels, bottles and all visible evidence of illegal drinking were hidden outside the premises.

The resident's lounge, which was used for late-night drinking, was a cold, damp, sparsely furnished room with wooden chairs and a small, inadequate fireplace. The main picture over the mantelpiece was the traditional representation of the Sacred Heart—a long-haired adult Jesus with outstretched hands. The predominant part of the picture was the flaming heart. Surrounding the picture were many photographs of celebrities whom Kruger had met on his American travels, or who had visited his hostelry. All were autographed with generous dedications to Kruger. The story was told of how Brendan Behan, after a certain amount of drink, had removed the picture of the Sacred Heart from its frame and added the inscription, 'To Kruger from Jesus Christ', before carefully reframing the image and returning it to the wall.

Irish was the spoken language of the house. For me, it was a revelation to hear people use Irish as a living language in this practical way. Kruger's was a popular place for those who wanted to improve their knowledge of the Irish language in a friendly, if slightly primitive, atmosphere. I once met a young bus conductor from Liverpool there. He had no Irish connection whatsoever, but spoke the language he had learned in Kruger's much better than I ever could. My own respect for and liking of Irish grew and I learnt to speak the language better during my few brief visits to Kruger's than I had ever done at school.

*   *   *

It was just after my twenty-second birthday that we discovered Angela was pregnant. We were upset, confused, uncertain and downright scared of what the future might hold. After discussing the options available, we decided to become engaged. I was unhappy with the situation, but there seemed to be no alternative. Although I loved and cared about Angela and our future child, I did not really want to marry at that time. But within a few months, I was a husband and expectant father. The ceremony was performed by a kindly priest, Fr John Moloney, and it took place in the early hours of a July morning in Dalkey's Catholic Church. 'Shotgun' weddings were invariably hush-hush affairs that took place early in the morning, when few people were around. The best man was my friend, Colman Doyle. His wife Eileen was matron of honour. Angela wore a bright green linen outfit and I a dark lounge suit bought for the occasion from Paddy Barron's brother, Sean, then a sales assistant in Bests, men's outfitters in O'Connell Street.

After the ceremony we went to Colman and Eileen's flat in Dalkey. There we enjoyed a full Irish breakfast, which Eileen cooked and served up to us. Later in the day the four of us had lunch in the Glenview Hotel, overlooking the Glen O' The Downs in Co. Wicklow. That evening, Angela went to work on a late duty in Ryan's Car Hire office, while I joined Terry O for our usual nightly routine. Terry was aware of the situation, of course, but it was only when I reached the office that I told him about the wedding. When we finished work he took me to a famous night-spot, the Green Tureen on Harcourt Street. There the two of us were joined by the owner, Belfast man Cecil Frew. We had champagne, drinking from the flat glasses fashionable at the time. Reluctantly, I returned to Angela's flat in Pembroke Road, Ballsbridge. It was our wedding night, but I felt that, like Terry, I too might be unhappily married. My own family was unaware of my changed circumstances, although Angela's parents knew the score. They understood and we sometimes spent a night or two in their fine but somewhat run-down home, Clonicavant House, outside Killucan in Co. Westmeath. Angela's sisters, Moyra and Paddy, were also understanding and supportive.

Alongside the decision to go ahead with our marriage, we also agreed to emigrate. This would achieve two objectives: first, it would take us away from Dublin and out of the public gaze for some time; secondly, it was probably my last or only chance to realise my dream of reaching Hollywood. A television service for Ireland was becoming increasingly likely, so if my ambition was to work in that medium, this was an opportune time to seek experience abroad.

Our first thought was to contact Basil King and check out the possibilities of employment in Vancouver. Basil and Lena, who had just given birth to their first daughter, Lorraine, were now well established there. The plan was to follow in their footsteps and gain a foothold on the North American continent before eventually moving to the United States. Basil's reaction was neither positive nor encouraging: he replied by telegram, informing us of a series of strikes in the province of British Columbia and advising us to try another part of Canada. At that point the die was cast, however, and Vancouver was our destination. I sold the goodwill of the business, my Linhof camera and all the studio equipment to Tony O'Malley, the man who had been instrumental in starting me out on my photographic career. The wheel had turned full circle. Tony had decided to leave Independent Newspapers and work as a freelance photographer. Now I was doing *him* a favour.

Angela and I packed our belongings and prepared to sail for our new home in the New World. A few days before we left, my colleagues in the *Irish Press* held a send-off party in the White Horse pub, beside the office. The most practical present we received was a large, expanding suitcase. It was the gift of Dominick Coyle and it served us well in our travels over many years. Our main item of luggage was a large cabin trunk given to us by my old school friend, Noel Barron. He was now working in Murray's Car Hire, the other large car rental company in

Dublin. Noel had received the trunk as a gratuity from a visiting American. It too served us well, doubling as a cradle when our daughter had outgrown the bedroom drawer that accommodated her for the first few weeks of her life! The most treasured present I received was a Waterford Glass piece from Kay Toal. The day before our departure we met very briefly outside the Mansion House, where Kay was modelling in a fashion show. She had become a true and trusted friend; saying goodbye to her was not easy.

The day before our departure, Terry O'Sullivan had written a valedictory piece in 'Dubliner's Diary' under the heading, 'Good Luck'. It read:

> Here with regret I say goodbye and good luck to a young man who, for almost four years, was the other half and many times the better half of this column, for photographer Sheamus Smith leaves for Canada tomorrow, where, with his wife, he goes to live in Vancouver.
>
> The best tribute I can pay this very young and very successful photographer is that in more than one thousand nights and several hundred days of work on 'Dubliners' Diary' he acquired a reputation for an unshakable reliability that was remarkable.
>
> Many readers and all his colleagues here will join with me in wishing Sheamus and his wife Angela every success in the New World.

Reading this in the paper was the first indication my family had of our marriage. It was a great shock to my mother, who I suspect knew the reasons for the secret wedding. She was heartbroken that her son was leaving Ireland, possibly never to return. After our marriage I continued to live with my mother in the apartment in Drumcondra. As my work often took me away from home, spending an occasional night with Angela did not arouse suspicion as to my circumstances. My family knew that we were engaged and expected us, like Basil and Lena King, to marry in Canada.

In early September 1958 we set sail for Canada. On the evening of our departure, Terry O brought us to the Liverpool boat in the 'Dubliners' Diary' car. As he shook hands, he gave me a big hug. For me it was a moment of great sorrow. Terry kissed Angela passionately and we climbed the gangway onto the ship. Colman Doyle also came to the quayside to say goodbye. He brought a large brown envelope, which contained some excellent fashion photographs taken by him. Handing it to me, he mentioned that he thought the portfolio of my work might be a little thin on good fashion pictures and felt that this contribution might help. It was a lovely thought. I carefully placed the envelope on the top shelf of the wardrobe in the ship's cabin. Next morning, I forgot to retrieve it. I never had the heart to tell Colman that his generous gesture was no help to me. Those pictures may have sailed many times between Dublin and Liverpool before the envelope was finally discovered.

*   *   *

In Liverpool, the next morning, we boarded a pristine white ocean-liner, the *Empress of England*. That afternoon she sailed for Greenock, in Scotland, and thence to Quebec, on Canada's western shore. There we docked for a day before moving to Montreal. I had twice visited the giant cruise-liner the *Coronia* when it called at Dún Laoghaire while cruising in Europe, but this was my first time to travel on such a large ship. Crossing the Atlantic in autumn was another adventure. Angela had made the crossing as a child when her family returned from California, where she was born, but she had no memory of the experience. The standard of food, accommodation and facilities on the vessel was outstanding. We treated the voyage as our honeymoon. The outside cabin on an upper deck had a large double bed, two huge portholes, en suite bathroom and a comfortable sitting area. The ship's restaurant resembled that of a top-class luxury hotel. The varied menus were a gourmet's delight and included items such as fillet steak for breakfast. Bouillon was served on deck each morning, with afternoon tea at 4 p.m. in the same place. The wine list was extensive and prices duty-free, so we could afford to indulge ourselves each evening.

The journey took a week and was pleasant, except when we encountered rough sea for about twenty-four hours. Then the large ship was tossed about like a cork in waves the size of which I had never imagined could exist. After five days at sea our first sight of land was the island of Belle Isle, off the east coast of Newfoundland. Passing that we sailed through the Gulf of St Lawrence and into the St Lawrence River, with the province of Quebec on the starboard side and those of New Brunswick and Nova Scotia to our left.

We docked in Quebec, where there was time enough to go ashore. Standing high on a promontory overlooking the mighty St Lawrence River is the magnificent Château Frontenac; this was our first impression of Canada. We went on foot to visit this huge, medieval-looking hotel, which is located in the old part of the city. It was there that the three world leaders, Stalin, Roosevelt and Churchill, met for talks following the ending of the Second World War. The classic photograph displayed in the lobby of all three seated together was taken on the adjacent Terrasse Dufferin. We had tea in the vast hotel lounge before continuing our walk through the winding streets and alleys of Old Quebec.

The next leg took us to Montreal: the point of final disembarkation. There was no time to explore the city before we boarded the Canadian Pacific Railway train, which would take us, over the next seven days and six nights, to our new home in British Columbia. The ultra-modern train had an observation lounge, a fine dining car and excellent sleeping accommodation. We were welcomed on board by an enormous black gentleman in uniform, complete with the small peaked cap worn by railway conductors in the movies. A kind, genial person, he made a particular fuss of us. It was one of the first differences I noticed from home. In the Dublin of the 1950s, the few black people one met were invariably medical students or recently qualified doctors. Apart from Charlie, the car-parking attendant outside the Gresham Hotel, who was one of the city's characters, I had never seen someone of African ancestry performing menial tasks before. The train, like much of Canada at the time, was 'dry'. There were no bars. So the bottle of Hennessy brandy we had been given by Dominick Coyle in Dublin came in very handy!

Travelling across Canada was like re-reading the brilliantly descriptive letters of Basil King. As the litany of station names came to life, it was familiar territory: Ottawa in Ontario; Winnipeg in Manitoba; Regina in Saskatchewan; and, shortly afterwards, the quaintly named

Moose Jaw. The train's observation coach had a 360° spherical glass dome where the passengers could sit and watch the changing panorama. In Alberta, the train made one of its longer stops in the tiny town of Medicine Hat and we had breakfast in the station. Then it was on to Calgary and across the Rocky Mountains to another meal stop in the beautiful ski-resort of Banff. We enjoyed the stunning scenery of the snow-capped Canadian Rockies as we crossed the Continental Divide and left Alberta for the Province of British Columbia. The train then entered the twin spiral tunnels, marvels of engineering built in 1908. The superb alpine vistas continued as the train descended to hug the banks of the mighty Kicking Horse River, before entering British Columbia near Kicking Horse Pass. We travelled through Salmon Arm, the large city of Revelstoke and on to Kamloops before climbing again into the Monashee Mountains. In Eagle Pass we saw the historic site at Craigellachie, where the legendary 'last spike' was driven to complete the transcontinental rail-link on 7 November 1885. Then the train continued west to follow along the Thompson and Fraser rivers, named after two nineteenth-century Canadian explorers, before reaching our final destination—Vancouver.

We were met off the train by Basil King and stayed for the first weeks in Basil and Lena's home in New Westminster, on the banks of the River Fraser. Angela and I were anxious to be independent, however, so we moved to a small flat as temporary accommodation. It was my good fortune that Basil's colleague, a young Australian photographer, had just broken his leg while skating during a coaching session with the local professional ice hockey team. That meant there was a temporary vacancy in the photo department of the *British Columbian*. I immediately had a job.

Basil was contracted to supply all the photographs for the news-paper. Payment was on a fee-per-picture basis. Together we provided twenty-four-hour coverage for news and other events by dividing the duties into alternating twelve-hour shifts. Basil was more than generous; he paid me exactly the same rate as he himself received. Our office accommodation was provided by the newspaper, so overheads were low, which meant we could earn a decent wage. In a very short time Angela and I found a small, newly built duplex apartment. We were to be the first occupants. Living on the other side of the duplex was a young, recently married French/Canadian couple, Claude and Hélène Fournier. Hélène, a local girl, was bilingual, like all the French-Canadian community in British Columbia. Claude had come from Trois Riveries, the small town in Quebec we had sailed past on our journey up the St Lawrence River. A native French speaker, he was just starting to learn English. We introduced them both to Irish coffee on our first St Patrick's Day in Canada. I also acquired a large 1954 Chevrolet car in fine condition. This would see us through the duration of our stay in Canada and the United States.

As we adjusted to our new life, we did not lose touch with Ireland. Each week my mother sent copies of the previous week's *Evening Press*. Terry O wrote long letters twice a month, in pencil on copy paper, giving us all the other news, a practice he continued over the next three years. One thing that surprised me was the lack of worldwide news in the local or national Canadian newspapers. It was the *Evening Press* that kept us reliably informed on international matters. We did not have television, relying instead on the Canadian Broadcasting Corporation's excellent radio service.

* * *

On the evening of Friday 12 December 1958 our daughter was born in St Mary's Hospital, less than 100 yards from our home. We were always certain that our baby would be a girl, so it was no surprise when she arrived. Her name was predetermined, too. She would be called Terry, after our dear friend and my mentor. Within a few days of her birth Teri's long dark hair was replaced by new baby-blonde locks. She was a beautiful child and we both rejoiced in her presence. Like her father, she later changed the spelling of her name, preferring the trendier Teri. She became a Canadian citizen at birth and proudly remains a Canadian.

There was not enough money to buy a proper cradle, so Teri spent her early weeks in a bedroom drawer. From this she graduated to new sleeping quarters in Noel Barron's cabin trunk. But at six months she got a luxurious, brand new cot, bought on hire-purchase. Before reaching that age she was taken to her first film at the local drive-in movie theatre. Drive-in cinemas, which only operated during the summer months in British Columbia, were a new experience and something we had seen before only in American movies. The giant, open-air screen dominated what was really a sophisticated car park. The cars lined up in bays. A loud speaker with an individual volume control was clipped onto the inside of the car's front window, and popcorn, snacks and soft drinks were available. It was an excellent way of going to the movies with a small baby.

*   *   *

Basil King and I were free on alternate weekends. Apart from covering any news stories that broke and Saturday night's professional ice hockey game, the working photographer provided a full picture page of the weekend events for the following Monday's paper. These could vary from a rodeo to a car rally, skiing in the mountains north of Vancouver to an unusual annual event, such as the crowning of the King and Queen at Sunny Trails, the local nudist colony. For this event the photographer was obliged to remove all his clothes before entering the area. The strangest sight, and one that would really have made the best picture of all, was of a naked photographer with a heavy press camera and the large battery of an electronic flashgun on his shoulder! Despite our heroic efforts, the only picture the newspaper ever published was a close-up 'head and shoulders' of the winning couple.

Photographing sports on a regular basis was new to me. Canadian football is similar to its American cousin, a sport that, like rugby, I neither understood nor enjoyed. Professional ice hockey, on the other hand, became one of my favourite assignments as I developed a passion for the game. We also covered sports then unknown in Ireland, like curling or box lacrosse—a professional game that is played in an indoor arena and is a cross between hurling and tennis. During their tour of Canada in 1959, the British Lions rugby team played in Vancouver. I was covering the game and the captain of the team that day was none other than Tony O'Reilly. He was very surprised to see me there.

*   *   *

The giant Pattullo Bridge stretches across the Fraser River to connect the city of New Westminster with the District of Surrey, an extensive suburban area. This bridge was much favoured by those wishing to commit suicide. I often photographed bodies of victims as they were retrieved from the river. The federal police force, the famous Royal Canadian Mounted Police (RCMP), was responsible for law and order in the District of Surrey. It was in charge of the remains of victims of suicide or drowning which were washed up on or retrieved from their side of the wide Fraser River. New Westminster's City Police, a force then not up to the standard of the RCMP, was responsible for similar victims on their side of the imaginary line dividing the waterway. It was alleged that under cover of darkness, New Westminster police were often responsible for diverting bodies away from their side of the dividing line to ensure that they came ashore in the territory of the Royal Canadian Mounted Police!

By far the biggest news story during my sojourn with the *British Columbian* was the visit to New Westminster of Queen Elizabeth II and the Duke of Edinburgh on 15 July 1959. Basil and I both worked that long day, covering every official function in leap-frog fashion. My day started with the arrival of Her Majesty and Prince Philip at the local station, on board the royal train that had taken them across Canada.

The city of New Westminster had many fine traditions, one of which was the May Day Festival, celebrated annually since 1870. It is the oldest continuous annual event in the province of British Columbia. The royal couple's welcoming ceremony was a demonstration of Maypole dancing. After that I covered several locations around the city. Queen Elizabeth and Prince Philip drove in an open car through the crowd-lined streets and avenues, accompanied by a motorcycle escort of scarlet-coated Royal Canadian Mounted Police. It was described by a Buckingham Palace spokesman as 'the busiest [day] the Queen has ever faced'. Looking back now, nearly fifty years later, one is struck by the almost complete lack of security. Press photographers didn't use telephoto lenses, so we were allowed to walk right up to the monarch. Many of my pictures were taken at a distance of no more than 3 feet away. It was deemed quite appropriate to address the Queen with words such as, 'Look this way please, your Majesty.' Prince Philip was also amiable and co-operative with the press corps. The long day ended with a late evening performance of 'The Chocolate Soldier', attended by the royal couple. This was held in an open-air theatre specially erected at the local football ground. Queen Elizabeth was resplendent in a jewel-encrusted, heavy, white satin gown. Diamonds and pearls in her tiara were repeated in her necklace and pendant earrings and a white mink stole topped her gown to keep off the chill of the July evening. It had been an exhausting but successful day—for the Queen and for me!

*   *   *

Early in 1959 the University of British Columbia in Vancouver announced a new course in film and television. Applicants were invited to apply for a scholarship scheme. I submitted an application and was awarded a bursary funded by the local Koerner Foundation. As well as day and evening lectures, practical filming sessions took place over weekends. The opportunity to change my work schedule at random meant I could do both easily. The small group selected for this, the first ever course at the University of British Columbia (which now boasts a very successful film school), was all Canadian with the exception of myself and another immigrant, Welshman Russell Jones. Russell and I worked well together and over the summer period enjoyed making a short film on the subject of racial prejudice. I finally felt that my long-held dreams now had some possibility of being realised.

Chapter 7

THE LONG LADDER
TO HOLLYWOOD

O nce I had completed the film course, it seemed like a good time
to move further towards my ultimate goal of working in
Hollywood. After spending our second Christmas in New
Westminster, we packed our meagre belongings into the old cabin
trunk and various suitcases, loaded everything into the car and set off
early one January morning in 1960 on the long journey south to Los
Angeles.

As the spouse of an American citizen, I had no difficulty getting a
work permit upon entering the United States as an immigrant. We
drove through the state of Washington, into Oregon and then into
Northern California, where we stayed two nights in San Francisco.
From San Francisco we took the Pacific Coast Highway south through
places we knew from the movies: Monterey, San Louis Obispo, Santa
Barbara and through Santa Monica to our final destination, Manhattan
Beach, just south of Los Angeles where we stayed with a friend.

Finding work in Los Angeles was not easy. I knocked on all the
studio doors—or, more correctly, called at the security areas where
uniformed security guards controlled the barrier that admitted or
denied access to the sacred ground beyond. I watched with envy as the
sleek convertibles and stretch limousines drove under the raised barrier
and the guards saluted the passengers. The barrier remained firmly in
place when I drew up in my old Chevy.

I had been given an introduction to John Ford. The meeting had
been arranged from Dublin by his friend, Lord Killanin. Although he
had the reputation of being tough, and indeed a bully, he was friendly

to me on that occasion and claimed to remember our meeting in Co. Clare when he was shooting *The Rising of the Moon*. He told me that when he first came to Hollywood, in 1914, the movie industry was run by the Irish, meaning Irish-Americans, and the Jews. Sadly, he reflected, the Irish had sold out to the Jews at an early stage of the film industry's development. He was now the only Irishman left. The son of emigrants, Ford (whose real name was John Martin Aloysius Feeney) was born in the seaport town of Portland, Maine. He was furiously proud of his Irish ancestry. He explained that he was in the early stages of pre-production on his next film, *Two Rode Together*, a western that would star Richard Widmark, James Stewart, Shirley Jones and Linda Crystal. He promised to find me some job on the unit when shooting commenced, but said that it would be twelve to eighteen months from then. With a wife and a fourteen-month-old child, immediate need was more pressing. I thanked him and moved on.

Without work and with dwindling resources, we were still optimistic and confident enough to move from the relative security of our temporary accommodation at Manhattan Beach. Finding a place to live with limited means was depressing. I searched alone, driving around the Hollywood area and stopping at apartment houses where accommodation was available. Everything that came within our price range was small, run-down and far from desirable. To raise my spirits, I sometimes viewed properties that were far beyond our means. After a week of searching I found a suitable place in a slightly faded, small apartment block on Los Felix Boulevard in Hollywood. I had always wanted a Hollywood address, so 4327 Los Felix Boulevard, Hollywood 27 was just fine by me! At $100 a month the rent was just within our budget. On my annual return visits to Los Angeles, I always go to see this small, wooden-framed apartment block. It is still occupied, which is remarkable as many of the upmarket high-rise apartments built there years later have been replaced more than once since we left in 1961. Los Felix Boulevard was then, and remains still, one of the most prestigious addresses in Hollywood. The legendary Cecil B. de Mille lived just down the street from us in a magnificent mansion surrounded by tall mature trees, with railings and high gates.

Angela was also seeking employment. She soon found a good job as an assistant in the Bridal Boutique, the specialist wedding-dress department of Bullock's Wiltshire. A few weeks after we moved into our Hollywood apartment, Eamon Murphy, a photographer from Dublin, his wife, Betty, and young son, Frank, whom we knew in Vancouver, decided to follow our example and seek their fortune in Los Angeles and shortly thereafter they arrived to stay with us. There were now two couples and two small children living in a one-bedroom apartment and the only breadwinner was Angela. Between looking for a job and driving Angela to and from work, I took care of the home and Teri. Eamon was also looking for work. He did not own a lounge suit, so in the afternoon he borrowed the one I wore in the morning for my job interviews. One day, unbeknownst to each other, we both had an interview with the same prospective employer. Wearing the dark green lounge suit, I attended in the morning. Eamon changed into the suit after lunch and went along for his appointment in the afternoon. The gentleman who interviewed us both mentioned to Eamon the unusual coincidence of having two Irishmen applying for the same job … and dressed identically … in green. Neither of us got that job.

There was a petrol station close to our apartment owned by an Englishman from Yorkshire. On learning of my situation through a few judicious questions, he firmly refused to take any money for gasoline until I found employment. I did not even know his name, but certainly appreciated his generosity. Eventually I found a reasonably good job with a fashionable photographer in Beverly Hills, a Jewish gentleman named Sergis Alberts. His studio was near the designer paradise of Rodeo Drive, featured in the movie *Pretty Woman* and then, as now, the shopping Mecca of the stars and visited by all the top names in Hollywood. Alberts had photographed Elizabeth Taylor's first marriage to Nicky Hilton, heir to the Hilton Hotel Group. The wedding pictures were on display in the reception area.

Sergis Alberts' attitude to his staff resembled that of a bad Kentucky plantation owner toward his slaves. Personnel turnover was rapid. I created something of a record by remaining with him for four weeks. Then more interviews, answering advertisements for all sorts of jobs: gas-station attendant; assistant in a law firm (unsuccessful because I had never heard of William Blackstone, who apparently was an important influence on legal systems throughout the English-speaking world); and a sales assistant in the men's outfitting department at one of Los Angeles' largest department stores. To my amazement, I was successful in the latter application, despite never having had the experience of buying an item of men's clothing since leaving Ireland.

Bullock's Downtown in the city centre of Los Angeles is a sister store of the Bullock's Wiltshire in Beverly Hills, where Angela worked. Together with a small group of mixed ethnic backgrounds, I reported there for an intensive two-day training course one Monday morning. By Tuesday evening we were all sufficiently skilled in the art of selling to take to the shop floor and face customers. However, before leaving for work on Wednesday morning, I received a telegram offering me a job on a Walt Disney film then in production in Arizona. After the interview some weeks earlier, I had entertained little hope of a positive outcome. The personnel officer of Bullock's Downtown store expressed regret at my inability to take up a career in the retail trade, but generously sent on a cheque in payment for my two days' attendance at the training course.

Later that day I boarded a Trailways long-distance bus bound for Sedona in Arizona. Set at an elevation of 7,000 feet in the foothills of the Mogollon Mountains, the ancient home of the Apache Indians, Sedona in the 1950s was a tiny, cool mountain village. Off the famous Route 66 that crosses the United States, Sedona is close to the Grand Canyon and the Painted Desert. Location for many of the black-and-white western movies of my youth, the landscape was immediately strangely familiar. In real live colour, however, the famous red rocks of Sedona against the clear blue sky created a breathtakingly beautiful panorama, indeed one of the most dramatic I have ever seen.

The journey to Sedona from Los Angeles took about twenty hours. I was the only passenger to leave the bus outside the western-type saloon in the centre of the tiny village. I really felt that I had stepped into the scene from a cowboy movie. A timber deck in front of the saloon had wooden rails to which horses could be tethered. The timber building was the local saloon, grocery store, post office and bus stop in one. The bus departed into the low, late afternoon sun, raising a cloud of red dust as it gathered speed along the otherwise deserted road. I was left standing there, alone, with my small suitcase. I suddenly remembered the evening my father had left home and walked up the gang-plank onto the mail-boat in Dún Laoghaire to seek work in England. I felt vulnerable. My family and friends were far away. I was really alone for the first time in my life.

My reverie was interrupted by the arrival of a large automobile driven by an attractive lady. She was the wife of Tom McGowan, the film's producer/director, and had come to take me to the motel where the film unit lived. Sedona Lodge Motel was a slightly run-down, sprawling complex that consisted of about thirty single-storey timber cabins, with ramshackle outhouses at the back. There was no restaurant. The motel nestled under a tall mountain and was about three miles from the town. The faded painted sign near the entrance proclaimed its glorious past as the location for a plethora of famous western films, the most recent being the 1950 classic, *Broken Arrow*.

I was a camera assistant. Bob Brooker, the Director of Photography, was a young man who had served in a US Army film unit. He was a good person to work with and taught me a great deal. One of the actors was a New Yorker, Bob Becker, who had studied at the Royal Academy of Dramatic Art in London. He spoke with a phoney English accent. There was another professional actor, Jorge Montoro. In his native country, he had been an actor in the National Theatre of Peru in Lima. All three played cowboys on the cattle trail. The female interest was a raven-haired Mexican actress named Maria. The only well-known member of the cast was the older Rosita Fernandez from San Antonio in Texas. Known as 'the Flower of San Antonio', she had played in *The Alamo* with John Wayne and Richard Widmark.

The film, *Sancho the Homing Steer*, told the story of an orphaned Mexican steer that gets lost and must find his home. In the United States it was screened over two one-hour shows on the 'Wonderful World of Disney', a weekly network television programme. The film had a cinema release in Europe and was screened by RTÉ in the 1970s. The main shooting location was in Arizona, but we also filmed in Texas, New Mexico and Utah to show a diversity of territory as the steer roamed the countryside alone in search of his home.

As was then the practice for low-budget films in the US film industry, the crew was non-union, which explained how I became involved so easily. The Walt Disney Studios in Hollywood sent the money for our wages to the producer each week, and he would pay the contract figure he had negotiated with each individual. We all knew this was at best 50 per cent of what was provided by the studio for all of us. But the experience was great. We were a happy bunch of people who enjoyed working together.

Our wake-up call was at 3.30 a.m. every morning. Preparing breakfast was one's own responsibility. Every morning as we left the motel in the pre-dawn darkness, Jorge would peel a lemon—his only breakfast. As he tasted the bitter fruit, his exclamation was always the same: 'Life,' he would say, 'she is sheet!' We were on the road by 4.30 a.m. to drive nearly three hours and 120 miles south to the location, which was that of a typical western movie. It had a winding river, high mountains and vast expanses of land without any human habitation. Rattlesnakes and deadly scorpions were plentiful, so we learned to tread carefully. Each day at 10.30 a.m. we drove to the nearby small town of Scottsdale for lunch, returning immediately afterwards. We finished work at about 4 p.m. Sunday was our only day off.

On Saturday evenings we would walk the 2 miles of narrow, one-lane roadway from our motel into Sedona. There in the local saloon a member of our crew, Kenny Gale, played the honky-tonk piano to entertain the customers. I sometimes read from a book of Yeats' poetry. The reward for this was a supply of small bottles of Guinness. This was the only export Guinness available then: it came in a quarter bottle, similar to the wine sold in bars today. It had a heavy, sticky consistency and one could be certain that it had been standing on the shelf behind the bar for years. Late at night, under the light of the stars, we returned to our motel, walking in single file, our arms outstretched with hands on the shoulders of the person in front. This was to avoid attack by the rattlesnakes, which at night were likely to coil up on the warm surface of the empty road. The only one who could not afford cowboy boots, I walked in the middle of the line. A rattlesnake would always strike at the leading walker, who had the protection of his knee-high leather boots.

My other friends were the Apache Indians who worked as extras on the film. They were fine people and superb horsemen, but they were treated badly by the production company. They were obliged to live communally in the dilapidated motel outhouses and not encouraged to mix with the rest of us. An early sequence in the film called for a number of Apaches to be shot and fall dramatically from their horses. Most of the young braves volunteered for this spectacular scene in order to demonstrate the fine quality of their horsemanship. When I questioned an older man about his reluctance to appear in the scene, he explained that an Indian who dies early in the movie cannot be seen again. For this wise man, sustained employment was more important than a moment of spectacular glory!

As in all movies where an animal plays a major part, we had three identical Mexican steers: one placid and well-trained, another more highly spirited and the third totally wild. Depending on the mood required, different animals were used in various sequences. Without the protection, or indeed restrictions, of a trade union, members of the unit were expected to be versatile and turn their hands to anything. We built a small adobe farmstead and beside it re-planted a field of fully grown corn. The mature corn plants had been transported in a refrigerated truck from miles away in a warmer part of Arizona. Re-planting the corn stalks, which stood over 6 feet tall, took a full day. The next morning the wild steer was released into the field. As the scene required, he completely demolished the neat rows of plants in minutes.

To capture the atmosphere and different terrain of the landscape, we travelled with the quiet steer from Arizona to New Mexico and Texas. That journey took us from our base in Sedona to Albuquerque in New Mexico, then south alongside the majestic Rio Grande to San Antonio and further south again along that great river to the West Texas town of El Paso. Spending a night in that border town afforded us an opportunity to visit Ciudad Juarez on the Mexican side of the border. A ramshackle place, Juarez was a typical border town and certainly not representative of Mexico. Money could buy you pretty much anything in Juarez. I ignored the exhortation of the touts on the street to 'Come and see the girls', so their next offer was, 'Maybe come and see the boys?' Not receiving any response to this either, the final offer, with a sidelong look at my beard was, 'Come and see the barber shop'!

*　*　*

As my twenty-fifth birthday approached I was offered another job back in Los Angeles. The Trailways bus from Phoenix did not depart until 8 p.m., so I spent the late morning avoiding the stifling heat by browsing in one of the large, air-conditioned department stores, where I bought some presents for Angela and Teri. Leaving the store and walking out onto the street was a shock to the system: it was like entering a hot oven. Fortunately, I had decided to buy my bus ticket in advance of the journey. Arriving at the bus station, I discovered that the fare from Phoenix was more than I had paid to get to Sedona. I did not have enough money for the ticket. Back at the department store, the sales assistant was most helpful and refunded cash for the items I returned. There were still some presents left for the family. After buying the bus ticket I was left with 25 cents to spend until I reached Los Angeles. I went into an air-conditioned beer parlour at 2.00 in the afternoon. Drinking one glass of beer, which cost 15 cents, very, very slowly, I remained there and away from the heat on the streets until 7 p.m. In the middle of the night the bus stopped somewhere in the desert and I used my remaining 10 cents to buy a coffee. That was my only sustenance before reaching home.

My new job in Los Angeles was as a photographer/cameraman in the photo department of Cannon Electric, a long-established company that manufactured complicated electrical contacts used in aircraft and space exploration vehicles. The work was interesting, but not very exciting; it was not to be a lifetime career. Angela and I were now well settled. We both had good jobs. Teri was looked after during the day by an Irish family who had settled there many years earlier. We were close to good restaurants, shopping and there was no shortage of cinemas, of course. Griffith Park and its outdoor theatre was just down the road and the famous Hollywood Bowl was close by. There, one beautiful summer evening, Angela and I attended a concert at which Leonard Bernstein conducted George Gershwin's haunting 'Rhapsody in Blue'.

At this stage Angela and I were getting on well together. Living and doing things like the average family of the time, we were content if not madly in love. Watching Teri grow up was a great joy for both of us. We had Irish and American friends; occasionally people such as Angela's sister, Paddy, came from Ireland and stayed with us. We were happy with our lot, but constantly aware of our determination to return to Ireland. Hollywood, with its many charms and idiosyncrasies, had been good to us. We had seen the sights, but with the imminent birth of Ireland's first television station, home was the place of our future. I yearned to be back in Ireland with people I loved. I felt we both needed the support of friends and family. While we never had any serious rows, our relationship was becoming strained and in my heart I knew that our marriage was unlikely to last.

*   *   *

The period during which we lived in Hollywood was an exciting time in the United States. The United Nations was going through a turbulent period. Russian leader Nikita Khrushchev took part in General Assembly debates, as did Fidel Castro. Tension was sometimes raised to boiling point and tempers raged. Once, when Khrushchev had removed his shoe and was banging it on top of his desk, the President of the Assembly, Irishman Freddie Boland, broke his gavel in an effort to control the debate. We watched it all on our little black-and-white television set.

The 1959 revolution in Cuba, led by Castro and Che Guevara, had deposed the fascist dictator Fulgencio Batista, a puppet leader controlled by the Mafia. The thirty-three-year-old Fidel Castro was now his country's leader. He appeared frequently on US television. Castro spoke English well—a practice he discontinued in public many years ago. Since the Cuban revolution I have admired Fidel Castro and been impressed by the manner in which he has led his people. My principal motivation in attending the 8th Cuban Film Festival in Havana in 1986 was the possibility of meeting Fidel Castro; it was the President's custom to receive and personally welcome delegates to the festival. At the last minute, the time of the reception was altered. Unfortunately, I could not be contacted. My opportunity to meet a man I consider to be one of the world's great leaders was lost.

The year 1960 was a US Presidential Election year. The television coverage of the Democratic Convention, which was held in Los Angeles, was gripping. After much debate the party ticket of John

Fitzgerald Kennedy and Lyndon B. Johnson emerged. Then we witnessed the first-ever television debates between the protagonists: the charismatic JFK and the Republican Vice President, Richard Nixon, a native of California. One of Bob Hope's jokes on his weekly television show from Hollywood was: 'And the Republican candidate is a local boy, Richard Nixon. Right now they're building the log cabin he was born in!'

The wholesome golden-boy image of the handsome John F. Kennedy, with his ready smile and easy manner, far outshone the shifty appearance of Richard Nixon. Like all our friends and most of my colleagues, we were Kennedy supporters, although as she was a US citizen, Angela was the only one who could actually vote for JFK. The election campaign and result were covered extensively on the three national television networks. It was an exciting time to watch the history of America unfolding.

*   *   *

When we received the news that a national television service was due to be launched in Ireland in January 1962, that determined our next move. On the first Monday in May 1961 we again packed all our belongings and prepared for the long journey home. Noel Barron's reliable old cabin trunk, which had most recently been pressed into use as an improvised table in our apartment, was sent by rail to our port of embarkation in New Jersey. We said our sad farewells to those who had come to mean so much to us during our stay, then we left Los Angeles, heading southeast along Route 66 for Arizona. Before leaving I got new tyres for the car at a cost of $80 and bought a 'water bag'. This canvas bag held about 3 pints of water and was vital in case the engine overheated while travelling through the desert. Evaporation through the canvas kept the water cool.

The boot and back seat of the car were crammed with our belongings. All three of us travelled on the wide front-bench seat. The water bag with its rope handle hung from the mascot on the car's bonnet. We felt like pioneers in an old western movie. The first night of our journey was spent in a motel in the Californian desert. Next day we continued along Route 66 to the majestic sight of the Grand Canyon. Then through Northern Arizona to Sedona, which had been my home while working on the Disney film a year earlier. We rejoined Route 66 and headed off through New Mexico, bypassing a town called Moriarty in order to stay in Santa Rosa. Driving through Middle America was quite boring: long, straight concrete highways stretched for miles, disappearing into the distant horizon. Unlike the drive from Vancouver to Los Angeles, there were neither trees nor sea to break the monotony. We travelled about 400 miles each day, choosing one of the many motels available for the night before the light faded. On we went, through Northern Texas, Oklahoma and Missouri, where, west of St Louis, we came across the small town of Cuba. A sign on the outskirts read: CUBA—No Castro here. We did not stop. In Illinois we visited Chicago briefly before continuing on through Indiana and Ohio, towards the southern shore of Lake Erie and Cleveland, across the states of Pennsylvania and New Jersey and finally to New York. There we found a small hotel. The next morning I sold the car for $100—slightly more than I had paid for the new tyres in Los Angeles ten days earlier; it would have cost more than that to park it while we stayed. Three days later we set sail from New Jersey on the Holland America Liner, *Maasdam*, whose first port of call was Galway.

Leaving New York on a hazy May morning, we watched from the ship's deck as Ellis Island and the great Statue of Liberty slid by. Eventually the New York skyline grew smaller, then disappeared beneath the horizon. We were surrounded on every side by endless billows of grey water.

Chapter 8

THE IRELAND OF TELEFÍS ÉIREANN

The dependable Terry O came to collect us from the ship in Galway in an even larger car than usual. We were overjoyed to see him. We had thirty-two pieces of luggage, a lot of it presents for the family. There was a soft leather handbag for my mother, which she used for the rest of her life, and a large leather suitcase and a beautifully presented long-play record of Shostakovich's Leningrad symphony for Terry O. Noel Barron's cabin trunk, which had proved useful in so many ways and which he never expected to see again, would be safely returned to its owner. Our total cash assets amounted to $135. Clearly we had not made our fortune in America, but we had had a great time there and achieved our objective.

Terry took us to the Great Southern Hotel in Eyre Square, where our old friend the manager Brian Collins was on hand to greet us. A large log fire blazed in the fireplace at the end of the hotel lobby. Teri had only ever seen bush fires in the Hollywood Hills behind our home, so when she saw this conflagration she cried out, 'Jesus, the house is on fire!' Obviously a well-brought-up two-and-a-half-year-old!

* * *

Back in Dublin, nothing seemed to have changed. I called to see my former boss, Bob Dillon, and he immediately offered me my old job. Within a few days of our return, I was back working with Terry O'Sullivan on 'Dubliners' Diary', but I regarded this as a stop-gap situation. My real ambition was to find a place in Telefís Éireann.

It was a good time of the year to be working on 'Dubliners' Diary'. Terry O was always keen to travel around the country during the long days of summer, so he decided to cover the opening of Cork Airport, which was an occasion of immense importance to the nation's second city. The inaugural flight, on an Aer Lingus Viscount, carried Taoiseach Seán Lemass, Minister for Industry and Commerce—and Cork's favourite son—Jack Lynch, accompanied by his wife Máirín, other dignitaries and members of the press. The public relations were handled by Frankie Byrne, who had a pathological fear of flying. On the flight from Dublin to Cork, Frankie sat beside me and Terry. Before we took off, she produced a small bottle of Cork gin from her handbag, which helped to alleviate her distress.

In Cork we were met by the Lord Mayor, supported by local and national politicians and the inevitable brass band. The official ceremony was followed by a formal lunch, after which guests were free to explore the city. Paddy Barron was a cameraman for Independent Television News, while Seamus Corcoran, my old friend from schooldays, was filming for BBC Television News. After lunch we three set out on our own voyage of discovery, which primarily involved visiting many of the well-known hostelries in the city. Seamus left early to spend some time at the new airport before our return flight. When Paddy Barron and I arrived at the airport, feeling no pain, it was to see the Aer Lingus aircraft poised for take-off. There was no airport security to prevent us running out onto the runway. Our efforts, which involved shouting and waving arms, were to no avail as the Dublin-bound flight rose into the air a mere few feet above our heads.

When we sat into the taxi outside Cork Airport and asked the driver to take us to Burgh Quay, he enquired as to where that might be. We promised to direct him when we reached Dublin and promptly fell asleep. Paddy and I shared the cost of the taxi. We were embarrassed by our indiscretion, but relieved that none of our fellow passengers—all of whom, it has to be said, were well fortified themselves before the departure from Cork—had missed us.

*   *   *

Telefís Éireann was now at an advanced stage of preparation for the launch date of 31 December 1961. The daily newspapers carried advertisements for different jobs on offer, and, like many other hopefuls, I applied for several. A television training school for technicians, studio cameramen, floor managers and vision-mixers was set up in the Marian College in Ballsbridge, and temporary studios were erected around the city. These were used to try out programmes and carry out 'dry runs', which also provided experience for the trainee technicians.

Chairman of the Telefís Éireann Authority was the well-known BBC broadcaster and Dubliner, Eamonn Andrews. The Director General of the new television station was an American, Ed Roth. Former BBC television producer Michael Barry was Controller of Programmes, which made him the person with most influence over the new station's output. Two former Radio Éireann radio producers, James Plunkett Kelly, who later wrote *Strumpet City*, and Gerard Victory, a music composer, had completed training courses with the BBC in London. They were joined by producer/directors of varying experience and talent, who came primarily from the UK. Don Bennetts was a self-confident young Australian. Others came from the American networks or, like Patrick Kearney, Assistant Controller of Programmes, and producer Tom McGrath, had returned from Canada. The same sources provided experienced technicians, such as Irishman Tony Barry, a studio cameraman, and Tom Kelly, Head of Lighting. Local people who held prominent positions were Maev Conway, a former schoolteacher who was Head of Children's Programmes, and the well-known journalist and radio commentator Michael O'Hehir, who was appointed Head of Sport. Jack White, a journalist from *The Irish Times*, was Head of Current Affairs. Stuart Hetherington had left the camera department of Ardmore Studios to become the newsroom's leading film cameraman. The Head of News was Pierce Kelly, a former Chief of Staff of the IRA, then always referred to in the media as 'an illegal organisation'. James Pearse McGuinness, another former IRA activist and editor of the *Irish Press* before he left to work in San Francisco, was Editor of the station's first programme journal, 'The RTV Guide'. He later succeeded Pierce Kelly as Head of News. The Editor of Television News was Des Grealy, a delightful man who was in the RAF and saw action in the Far East during the Second World War. The redoubtable Hilton Edwards was Head of Drama.

One of my attempts to find a place in Telefís Éireann was via Marie Keane, the Abbey actress whom I knew from my 'Dubliners' Diary' period. She arranged a meeting with Hilton Edwards, whom I had photographed a number of times but did not really know. Hilton was a charming man who was immersed in theatre and seemed to care about little else. He received me graciously and suggested that I might assist him in adapting Ibsen's play, 'A Doll's House', for television. I explained that I had neither the ability nor the interest in doing this. He wished me well in my other attempts to join the station and we parted amicably.

There are some great stories about Hilton, one of which I'll share. During his early days as Head of Drama, he took a trip with a junior technician to check out a filming location in the country. The younger man was delighted to have the privilege of driving someone of Hilton's stature in his brand new car. Although he had no interest in such things, Hilton, being a person of impeccable manners, was polite enough to express his amazement at the car's various features. Driving down a quiet country road, Hilton, an inveterate cigar smoker, produced his cigar case. As he placed the cigar in his mouth, the young technician was delighted to point out that his car also had a cigar lighter. This he instantly activated and passed to Hilton. 'Thank you, dear boy', said the great theatrical personality, lighting his cigar. Then, before the driver had even noticed, Hilton had wound down the car's window and flung what he assumed to be the disposable cigar lighter into the roadside ditch!

*   *   *

While construction work continued on the new television centre in the grounds of Montrose House, in Donnybrook, the main body of the newly recruited staff was based in temporary offices in Clarendon Street. Administration, engineering and programme staff shared the same building. The newsroom staff was the first to occupy the partially completed building in Donnybrook.

The first interview I attended was for a job as news film cameraman. I was not successful, but my disappointment was short-lived. The next day News Editor Des Grealy, who was chairman of the interview board, telephoned me to say that I should not worry as the new station had other plans for my future. A few days after an interview for the post of lighting film cameraman, I received a letter announcing that I was the successful candidate. The initial pay was £1,250 per annum—a generous salary at a time when newspaper photographers were earning £500 a year. The other lighting cameraman in the programmes division was Michael Monaghan, who was a genius in all matters technical. Our boss was William F. Harpur, Head of Film, who would feature in my later life.

*   *   *

Working for the embryonic Telefís Éireann was a joy—it was also the first time in my life that I was in permanent and pensionable employment. We rented a small house in Sandycove. Up until now, Angela and Teri had been living with Angela's parents in Co. Westmeath, while I stayed with my mother and sister who lived over their chemist shop in Kimmage; my father was still working in London. For our little family, the future was looking bright.

The first important assignment for both Michael Monaghan and me was filming the inaugural address by President Éamon de Valera. This would be the opening programme of the new television station. I had been to Áras an Uachtaráin several times during my tenure with the *Irish Press*, to cover the presentation of credentials by newly appointed ambassadors; Sean T. O'Kelly was President at that time. These formal assignments were for photographers only. Any conversation between the President and the new ambassador was considered private, therefore reporters were excluded. Usually when the ceremony was over and the principal guests had departed, President O'Kelly—a jolly little man who was a lifelong friend of de Valera—invited the photographers into his pantry for a glass or two of whiskey, an indulgence he enjoyed himself. President de Valera was a more austere figure than his predecessor. Although I had seen him in Ballaghaderreen when I was a schoolboy and met him in his role as Taoiseach, he had always been a distant person. He was now almost totally blind.

Michael and I set up our cameras in the President's office. Experienced speaker that he was, de Valera performed flawlessly, completing the Irish and English versions of the address. That first programme was followed on the opening night by a live broadcast of Benediction conducted by the Archbishop of Dublin, John Charles McQuaid. After the ceremony, which took place in the smallest television studio, the Archbishop quietly asked the senior floor manager, Peter Collinson, if his performance had been satisfactory. Peter, a cocky young Englishman with no knowledge of the esteem in which the Archbishop was held, or the fear he engendered in his flock, gave a thumbs-up sign and simply replied, 'Swinging, Vicar'. I doubt it was a form of address with which the venerable McQuaid was familiar.

Within a few days of beginning with Telefís Éireann I met a young man who would have a huge influence on my future life. Micheal Johnston was about my own age. A graduate of Cambridge University, he was also prominent in college rowing circles. Later, he went on to train the Garda Rowing Team and became an accomplished radio and newspaper rowing correspondent. Micheal trained as a television producer/director with the BBC in London. He had worked mostly on 'talks programmes' under the legendary Grace Wyndham Goldie and at one time had been responsible for Patrick Moore's phenomenally successful astronomy programme, 'The Sky at Night'. Micheal's father, the playwright and author Denis Johnston, was the first Controller of Programmes of BBC Television. His mother, Shelah Richards, was the former Gate Theatre actress and now a producer in the Drama Department of Telefís Éireann. A large, handsome man with a boyish face and youthful demeanour, Micheal's chosen mode of transport was a Lambretta motor-scooter. Dressed in a khaki-coloured duffle-coat with a long Cambridge University scarf wrapped twice around his neck, the ends trailing in his slip-stream and, unusually for those days, wearing a white crash helmet with a peak in front, thus Micheal travelled to the office, social events and meetings.

Micheal was the Producer/Director of the farming programme, 'On the Land'. Although uncharacteristic of his own background or experience, he immediately established an excellent working relationship with the Department of Agriculture and the various farming groups in the country. The programme's original presenter/advisor was Paddy Jennings, an agricultural advisor in North County Dublin who hailed originally from Co. Mayo.

I was assigned to work as a film cameraman with Micheal on the farming programme for two days each week. My first assignment was filming sugarbeet harvesting in Co. Carlow. This is a late autumn or winter operation, usually carried out in rain-sodden, mucky conditions—very dirty work. The wellington boots and protective clothing issued by our new employer were essential for such an undertaking. However, the farmer with whom we were filming decided that, as this was his television debut, he should dress for the occasion. He wore a navy suit and well-polished, tan-coloured shoes. Micheal gently but effectively persuaded him that his ordinary working clothes would be more appropriate!

In the spring of 1962, Telefís Éireann's original building, designed by the architects Scott Tallon Walker, was almost complete. Gradually, personnel based in Clarendon Street took up residence there. I moved into a corner of the larger first-floor front area, which housed the programme division. Along with Pauline Kelly, Micheal's production assistant, we were, in effect, the farming programme team, although my own commitment to 'On the Land' was still just two days each week.

For one of the early programmes we filmed the birth of a Friesian calf on the farm of a young man named Fraser McMullen in Clontarf, a few miles from Dublin city centre. Yes, that's right, in 1961 there was still at least one farm in Clontarf! At the suggestion of Fraser—a dairy farmer with no interest in a bull calf—the programme team bought the calf at a very reasonable price. We named the animal *Bealach a Seacht*, after the station identification of '*Telefís Éireann, Bealach a Seacht*' (Channel 7), which were the words that opened each evening's television presentation. Fraser McMullen agreed to look after our new calf until maturity, which enabled us to film progress reports as *Bealach a Seacht* grew up. These became a regular and extremely popular feature of 'On the Land', particularly with urban viewers, who were equal to, if not larger than, the rural audience for the programme. *Bealach a Seacht* remained a bull until he was sold for slaughter. The programme team, which formed the owners' syndicate, made a modest financial gain from the enterprise.

* * *

I also worked on 'Broadsheet', the nightly weekday magazine programme. Its editor, P.P. O'Reilly, a former commentator for Radio Éireann, possessed a mellifluous voice. Others who presented items on the programme included *Irish Times'* reporter, Cathal O'Shannon, Brian Cleeve, John O'Donoghue, a former army officer, John Skehan, who had a distinctive, deep voice and a young academic, Brian Farrell. Lord Killanin and Rory Childers, grandson of the patriot Erskine Childers, were occasional interviewers.

Peter Ustinov often recalled participating in a live interview with Lord Killanin in the small 'Broadsheet' studio. Behind his interviewer was a man holding a large, very disturbed, noisy kestrel, who was the subject of the following item. Jim Fitzgerald, previously a well-known actor and theatrical director, was cast in the unlikely role of Producer/ Director of the programme. Jim was a small, fiery man with a booming theatrical voice. He applied himself with great enthusiasm to providing the sometimes frivolous items required for a nightly magazine programme. One such was about a man I had met while working for 'Dubliners' Diary'. He owned a small factory that manufactured burglar alarms in Leixlip, Co. Dublin. As a hobby, he kept pet monkeys. Jim Fitzgerald devised a hilarious item in which the monkeys appeared to assemble the burglar alarms!

Another more serious item I filmed, with Jim Fitzgerald as director, was an interview with Sylvia Beech, the first publisher of James Joyce's *Ulysses*. This film was restored and re-broadcast by RTÉ in 2005. The interview took place in the garden of architect Michael Scott's house, just under the Martello Tower at Sandycove, which is mentioned in the opening chapter of *Ulysses*. The interviewer was Niall Sheridan, who as a young man had known Joyce. Then a good age, Sylvia Beech was a tiny, grey-haired lady with a rather shrill voice. After a lifetime in Paris, she still retained her American accent. She was well dressed, in a conservative fashion. The interview told of her first meeting with James

Joyce in Paris and her agreement that the tiny publishing company she owned, Shakespeare and Co., would publish his book.

* * *

Our visit to the Norbentine Monastery at Killnacrott in Co. Cavan was just before Christmas. We filmed the Lord Abbot delivering the Christmas message to the nation on behalf of the Catholic Church. The Producer/Director was Pat Kearney. Sound recordist Jimmy Quin, electrician Sean Keville and driver Simon Weafer made up the rest of the unit. After dinner we prepared to set off into the frosty December night. Before leaving, the Abbot insisted on blessing the car and its occupants to ensure a safe journey home. That completed, Simon started us on our way by reversing the car from its parked position. He was unaware of a badly lit corner of the church building ... until we heard the crash. His comments on the worth and consequence of the Abbot's blessing were not what one might expect to hear on such hallowed ground in the week before Christmas!

* * *

Another producer/director who came from the BBC was the slightly eccentric Chloe Gibson. By our youthful standards, Chloe was an old lady even then. She had a strange, somewhat unkempt look and was forever dressed in a heavy black sweater and black trousers. She had a long, sharp nose and a cigarette always languished in the corner of her mouth and was never removed until it became a long length of grey ash, which invariably fell to land onto her black sweater. Her voice, ravaged by a lifetime of smoking, was that of a man. A recent convert to Catholicism, Chloe was, in the fashion of all converts to their newly espoused belief, more than enthusiastic about her religion. Either as a break from years of directing plays or in deference to her new-found faith, Chloe decided to produce and direct a film on the Catholic seminary, St Patrick's College, in Maynooth, which was then exclusively an institute for training young priests. Unlike the present-day university, there were no women or lay students on campus.

The film, *Men for the Harvest*, was shot over a period of thirteen months, culminating with the ordination to the priesthood of a large group of students. It followed the activities of the seminarians from the time they entered the college until they left as young priests seven years later. My abiding memories are of filming in the winter. We would leave Montrose in the dark and frost of early morning, with Simon Weafer guiding the camera car over treacherous ice-covered roads with his usual skill and dexterity. Filming outdoors was usually completed before darkness arrived. It snowed heavily some days. When this happened we went inside to do interior filming. Initially this caused a problem for one member of the crew. Pat Hughes, Chloe's young, female production assistant, was not permitted inside the college when the male students were present! Presumably Chloe herself was considered to be beyond the age of temptation or seduction. When the crew's names had been submitted for approval, the college authorities had assumed that Pat Hughes was a man. Now, Pat stood dutifully outside in the snow while we shouted out to her the information she required for the shot-list. It was a few days before one of the staff, a priest named Tom Fee, noticed her. He soon resolved the ridiculous situation and Pat was allowed to rejoin her colleagues. Later, Tom Fee became better known as Cardinal Tomás Ó Fiach, Archbishop of Armagh and Primate of All Ireland.

Each day we had a late lunch in the dining room reserved for visiting dignitaries. Food and wines were good and plentiful and Chloe entertained the company, which usually included the president, vice president and senior lecturers of the college, with tales of her previous adventures. One morning, in order to illustrate that students were free to leave the seminary at any time (the entrance gates were never closed), Chloe set up a scene in which we would film a young student walking through the open gates, carrying a suitcase with all his belongings. She selected a young man at random and asked him to get his suitcase and enact the scene for us. When he returned, we were pleased to see that he had in fact packed the suitcase suitably. It was heavy to carry and looked authentic. When the camera was rolling, Chloe shouted, '*Action!*' The student walked, as directed, out through the open gates. It took a few minutes for us to realise that he had not returned. When we went looking for him, he had disappeared. He never came back!

Another early venture with a religious theme arose from an invitation from Aer Lingus to 'Broadsheet' to travel to Tarbes in France. Located near the Pyrenees, on the border with Spain, this was the airport that served Lourdes, which was then a thriving route for the airline, with a steady stream of pilgrims. The television team consisted of the programme editor, P.P. O'Reilly, sound recordist Michael Francis and myself. Although the intention was to make a short item about Lourdes, I suggested to P.P. O'Reilly that we should make a thirty-minute documentary film on the subject. Being a Francophile, he agreed enthusiastically. Among those P.P. interviewed for our film in his adequate French were the Bishop of Lourdes and the nun who was matron of the large hospital that catered for sick pilgrims. In the finished film the voice-over English translations for these interviews were performed by Jim Fitzgerald, producer of 'Broadsheet', and by one of the programme's production assistants, Anne Leonard, who had translated the French interviews into English and had an excellent broadcasting voice. Jim, who was a profound agnostic and sometime self-confessed anarchist, derived great pleasure from being the voice of a bishop. The casting of the good sister's voice was more in character!

*   *   *

By far the biggest television outside broadcast undertaken by Telefís Éireann was coverage of the visit of President John F. Kennedy in June 1963. Equipment was borrowed from BBC Northern Ireland to augment the station's own limited facilities. There were live outside broadcasts from all the key points of the President's visit, starting with his arrival at Dublin Airport and concluding with his departure from Shannon Airport. Mounting a live outside broadcast was a mammoth task, especially as cameras were limited. The more mobile film cameras were used to extend coverage of the three-day tour.

I was assigned to film the President's visit to Wexford. Frankie Byrne, who had just launched her own PR company was in charge of Press

Relations. As one would expect, Frankie made an outstanding success of the job. To facilitate the White House Press Corps, international, national and local journalists, she arranged for the Department of Posts and Telegraphs to install 170 direct telephone lines in Wexford specially for the visit. This was an almost impossible task in those pre-mobile phone days. She was surprised, and indeed amused, that throughout the visit not one call was made or received on any of these telephones.

Despite the fact that the local bishop had died the previous evening, the locals in Wexford celebrated the visit of JFK with great enthusiasm. The town was in carnival mood, and song and story prevailed until late in the public houses. As Frankie Byrne entertained us in the bar of the Talbot Hotel, one reporter commenting on the racket from the street outside remarked, 'You'd never think that the bishop has just died.'

From Wexford I was due to travel to Cork, where President Kennedy was arriving the next day. After filming there I was scheduled to return to Dublin and have a few days off. However, Paddy Barron, who was working for ITN, asked me to continue on the Kennedy trail to help him out. At this stage I was totally hooked on the whole experience and was delighted with the opportunity to carry on. I had been a fan of President Kennedy since I first saw the young senator on television in the United States, and this was a rare opportunity. After Cork we drove to Galway, the penultimate stop on the presidential visit. Afterwards, as the two press corps helicopters were just about to take off, I jumped aboard the second one. The pilot did a head-count and finding that he had an extra passenger, his only comment was, 'We seem to have taken aboard someone who should have been on the other helicopter.'

My task was to film the final scene of the President's departure. As he approached the steps of Air Force One, he shook hands with the various dignitaries and then came over to me. Gay Byrne, the commentator on the live television broadcast, mentioned that the President of the United States was now having his final handshake, with Telefís Éireann cameraman Sheamus Smith. My mother, watching in Dublin, said it was one of the most exciting moments of her life and she spoke about it for years afterwards!

Chapter 9 ∿

CREATING
A SCENE

After almost three enjoyable years as a film cameraman, I was appointed a producer/director. At last I had realised my greatest ambition. I now worked on many programmes, the most memorable being the agricultural programmes 'On the Land' and 'Telefís Feirme' and the current affairs programme, '7 Days'. I also enjoyed all the others, including 'Discovery', a documentary series, 'Hurler on the Ditch', a political programme originally presented by *Irish Times'* political commentator John Healy, my old *Evening Press* colleague, 'The World of Film' with Gay Byrne, and my last series, 'My Own Place'. There was also a spell in the Sports Department and a number of single programmes, including one on the Cork Film Festival. The most consistent viewer of all my television output was my mother. She would enthusiastically watch programmes in which she had no interest whatsoever, anxiously awaiting my name on the end credits.

When 'On the Land', my first assignment as a producer/director, was taken off the air for a summer break, I was sent to the Sports Department. While I had no particular interest in sport personally, it was considered a good assignment. Michael O'Hehir was overall boss, with Philip Green his assistant. Other members of the team were Fred Cogley, Brendan O'Reilly, who was still an active athlete and Irish title-holder in the high jump and a great editor, Maurice Quinn, boxing commentator, Noel Andrews and my old friend Esther Byrne, now a production assistant experienced in outside broadcasts. Apart from watching Micheal Johnston directing an 'On the Land' outside broadcast from the RDS, I had little knowledge in this area.

Previously the Sports Department had only one producer, Burt Budin, an American who later directed 'The Late Late Show'. An outgoing character with a droll sense of humour, Burt was a consummate professional and had vast experience. He had produced everything from live drama to musicals, from current affairs to sport. Burt invited me to sit beside him at the control desk as he directed a live outside broadcast from the National Boxing Stadium. After a few rounds of the preliminary bouts, he suggested that I take his chair and, under his supervision, direct the programme for a while. During live sports outside broadcasts the director does the actual switching, or cutting, between cameras. There is no vision-mixer as in studio presentations. So apart from calling the shots and directing the cameras, the director must have an additional technical skill. Tentatively, I took over the master's chair. Burt watched over my shoulder and advised me for about five minutes. Then, to my horror, he said, 'Okay, you can do this. I'm going home.' I was petrified, but thanks to the support of the always brilliant outside broadcast crew, I finished the programme successfully. It was a great sense of achievement to have done my first live outside broadcast. Esther Byrne, who held my hand during those first nervous minutes, was a tower of strength and great support when we worked together on future sports programmes.

One of the highlights of my sojourn in the Sports Department was directing the Carroll's Irish Open Golf Tournament. The principal television commentator, Paul McWeeney, was golf correspondent of *The Irish Times*. A slight impediment in his speech added to the attraction of his informative, laidback commentary.

Michael O'Hehir, the department head, was a pleasure to work with, both as the boss and as a commentator at the racing outside broadcasts I directed. When leaving for the Carroll's Irish Open at Little Island Golf Course in Cork, Micheal gave me £100, which was a substantial amount of money. He said, 'That's for your expenses over the next four days. I do not want to see any of it coming back here!' He need not have worried; Esther and I had no difficulty spending it. From the beginning Esther Byrne signed all of Michael O'Hehir's correspondence and other documents with his name. Her version of Michael O'Hehir's signature was the only one recognised by the Administration Department. Once, in Esther's absence, I asked Michael himself to sign an expenses claim. It was returned unpaid; the signature was not genuine!

*   *   *

I was sad to leave all my colleagues in the Sports Department when the Controller of Programmes moved me to 'Newsbeat'. This Monday-to-Friday programme was the successor to 'Broadsheet'. The editor, Frank Hall, had moved from the newsroom to the programme division. Other 'Newsbeat' contributors included Cathal O'Shannon and Michael Ryan. Des Keogh and Ted Bonner, an expert on Egyptology, made occasional contributions to the early programmes; Des mostly did humorous items. Whenever there was a gap to fill in the programme, Ted could always be relied upon to come up with yet another new angle on the Tomb of Tutankhamen, the boy king who ruled Ancient Egypt and died at the age of eighteen. Our viewers learned more than they really needed to know about King Tut!

While working with the earlier 'Broadsheet' programme, Cathal O'Shannon had been spotted by the BBC. He was offered a contract to work in London as a reporter with 'Tonight', the BBC's nightly magazine programme. Even then regarded by many as a natural television personality, Cathal gave up his permanent job with *The Irish Times* and went to London. When 'Tonight' was axed by the BBC, he returned to Dublin and we met for a drink in the Shelbourne Hotel. Cathal was elated: he told me that he need never work again. On leaving the BBC, he had received an enormous amount of money. They had given him a cheque for £7,000. Values have changed since the early 1960s!

Dominant among the production assistants on 'Newsbeat' was Marianne Crowley. A strong-willed, amusing, lovable and extrovert red-haired young lady, she liked to give the impression of being the programme's real boss! Marianne was friendly with the Programme Controller and his wife. She referred to them both by their first names, Gunnar and Gillian, knowing well that this intimidated the rest of us.

*   *   *

In 1964 'The World of Film' was presented by Gay Byrne. It was the successor to 'Kino', Telefís Éireann's first film programme, and consisted of film clips and studio interviews. 'The World of Film' was my first attempt at developing a programme from scratch. The set designer was Welshman Alan Pleass. The black-and-white set, based on large-scale film frames, was quite spectacular. On my suggestion the presenter and guests sat on the canvas-and-wood folding chairs used on movie sets. Each chair had the individual's name printed on the back. To this day a publicity photograph of a young Gay Byrne sitting in the presenter's chair is frequently published—and incorrectly described as being from 'The Late Late Show'. One of the first guests interviewed on 'The World of Film' was the Irish Film Censor and Director of the Cork Film Festival, Dermot Breen. Dermot, whom I already knew as Director of the Cork Film Festival, became a friend and he regularly invited me to screenings of films he thought might be controversial enough to be cut or banned. Little did I imagine that twenty-two years later I would be sitting in his chair as the Irish Film Censor.

*   *   *

It was Micheal Johnston who first introduced a young academic, Justin Keating, to television. Justin was a senior lecturer in veterinary medicine in Trinity College, Dublin, but proved to be a natural broadcaster. He was small in stature, but the camera loved him. He was articulate, friendly and a born communicator. In 1966 Justin Keating won a Jacob's National Television Award for writing and presenting the educational farming television programme 'Telefís Feirme', which I produced and directed. In 1969 he stood as a Labour party candidate and was elected to Dáil Éireann. He became Minister for Industry and Commerce in the Fine Gael/Labour coalition government of 1973. He continued to be a regular participant in political programmes and remained a popular television personality. After his defeat in the 1977 General Election, he briefly presented a weekly television talk show before returning to academic life.

Justin, who later became Head of Agricultural programmes, devised a unique educational farming programme. 'Telefís Feirme' was aimed primarily at young farmers, who watched the programme in groups set up by Macra na Feirme (the young farmers' organisation) throughout the country. I was happy working in 'Newsbeat' when Justin Keating asked me to return to agricultural programmes and become producer/director of the 'Telefís Feirme' series. Mainly a studio presentation, 'Telefís Feirme' afforded Justin plenty of scope to demonstrate his extraordinary ability as a presenter and communicator. A vital element of our team was the film-maker and artist Gerrit van Geldren. Gerrit designed and made brilliant animated graphics, which he worked by hand from behind the studio set. 'Telefís Feirme' was the first RTÉ programme to have an animated film of a farm gate swinging open for the main title. It was animated and filmed by Gunther Wulff, a young German who had set up a film animation studio in Dublin. Although crude by today's standards, we were all very proud of that achievement.

The first series of 'Telefís Feirme' ran for thirteen weeks. At the end of that time Justin Keating set an exam for those participating in the Macra na Feirme viewing groups. As a prize, the young farmers who received top marks in the exam were taken to various farms in Denmark. Justin and I, along with Seamus Deasy, his brother Brendan, then a young sound-recordist, and my production assistant Nuala Malone, accompanied the winners and filmed the event. A problem for the cameraman and for me was that while most of the young farmers, which included an attractive young lady, were in their early twenties, one was more mature and losing his hair. Filming this 'young' farmer without showing the top of his head was sometimes difficult!

When I became a producer/director, my job as a film cameraman went to Godfrey Graham. Godfrey and I often worked together on 'On the Land' programmes. When filming the launch of Kerrygold butter on the UK market, the team travelled to Manchester with Tony O'Reilly, then Managing Director of An Bord Bainne. On the flight from Dublin, Production Assistant Maura Lee bought two bottles of duty-free perfume—twice the permitted allowance. To avoid problems with customs officials back in Dublin, Maura asked Godfrey to carry one bottle of her contraband fragrance in his suitcase. Being the gentleman that he is, Godfrey could not refuse. When packing his suitcase, he carefully wrapped the perfume in his pyjamas. After clearing customs at

Dublin Airport, Godfrey discovered that the perfume had leaked all over his pyjamas! Had this happened to anyone else, it would have been a major catastrophe, with little chance of explanations at home. But Godfrey, decent and good-living fellow that he was, knew that his young wife Sheila would accept his explanation and never doubt his fidelity.

* * *

In the early 1960s the Cork Film Festival was in its prime. The Director, Dermot Breen, who later became Film Censor, was a man of great flare. He was known and respected throughout the international film world, as was his charming wife, Veda. Back then, evening events at the film festival required formal dress. The atmosphere was one of style and elegance; torn jeans and woollen sweaters were never in evidence then. Whatever programme I was involved with, I always managed to arrange filming in or near Cork City during the Festival. On one such occasion we stayed at the Victoria Hotel. Truly Victorian in every sense of the word, this establishment was the least fashionable of the city's top four hostelries, but the members of the staff were very friendly. The head-waiter, who also doubled as the *sommelier*, was getting on in years and was a bit doddery. Whenever a guest ordered a bottle of wine, this gentleman would open it with the appropriate ceremony. After sniffing the cork, he would pour a generous glass, which he tasted and pronounced satisfactory. Before serving the guests he placed his glass on the piano. Whenever he topped up the diners' glasses, he never omitted to do likewise with his own!

In those early days of television, Telefís Éireann crews were treated as VIPs. One evening Dermot Breen invited us all to the Film Festival club, where formal attire was *de rigueur*. Our driver, Simon Weafer, and sound-recordist Colm O'Byrne were unprepared for such an eventuality. Not deterred by this inconvenience, I brought the problem to the attention of the man who had imbibed so much of our wines— the hotel's head-waiter. His immediate solution was that our two colleagues could borrow dress suits which the hotel kept for use by casual waiters. Although many sizes too big, Simon's suit was passable, as was Colm's jacket. The problem was that the only black trousers available for him had been the victim of hungry moths. The white skin of Colm's legs shone through the holes like twinkling stars in a frosty winter's night sky. Inspiration struck again!

We got black shoe polish and covered Colm's legs with it in the appropriate places. In the dim lighting of the festival club, the moth holes were never noticed. Simon's over-sized jacket presented another problem, however. As he attempted to shake hands with the Lord Mayor, to whom he had been introduced, his proffered hand disappeared as the gathered-up sleeve extended to its full length! To prevent a repeat experience, Simon turned up the sleeves of his jacket to reveal the lining, thereby anticipating a style that became popular in men's fashion thirty years later.

During one Cork Film Festival we shot a programme on the woollen industry for the documentary series 'Discovery'. This was filmed primarily at the Sunbeam Woolsey knitting factory in Cork. Simultaneously, we made a half-hour programme on the festival itself. Such was the enthusiasm of the crew in those early days that no one complained about working all day and then dressing up in formal eveningwear to continue well into the small hours of the next morning. The cameraman on this particular test of endurance was Stuart Hetherington. A brilliant exponent of his art, Stuart was great company and my favourite staff cameraman, just as Seamus Deasy was always my first choice when a freelance cameraman was the option. Paddy Gallagher, who wrote the script for the 'Discovery' programme, learned during his research that in olden times the British Chancellor of the Exchequer had sat on a woolsack in parliament, to emphasise the importance of this commodity to the economy. After a late night at the Film Festival club, Paddy, like the rest of us, was somewhat the worse for wear the following morning. When we arrived at our location in the knitting factory, Paddy, emulating the British Chancellor, found a comfortable seat on a woolsack. A little later, when Stuart's camera emerged from behind a huge loom, the image of Paddy Gallagher fast asleep on the woolsack filled the viewfinder.

To celebrate her birthday, I took my production assistant, Nuala Malone, to the Oyster Tavern, then Cork's premier restaurant. After dinner I paid the bill by credit card, a practice that was nothing like as common as it is today. Late that night a fire destroyed the fine old restaurant. It was weeks before it became apparent that the credit card records were lost in the flames; I never received the bill for our splendid evening.

*   *   *

During filming of a 'Discovery' programme on the Ward Union Hunt, near its headquarters in Ashbourne, Co. Meath, cameraman Ken Murphy got a brilliant shot of Government Minister Charles J. Haughey on his horse, jumping a five-bar farm gate. As we followed the baying hounds and galloping hunt across the frozen fields of Co. Meath on a Saturday afternoon, Ken fell from the back of the four-wheel-drive vehicle we were using as a camera car. Stopping would have meant losing the hunt, so Simon Weafer and I, who were also operating cameras on the back of the car, continued the chase. We left a frozen and bruised Ken to find his own way back to the Hunter's Moon—the pub that had been our base for the previous week. The boisterous party in the Hunter's Moon after the hunt provided some great footage for our film.

*   *   *

In 1969 I was very contented back in agricultural programmes. 'On the Land' was once again my responsibility. Over my years as a film cameraman and as a producer, I had acquired many good friends in the farming community. Joe Murray, the new head of the department, was amiable and the team worked well together. Ted Nealon did a short farm news programme, which was transmitted before 'On the Land' early on Sunday afternoons. We also had a rather folksy short farm comment programme that focused solely on Joe Bruton, a fine, impressive-looking man and one of the country's most extensive and successful cattle farmers. Early in my 'farming' career I visited Joe's home in Co. Meath one morning. I was surprised to meet a milkman delivering milk to the door. Stocked with hundreds of beef cattle, it seemed odd to me that there was not a single cow to be found on the

Bruton farm. Joe Bruton's two young sons, John and Richard, were schoolboys then. Later, as Taoiseach, government ministers and Deputy Leader of Fine Gael, both would leave their mark on Irish politics.

*   *   *

'Hurler on the Ditch' was an early political television programme. It was the brainchild of *Irish Times'* political journalist, John Healy. He wrote the script and was the original presenter. Although a fine, opinionated writer, John was not good on screen. Brian Farrell, then acknowledged as a younger Irish version of the prodigious BBC television commentator Robin Day, replaced him.

The programme opened with a compilation of national and provincial newspaper cuttings with a linking script and commentary. This was followed by a discussion of the week in politics with the main political correspondents of the newspapers. The panel usually included Michael Mills, political correspondent of the *Irish Press*, who went on to become Ireland's first Ombudsman, and Michael McInerney, his opposite number in *The Irish Times*. It was a very timid programme. Politicians never appeared. It would be some time yet before Muiris MacConghail would change the face of political broadcasting in Ireland forever with his groundbreaking '7 Days' programme.

Chapter 10 ∿

THE DAYS AND NIGHTS OF '7 DAYS'

olitical broadcasting in Ireland was to change forever with the first broadcast of '7 Days'. The steady hand of editor Muiris MacConghail was firmly on the rudder, and he must take much of the credit for the impact this innovative programme had on the station and on the viewers. It was a strong format and well delivered, and very quickly '7 Days' became RTÉ's flagship current affairs programme.

When Muiris MacConghail invited me to take over from Dick Hill as Senior Producer, I was surprised. I had known and liked Muiris since we had made a film together some years earlier and later in 'Newsbeat'. While I was sorry to leave my colleagues in agricultural programmes, Muiris' invitation was not one I could turn down. It meant working closely again with my old collaborator, Esther Byrne, who was Chief Production Assistant.

Shortly before I joined the programme team, '7 Days' had been involved in a number of controversial programmes. The Director General, Kevin McCourt, under whose watch the titles of Radio Éireann and Telefís Éireann were combined into the now familiar Radio Telefís Éireann (RTÉ), had decided to remove '7 Days' from the jurisdiction of the Controller of Programmes, Michael Garvey, and place it instead under the Head of News, Jim McGuinness. This had caused disquiet among certain members of the team, but problems had been resolved by the time I came on board.

Not long after becoming a team member, I was given the opportunity to spend some time in Paris, where two major current affairs stories were running simultaneously: the talks following the end of the Vietnam War and the violent student riots. Cameraman Stuart Hetherington, production assistant Anne Logue and commentator John O'Donoghue covered these assignments with me. In those days the film we had shot each day was returned to Dublin for processing. Courier services did not exist, so every evening, before dinner, Anne Logue and I would drive to Le Bourget Airport with our film and shot-lists. There we would hope to find someone we knew who was travelling home on the Aer Lingus evening flight to Dublin. Once we had identified a 'courier' we would ask them to take the film, which would be collected by an RTÉ messenger at Dublin Airport. Aer Lingus flight and cabin crews were much smaller in numbers than today, so we knew most of them, too. Anne Logue shared her flat with an Aer Lingus hostess and I knew some of the pilots. This system, although unorthodox, worked perfectly.

One evening we were at the airport on our usual quest when I spotted the familiar tall, gaunt figure of film director John Huston waiting to check-in for the Dublin flight. Although we had met briefly when I photographed him at St Cleran's for the *Evening Press*, he was unlikely to remember me more than ten years later. Nonetheless, I introduced myself, explained our situation and asked him if he would carry the results of the day's work to Dublin. He enthusiastically agreed, insisting that, as he had a driver waiting for him at the airport, he would deliver the film to the '7 Days' office personally. I telephoned Muiris MacConghail to inform him that the film would be delivered, but did not reveal the identity of its courier. A few hours later Muiris could hardly believe his eyes when John Huston, a hero of his, walked into the office with our cans of film under his arm.

Muiris was anxious to introduce new talent and new faces onto the programme. From his work on 'Newsbeat' he was aware of the potential Bill O'Herlihy showed as a reporter/commentator. He knew that Bill and I were friendly, so the task of persuading Bill to leave his beloved Cork and join the '7 Days' team was given to me. It took several meetings and telephone calls before our prey finally capitulated.

David Thornley, a brilliant young TCD academic, had also been recruited to '7 Days' and he suggested that Muiris should interview a bright young graduate and former student of his, Rodney Rice. Belfast-born Rodney had none of Bill O'Herlihy's reservations about joining '7 Days' and accepted the offer of a job with enthusiasm. Another fine personality who became a '7 Days' presenter was Denis Mitchell. He later left television to take up a career in law, eventually becoming a judge in Hong Kong.

Among the producers working on '7 Days', the most talented were two young UCD graduates, Colm Ó Briain and Niall McCarthy. Shortly after I joined we got Paddy Barron assigned to the programme as permanent film cameraman. Paddy's experience, confidence and ability to identify and pursue news and current affairs stories were a huge asset. He considered himself better at the job than most of the '7 Days' reporters or producer/directors, and frequently proved that assessment correct! Paddy's experience and expertise in directing films also carried some of those to achievements they would never have reached on their own ability. From his newspaper days and work with ITN and Canadian television, Paddy knew Northern Ireland and its politicians intimately. He had a good relationship with Dr Ian Paisley, who trusted him. When Paddy was involved, Dr Paisley was always available for interviews.

Paddy Barron was a remarkable person to work with. A story on Dr Patrick Hillery, then Minister for Foreign Affairs, who was about to take up the post of Ireland's first EEC Commissioner, brought us to the Minister's holiday home in Lahinch. Paddy, who had married one of my former production assistants, Nuala Malone, who came from Co. Clare, was keen to impress his new in-laws, who he would visit during the filming. Instead of driving the large and dull camera-truck in which he normally travelled, Paddy brought along his top-of-the-range Mercedes car. The road tax on the vehicle had expired, but Paddy was undeterred by such detail. He simply switched the tax disc from the camera-truck to the car. The irony was that when we were about to film with Dr Hillery on the beach at Spanish Point, Paddy asked the gardaí on protection duty with the Minister to keep an eye on his car. Luckily, their eyes did not alight on the fraudulent tax disc!

Working with Muiris as second-in-command of this twice-weekly current affairs programme was one of the most stimulating and exciting experiences of my life. Muiris and I were a good combination:

he was a genuine intellectual with great ideas and incisive editorial skills, while I was a competent organiser with technical skills and experience of film-making and outside broadcasts.

At that time there were only three political parties represented in Dáil Éireann, along with a handful of independent deputies. We knew all the politicians by their first names. One of the year's highlights was reporting on the annual Fianna Fáil and Fine Gael Árd Fheiseanna, usually held in Dublin, or the Labour party's Annual Conference, which moved around the provincial cities. The Labour party's conference always had the liveliest discussions. It was the only party that held a secret session during its annual conference. All media was excluded while the delegates held their discussion behind closed doors. The organisers overlooked the fact that the outside broadcast unit's microphones were still in place and could be turned on at any time from the control van. Muiris and I would sit in the OB unit, with the technicians, listening in. The most dramatic party conference of all those we attended was the 1971 Fianna Fáil Árd Fheis held at the RDS in Dublin. This followed the 'Arms crisis', which had divided the party, and the Árd Fheis was the scene of an unpleasant row between supporters of former Minister Kevin Boland and the party leader, Jack Lynch. As Boland attempted to address the delegates from an elevated podium, he was restrained by the platform chairman, Patrick Hillery, who uncharacteristically lost his temper, jumped to his feet and waved his arms in the air shouting, 'Ye can have Boland, but ye won't have Fianna Fáil'. That television footage appears regularly on historical programmes.

The combination of David Thornley and Ted Nealon made a formidable two-man studio team. They regularly interviewed the political party leaders. David Thornley was a larger-than-life individual with an intellect to match. Born in England, where he was educated at St Paul's School in London, the *alma mater* of Peter Ustinov and British Prime Minister Edward Heath, he later moved to Dublin. In 1964 David became the youngest ever fellow of Trinity College, Dublin, where he was awarded his MA and PhD. Possessor of a fine tenor voice, David had competed in the Feis Ceoil and later won the Walter Ludwig Cup at the Royal Irish Academy of Music. He was also a former President of the

A well-dressed young film cameraman working on an interview with American singer Pat Boone, who was making a movie in Dublin in 1963. *Photo: Roy Bedell, RTÉ*

Directing a film in Paris with sound recordist Terry Gough, cameraman Stuart Hetherington and production assistant Nuala Malone. *Photo: Mick Murray*

On location with Cyprus Broadcasting Corporation crew in Paphos, Cyprus. *Photo: Yiannis Karoles*

With Belgian cameraman Jos de Cock and production assistant Anne Logue in the Netherlands.

Senior Producer of '7 Days' in the studio with Liam Cosgrave before he became Taoiseach. *Photo: RTÉ*

Outside Dublin District Court on 4 November 1968 with David Thornley and Sean Bourke. David and I posted bail for the man who sprang double-agent George Blake from a British jail. *Photo:* Irish Press

Controlling the television results
programme in the 1973 General
Election, an event that
changed my life. In the foreground
is co-editor Mike Burns.
Photo: RTÉ

Former TV colleague Justin Keating, who
emerged from the 1973 Election as Minister for
Industry and Commerce, before a '7 Days'
interview with Brian Farrell. *Photo: RTÉ*

Comedian Marty Feldman arrives to direct *The Last Remake of Beau Geste*, the first feature film to be made at the newly established National Film Studios of Ireland. *Photo: Jack McManus*

Official opening of the studio in November 1975. *L to R:* Author Freddie Forsyth, Director General Joe Malone, Chairman of Bord Fáilte P.V. Doyle, Minister for Industry and Commerce Justin Keating.

At the Cannes Film Festival with John Boorman, French director Bertrand Tavernier, authors Anthony Burgess and Graham Greene, and Irish Consul General Pierre Joannon.
Photo: Eddie Quinn

In Hollywood with old friend Eamon Murphy and former movie star Audrey Dalton, whose father, Emmet Dalton, was co-founder of Ardmore Studios.
Photo: Delmar Watson Photography

In Washington with Maureen O'Hara and writer Morgan Llywelyn, who wanted me to persuade Sean Connery to play the lead in the screen version of her book on Brian Boru.
Photo: Stuart Pohost Photography

Escorting Pat Lovell, Producer of *Picnic at Hanging Rock* and many other successful Australian movies, down the red carpet at Cannes in 1980. *Photo: Traverso*

Arriving at the Palais with Sheila in 1983. *Photo: Traverso*

Well-known Australian impresario and producer, Robert Stigwood, entertained Noel Pearson and me in his luxury accommodation aboard the cruise liner *The World* during the 2002 Festival. *Photo: Sheila Hampson*

With Suzanne Macdougald and the Ambassador, François Mouton, at Suzanne's birthday in the French Embassy. *Photo: Norma Smurfit*

Veteran Wheels! On location with *The First Great Train Robbery*. Carriage driver Sadie Murphy, from Gorey, Co. Wexford, with Sean Connery and President Hillery. *Photo: Frank Fennell*

On his first visit to the studio Des O'Malley, Minister for Industry and Commerce, tried out a Penny Farthing bicycle used in the same movie, while John Boorman holds the saddle. *Photo: Jack McManus*

Producer John Foreman presented the train used in *The First Great Train Robbery* to President Hillery, who kept it at the studio. Handing over a picture of the train I am accompanied by, from left, NFSI Director John Donovan, Producer John Foreman and writer/director Michael Crichton. *Photo: Frank Fennell*

At a reception during the Monte Carlo Television Film Festival: John Kelleher, Assistant Controller of Programmes RTÉ on left, Sean McBride and Muiris MacConghail, Controller of Programmes, RTÉ, with his wife, Máire. *Photo: Studio Mauro*

Dublin University Boxing Club, and was proud of the broken nose he had sustained when winning his colours for boxing in 1964. He drove around in an ostentatious, bright yellow Triumph convertible. It looked good, but because of the leaking roof, the floor of the car was constantly covered in water! Daily he could be seen, attired in bow-tie and blazer, smoking his pipe as he strutted with his distinctive swagger up and down Grafton Street. We became firm, if unlikely, friends. David described me as being 'totally apolitical'. However, he soon became aware that, like himself and Muiris, I too was a staunch supporter of the Labour party, having being converted to socialism by Justin Keating.

*　*　*

Susan Gageby, a tall, elegant and exceptionally intelligent university graduate, joined '7 Days' as a research assistant. The weekend before Susan started work with us, Muiris and I were covering a General Election Results programme in Northern Ireland. We stayed at the beautiful Dunadry Inn, near Belfast. On Saturday evening we invited two ladies of our acquaintance to the hotel's dinner dance. We were taken aback when into the dining room walked Douglas Gageby with his wife, Dorothy, and John Healy, all of whom we knew. Slightly embarrassed by what perception the highly respectable Gagebys might have of their only daughter's first employers, I asked Muiris what we should do. Without hesitation, and fortified by aperitifs, Muiris immediately crossed the floor to the Gagebys' table and invited Dorothy to dance. He clearly impressed her, either with his conversation or his dancing, as no comment was made on our obvious indiscretion.

Our live programme from Belfast on the Sunday evening was broadcast from a temporary studio set up on the stage of St Mary's Catholic Hall. The Reverend Ian Paisley had agreed to participate. Well into the programme, he had still not turned up. Believing that he would—in my experience he had always been a man of his word—we extended the programme. Finally, at the eleventh hour, the big man arrived. Afterwards he said to me in that laughing, good-humoured voice that is rarely heard in public, 'Mr Smith, I bet you thought I would never come to a Papish Hall'! We met a number of times. Unlike his public persona, in private I found Ian Paisley to be a soft-spoken, charming and amusing man.

Susan was an outstanding research assistant who contributed greatly to '7 Days'. Brimming with energy, enthusiasm and great ideas, she instantly became a valuable team player. Muiris and I had hopes that she would remain in television and become a leading commentator, of which she was more than capable. However, Susan's long-term ambitions pointed in another direction. When I now meet or read about the Honourable Mrs Justice Susan Denham, Judge of the Supreme Court, my mind returns to the Monday morning when she started her first job as part of the '7 Days' team.

Shane Kenny, a young reporter, also joined the '7 Days' team, as did John Feeney, an angry young man who later left to become a daily gossip columnist in the *Evening Herald*. In later years Shane Kenny became Government Press Secretary. Sadly, John Feeney died in a tragic accident when an aircraft flying journalists to the traditional launch of the Beaujolais Nouveau wine in France crashed over England. Others who joined '7 Days' as research assistants under my watch were Brendan O'Brien, who would become an influential investigative reporter, and Frank Dunlop, who went on to become Government Press Secretary, PR man extraordinaire and an author whose name was on everyone's lips as the result of his evidence at the Flood Tribunal.

*   *   *

One whose profile and media accessibility was greatly enhanced by his appearance on '7 Days' was Dr Patrick Leahy. Paddy was an outspoken liberal doctor who worked in Dublin's Ballyfermot Health Centre. Most of his professional life had been spent in England, where he had practised in Coventry. On his first appearance on '7 Days' he proved to be a natural television performer, and soon became a national figure. He challenged the attitude of the Catholic bishops to contraception, often quoting renowned theologians, yet took some pride in the fact that he had been at school in Tipperary with Dr Tommy Morris, then

Archbishop of Cashel. Paddy Leahy fought the cause and defended the rights of women fearlessly. He held strong views on such topics as euthanasia, of which he was in favour, and spoke out about the incidents of incest in the overcrowded living conditions of Ballyfermot, where he worked. He bravely and forcefully articulated the beliefs many held at a time when others were afraid to do so.

A small man with a slightly harsh voice and twinkling eyes, Paddy bore a remarkable resemblance to Pablo Picasso. Self-assured and astute by nature, he had a brilliant mind and a generous heart. He enjoyed working with patients who relied on social welfare, frequently giving much of his salary to help them out: mothers living with their alcoholic husbands, and large families struggling in the overcrowded and impossible conditions of small council houses. Any money he had left was either given away or spent on his friends. Paddy's wife Jean was an alcoholic, and he became an advocate and supporter of Alcoholics Anonymous. He personally looked after a number of alcoholics we knew in the media.

*   *   *

Some years previously, shortly after we had returned to Ireland and I had joined Telefís Éireann, I realised that our marriage was beginning to show signs of strain. I was away from home a good deal, but when I was there, Angela and I argued frequently. Angela felt trapped and complained about the lack of adult company. The truth was that, apart from the enjoyment of seeing Teri growing more each day, I did not enjoy being at home. I now realised the folly of marrying too young. Apart from Angela and my first adult girlfriend, June, I had not had the experience of going out with many girls before I got married. While my friends were sowing their wild oats, I was too busy working. There was something of a bohemian atmosphere among the workforce of Telefís Éireann and, for better or worse, I was bound to become involved. While young love blossomed successfully between many of the new recruits, there were also a number of illicit love affairs going on. It seemed only a matter of time before my relationship with Angela deteriorated even further. I was now involved with another woman.

Angela and I separated. Angela and Teri continued to live in our apartment in Clonskeagh; I rented a small modern apartment on Appian Way, near Leeson Street. Before I left home, Angela had started attending a new doctor recommended to her by a friend. Married with a family, he was a man of exotic tastes and expensive habits. He had a reputation for the manner in which he treated his female patients and his behaviour had been brought to the attention of the Medical Council on more than one occasion. This doctor contacted me and suggested a meeting at Dublin's exclusive Russell Hotel. To me it seemed a strange place to meet, but I went along. Although only a general practitioner, he told me that he was a highly qualified psychiatrist. Nursing a large gin and tonic, he discussed Angela's mental condition and explained that treatment would be expensive.

It was some days later that I learned my wife was having an affair with this doctor. In order to see our daughter, Teri, whom I missed very much, I proposed to Angela that we should make another effort to make our marriage work. She agreed. Immediately after we had paid a deposit on a new house in Killiney, I invited Angela out to dinner. She declined. Next day I discovered that she had spent that evening with her lover. Although we moved to Killiney, the relationship did not improve. My real motivation in returning to a family situation was to be with our daughter. For this I was prepared to end any other relationship. On discovering that my wife had no intention of keeping her promise, I felt no obligation to keep mine. We both continued our liaisons, she with her doctor and me with my own lady, although that affair had virtually run its course and we were drifting apart.

Arriving home to Killiney in the early hours of the morning after a '7 Days' programme in autumn 1969, I found the house deserted. Earlier in the day Angela had removed most of the furniture and the curtains from the windows. She fled with Teri to new accommodation, which had been pre-arranged. The brief farewell note ironically blamed my now former *inamorata* for her action. I did not see Teri again for weeks. When we did meet and went to a movie (from her earliest years, Teri loved the cinema) it was obvious that the eleven-year-old was undergoing indoctrination and now had little time for me. Angela forbade further meetings with Teri. The difficult decision not to legally seek visiting rights was based on the fact that I did not want to confuse our adolescent daughter. In the High Court an alimony settlement was reached; I continued to pay Teri's school fees and could influence where she was educated. I did not see her again for ten years. Teri was taken to live in the city with Angela and her doctor lover, who had left his own family. I never forgot the fun Teri and I had together and yearned for my daughter.

*   *   *

In preparation for the 1969 General Election, the Labour party leader, Brendan Corish, and his General Secretary, Brendan Halligan, recruited a number of high-profile candidates to stand for election. Most prominent among these were Conor Cruise O'Brien, Justin Keating and David Thornley. The party slogan was 'The Seventies will be Socialist', and most of our small group believed it would be so. (Reminiscing about those exhilarating days recently with Brendan Halligan, he commented wryly, 'And now the socialists are all seventy!')

I did not consider it a good idea for David Thornley to become an active politician. Knowing his personality and passion better than most, I thought he was more suited to the academic life that he loved and to political broadcasting, in which he excelled. I felt that becoming an ordinary member of Dáil Éireann would destroy David, or would allow him to destroy himself. It would be fine if he were to become Minister for Education, the job to which he aspired, but this was unlikely. Muiris MacConghail encouraged David to stand in the election, however, and his influence ultimately prevailed.

David was elected to the 19th Dáil for the constituency of Dublin North-West. This was a very safe Labour seat, previously held by the trade union official Michael Mullen. Later, whenever his political opponents wished to activate David's quick temper, it was only necessary to refer to 'The seat that Mickey Mullen lent you'. Incongruous as it seemed, this intellectual academic now represented a working-class constituency. But David, being David, was totally at ease with, and much loved by, his constituents, particularly those in the Finglas area.

An enthusiastic '*à la carte* Catholic', on Sundays he went to Mass and Communion in as many churches as possible in the constituency.

*   *   *

In August 1969 David Thornley and I planned a week's golfing holiday in Cork and Kerry. A friend, Owen Dawson, invited us to stay for a night in his large caravan, parked for the summer in Dunmore East. He had invited a number of his friends for the weekend and asked if we could give a lift to another guest. Neither David nor I had previously met the very attractive blonde lady, dressed in a tailored white trouser-suit, who met us. Sheila Hampson, whom I later learned made all her own clothes, was English and had been an Aer Lingus hostess for eight years. She had arrived in Dublin two months before I returned from the United States. Our conversation on the journey to Waterford ranged widely, and both David and I were impressed by Sheila's knowledge of politics, current affairs and her strongly held opinions. She was a stimulating person. We spent the afternoon with Owen Dawson and his friends under a cloudless sky, swimming and sunbathing on the rocks overlooking the clear blue sea at Dunmore East, and the next day David, Sheila and I drove to Cork, where we stayed in the Intercontinental Hotel and dined together. Sheila was scheduled to fly to New York, so she returned to Dublin by train.

David and I went on to meet Bill O'Herlihy, who had arranged for us to play at Monkstown Golf Club, near Cork. On our arrival Bill encountered an old friend, who was a member of the club. A scratch golfer, this man was preparing to practise on the driving range. However, he generously suggested that if he played the first hole with us, he could introduce us as his guests, thereby reducing our green fees considerably. Bill's friend took his stance on the first tee and was about to commence his back-swing when David interrupted to enquire what number his ball was, just in case there might be any confusion. Having informed us of the make and number of the ball, this accomplished golfer then drove it about 275 yards down the centre of the fairway. When it came to David's turn to tee-off, there were a number of 'fresh air' shots, leaving the ball undisturbed on its tee. Eventually Bill suggested that if

David removed the pipe from his mouth, his chances of connecting with the golf ball might improve. This worked. The ball travelled almost as far as the nearby ladies' tee! David continued to hack his ball up the fairway in short bursts. When we ultimately reached our friend's original drive, David had played twenty-two strokes. His ball, now much the worse for wear, certainly could not be confused with anyone else's!

The truth was, however, that David and I had lost interest in golf. Our hearts were elsewhere. We agreed to abandon our holiday and return home. We were both in love with Sheila and wanted to see her again as soon as possible.

Sheila was more amused by, than interested in, the attention being paid to her by these two quite interesting but very different and definitely unavailable suitors. She was in the 'off' stage of an 'on/off' romance with a man to whom she had been engaged. She was free to meet either of us. When Sheila returned from her transatlantic journey, two messages awaited her; it was less than a week after she had first met us. By this time, David, over-enthusiastic as ever, had dyed his hair blond to match Sheila's in the hope of improving his chances with her. That new hair colour lasted until finally, after the sustained efforts of Ted Nealon and myself, David agreed to return to his original colour the day before Dáil Éireann returned after the summer recess. In 1969 mature men, and particularly the Labour party's front-bench spokesman on Education, did not change their hair colour in such dramatic fashion. Touching-up the grey bits with black was acceptable, but that was the absolute limit. David's friends quite rightly felt that he would face ridicule from his fellow TDs if he appeared in the Dáil chamber looking like an overweight version of Adam Faith!

Sheila went to dinner with David, but thought better of further involvement when he produced the small handgun he frequently carried and threatened to shoot himself if she rejected him. It was somewhat dramatic for a first date, but David was given to such theatrical gestures. He had a fixation with guns and once shot at, but thankfully only slightly injured, a trespasser in his garden. He carried a double-barrelled shotgun in the boot of his car, even when parked in the grounds of Leinster House; security was less stringent then.

Travelling in my car with Micheal Johnston one day, David mentioned that he had a gun in his pocket. Moving uncomfortably to one side, Micheal explained that he was changing position so that in the event the gun went off accidentally, his manhood would remain intact! And so it was that although David and I continued to be close friends, in the end it was I who succeeded in wooing Sheila.

After seven turbulent years in Dáil Éireann and the European Parliament, David Thornley lost his seat in the 1977 General Election. The following year he died at the tragically young age of forty-two. His over-indulgence in alcohol had contributed to his being passed over for a Cabinet post when his academic colleagues, Justin Keating and Conor Cruise O'Brien, became ministers in the Fine Gael/Labour coalition government of 1973. Sadly, my intuition about David had proved correct.

*   *   *

Sheila loved Paris and spoke French well, but she wanted to improve her fluency. Accordingly, she arranged a transfer to the Aer Lingus office at Le Bourget airport and found a tiny apartment near the Bastille and the lovely Place de Vosges. As '7 Days' was off air for the summer, I took my car over on the ferry and stayed with Sheila for July and August. Living in Paris was idyllic. Close friends Sean and Olive Braiden, whom I knew when they lived in Brussels, were now in Paris. Sean was Aer Lingus Sales Manager for Europe; Olive, beautiful, charming and supportive, was too busy rearing a family to engage in any of the activities for which she would later become so well-known as a dynamic executive, social reformer and 'Queen of the Quangos'. We dined in good but inexpensive restaurants, enjoyed the splendid weather and frequently picnicked on the banks of the nearby Seine. One day, on the Île de la Cité, we saw Samuel Beckett sitting nearby. Thin, gaunt and craggy-faced, he looked exactly like the black-and-white image of his photographs; there was no colour in his appearance. He sat quietly, alone under the trees, the sunshine through the leaves creating a dappled pattern on his rugged face. Much as I would have loved to do so, interrupting his reverie to introduce myself as another Irishman would have been an intrusion. However, I later had contact with the great man. He wrote to me in February 1978. In his own tiny handwriting, the brief note on his simple card read:

SAMUEL BECKETT

Paris 5. 2. 78

Dear Mr. Smith

Just to say how pleased I am to hear from Monsieur Soussigne that you show an interest in his screen version of my "Trois Nouvelles" and how greatly I would appreciate any help you can give him toward the realization of this project.
With all good wishes,
Yours sincerely,
Sam Beckett.

* * *

Sheila and I were invited to the wedding of Paddy Barron and Nuala Malone in Ennis. Another guest at that wedding in the beautiful Old Ground Hotel was someone who had been the subject of a controversial '7 Days' programme two years earlier. Sean Bourke, a native of Limerick, had been an inmate of Wormwood Scrubs Prison in London in the 1960s, imprisoned for a relatively minor crime. There he befriended George Blake, the Russian spy and former official of the British Foreign Office in Berlin. At his trial in the Old Bailey in 1961, Blake was found guilty of spying and sentenced to the longest term of imprisonment ever imposed under English law: forty-two years. After his release from prison, Sean Bourke rented a flat nearby and continued to communicate with George Blake by means of a walkie-talkie radio. Together they planned Blake's escape, which was executed on 22 October 1966. After lying low in a flat a few minutes' walk from Wormwood Scrubs Prison—while the authorities, believing high-level KGB agents had engineered the daring escape over the prison wall, mounted surveillance on every port, airport and landing strip in Britain—Blake was driven in a second-hand dormobile by two friends to East Germany. From there he was taken to Moscow, where accommodation was provided by the Soviet authorities.

Bourke, who was now a fugitive from British justice, considered escaping to Ireland. Fearful of being extradited to Britain, however, he followed Blake to Moscow. There he lived in reasonable comfort while writing a book on the whole escapade. Bored with Moscow and the restrictions placed on his movements for the two years he lived there, Sean Bourke decided to return to Ireland and take his chances with the law. On 22 October 1968, the second anniversary of the jail-break, Bourke returned to Dublin on a flight from Amsterdam. In one of his characteristic master-strokes, Paddy Barron arranged for him to stay at the Gresham Hotel. He had the temerity to book himself into the adjoining suite, all the better to watch and protect his exclusive story and prevent rival television stations having any contact with Bourke until after the '7 Days' interview. Muiris MacConghail, Brian Farrell and I spent a great deal of time in the Gresham with the subject of our scoop. Paddy Barron filmed an interview there, to be used in the event of Bourke's arrest. This did not happen, so Brian Farrell was able to conduct a live interview on the next '7 Days' programme. Shortly afterwards, at 6 a.m., Sean Bourke was arrested in his hotel suite. He appeared in the Dublin District Court later the same morning, where an order was made under the Extradition Act of 1965 for him to be delivered to a member of the British Special Branch. An application for bail was refused and he was taken to Mountjoy Jail.

During the period we had been together, all of us had formed a good relationship with Sean Bourke and came to like him, as did David Thornley, who also met him before his arrest. With his usual ebullience, David decided we must visit our friend during the first few hours of his incarceration. A bag of goodies was assembled, which included chocolate, fruit, cigarettes and bottle of whiskey. At the front gates of Mountjoy we were admitted and went through a security check. The paper-bag containing our gifts was scrutinised and, with a wry smile and a raised eyebrow, the prison warder removed the bottle of whiskey and handed it back to us. No such luxuries in prison! The following day, after a successful application, David and I posted bail for Sean Bourke, pledging our homes as collateral in the process. Most of our colleagues thought we were insane to take such a risk for a petty criminal whom we hardly knew.

The following January, Sean Bourke's appeal against the extradition order was heard in the High Court. It lasted for more than a week. Judgment was given on 3 February 1969, when the President of the High Court held that the offence of helping George Blake to escape could be classed as 'an offence connected with a political offence'; the plaintiff was released. The State appealed to the Supreme Court, which five months later upheld the High Court decision. Sean Bourke was free at last. He settled in his native Limerick, where he became something of a celebrity. His book, *The Springing of George Blake*, was published in London in 1970. A copy he presented to me bears the inscription: 'For Sheamus Smith who displayed considerable moral courage by very effectively springing me from Mountjoy Jail one Monday morning— with sincere thanks Sean Bourke. June 1st. 1970.'

This story has a sequel. When arranging the jail-break, Sean Bourke had used a tape-recorder to record his two-way radio conversations with the incarcerated George Blake. Before leaving England, he had given this vital piece of evidence to his brother, Kevin, who lived in London, for safe-keeping. After regaining his freedom, Sean was keen to retrieve this tape-recording. Obviously as a fugitive he could not travel to the UK himself, so I volunteered to pick up the tape. At this stage we were all slightly paranoid and felt that we were under surveillance by MI5. The journey to Scotland, where his brother Kevin was now living, was made by a circuitous route in order to avoid detection by MI5 agents who might be watching any of Sean Bourke's associates. First, I travelled to London. There, in a working-class pub, I met a group who checked me out, then arranged the meeting with Kevin Bourke in Glasgow. Next morning I flew on a Pan-American transatlantic flight from London to Prestwick Airport, near Glasgow. There I met Kevin. In his little clapped-out van he took me to his home, a small, redbrick terrace cottage. While I waited in the tiny living room, Kevin went outside and returned with a lump hammer and a chisel. Remarking to me, 'You didn't come for a packet of fags, you know', he then proceeded to open a large hole in the chimney-breast. Concealed inside, wrapped in brown paper, was the reel of quarter-inch tape containing the recorded conversations between his brother and George Blake. With the precious package intact, I travelled by taxi to Glasgow Airport and returned directly to Dublin. Sean Bourke was delighted with the success of the mission. He received a fee of £4,500 from the *News of the World*, which printed a transcript of the conversations in an exclusive article.

As his fame and notoriety faded, Sean Bourke became increasingly reliant on alcohol. He died outside the caravan in which he lived, near the seaside town of Kilkee, on 21 January 1980. Kevin O'Connor's RTÉ radio documentary, 'A Death in January', broadcast on the second anniversary of Sean Bourke's death, was a fitting tribute to his extraordinary fellow Limerickman.

* * *

Sheila returned from Paris and resumed her flying duties on Aer Lingus transatlantic routes at the beginning of October 1970. Two weeks later, we were involved in a motor accident near Portlaoise in which Sheila broke her neck. She was taken by helicopter to the National Rehabilitation Centre in Dún Laoghaire. At the hospital, she was placed on traction. Lying immobile was difficult, but Sheila was a good patient. Every four hours she was carefully turned in the bed by hospital attendants to prevent bed sores. Each evening I cooked dinner at home and took it to the hospital, where we ate it together. Lying on her side with weights attached to her head by a pulley system, I had to feed each bite to Sheila. She drank wine from a special cup with a spout! After fourteen weeks of traction treatment, she was transferred to a wheelchair before learning to walk again. This was a joyous time for us as I was able to take her out to lunch on Sundays and afterwards wheel her along Dún Laoghaire pier. She wore a wig because her blonde tresses had been cut away to facilitate the traction treatment. After her release from the hospital, Sheila came to live with me.

* * *

One Tuesday evening Muiris MacConghail, Bill O'Herlihy and I were discussing possible items for the following Friday's programme. Bill pointed out that as it would be the fiftieth anniversary of the event, perhaps the programme should feature the famous ambush of the Black and Tans at Kilmichael, in West Cork, by the IRA flying column under Commandant Tom Barry. It was a brilliant idea! Early the following morning I was on the road to Cork. There I met the legendary guerrilla commander, Tom Barry. A slight, thin man, looking younger than his seventy-three years, he had the demeanour of a soldier and was nattily dressed. Soft-spoken, with a twinkle in his clear gentle eyes, he was smaller than I had expected. Together we drove around the countryside, rounding up the survivors of his famous West Cork flying column. All agreed to travel by train to Dublin to appear live on '7 Days'. One aging volunteer said with feeling, 'I followed him then. I'll follow him now. If he wants me to go to Dublin, I'll go.' Another showed me his souvenir of the ambush: a military tin hat with a bullet-hole in it. Yet another still had his rifle in the rafters of the house—shades of 'keeping the pike in the thatch'.

At noon on Friday, less than three days after formulating the original idea for the programme, all the remaining survivors of the ambush at Kilmichael were assembled at Cork railway station. Some had brought souvenirs; Commandant Tom Barry had brought his revolver. After seeing everyone safely aboard the train, I drove to Dublin at great speed, arriving at Heuston Station just in time to meet the Cork train. In the '7 Days' studio the group of survivors of the Kilmichael ambush were arranged on tiered seating, with their commander in the centre of the front row. Brian Farrell did a splendid interview with these aging heroes of the fight for Irish freedom; a few years later, nearly all were dead. When the programme was over, we accompanied Tom Barry and his men to their hotel. As Muiris and I were leaving, Tom Barry said, 'Why don't the three of us go up to the Park and shoot that bastard de Valera?' He was still a tough man, but I doubt if he was serious about harming our President!

* * *

At a meeting of European current affairs television producers in Brussels in 1973, I proposed making a special programme on our newly elected president, Erskine Childers. All were enthusiastic. The idea of a Protestant President in what was then perceived abroad as a fiercely Roman Catholic country was, to say the least, unusual. RTÉ would finance the programme and, under the exchange system that existed between us, offer it free to the other European television stations. Flushed with my colleagues' enthusiasm, I contacted the President on my return. He was eager to help and promised his full co-operation. During the course of the Presidential Election campaign some months earlier, I had met Erskine Childers several times. He had been the only member of the Fianna Fáil Cabinet who was always on hand when the government was in a crisis. After my meeting with the President, I discussed the programme with Jack White, RTÉ's Assistant Controller of Programmes. As he was a Protestant himself, I was confident of his approval. Imagine my amazement when he instantly gave the idea an emphatic thumbs-down, saying, 'We must protect that man from himself'.

My dilemma now was that, having given my commitment to the President and to my European colleagues, I had no resources to make the programme. In order to avoid embarrassment, I enlisted the help of my friends, Seamus Deasy and Rory O'Farrell. Both agreed to become partners in the enterprise, Seamus as film cameraman and Rory as editor. Together we borrowed £7,000 from my friendly bank manager, Jack Higgins in the Montrose Branch of the Bank of Ireland, to finance the project. Seamus Deasy's brother, Brendan, came on board as sound operator, while Brian Farrell signed up as scriptwriter/interviewer. In order to provide a variety of locations and events, we decided to shoot the film at a leisurely pace over the following year. The first location was the annual dinner of the Royal College of Physicians of Ireland, at which the new President and former Minister for Health would receive an honorary degree.

Over the following months we had a wonderful time working with Erskine and his wife, Rita, and their young daughter, Nessa. Brian Farrell interviewed the presidential couple in Áras an Uachtaráin and we filmed the President at some of the more colourful and interesting of his engagements. On a visit to Killarney, he travelled in the rarely seen Presidential rail-coach. Once, when filming the President using a scythe to cut the reeds on the bank of the pond near Áras an Uachtaráin, he called to his wife Rita, who was standing some distance away, to join him. She replied, 'Certainly not my dear. I'm not going near you when you have your weapon in your hand.'

Glendalough House, near Roundwood in Co. Wicklow, the home of the Barton family, was one of our summer locations. There the President took us on a tour of the extensive gardens and amused us with stories of the childhood adventures he had embarked on there with his cousins. The fine mansion was the ancestral home of the Bartons, a wealthy Protestant land-owning family. Robert Barton, the President's cousin, was the last surviving signatory of the Anglo-Irish Treaty. He died in 1975 at the age of ninety-four.

One Saturday evening, after our filming was complete but before we had started the editing process, Sheila and I had a dinner party in our apartment. Among the guests were Brian and Marie-Thérèse Farrell. In the early hours of Sunday morning, while we were still enjoying ourselves, I got a telephone call to say that the President had had a heart attack and died suddenly while attending the Annual Dinner of the Royal College of Physicians of Ireland. It was the same function at which we had started filming with him the previous year. Sobered by the tragic news, the party came to an abrupt end. I arranged to meet Rory O'Farrell in his editing room at dawn, a few hours later, and Brian was put on standby to complete his script. We worked right through Sunday and, thanks to Rory's skill and talent, had a really good film ready for scripting by late afternoon. Brian provided an excellent script, which we recorded that evening in RTÉ. By midnight our film, *A President for all the People*, was complete. RTÉ had little material on the President's short term in office. I took great pleasure in negotiating a fee in excess of £20,000 to broadcast our film the next evening. RTÉ paid us well for a programme that, if Jack White had agreed with my proposal, it would have had for nothing.

Erskine Hamilton Childers was laid to rest just seventeen months after his inauguration as President of Ireland. He had lived for sixty-eight years and truly was A President for all the People.

*   *   *

In 1969 we broadcast a '7 Days' programme that would change the lives of many associated with it. Presented by Bill O'Herlihy, directed by Joe McCormack and filmed by Paddy Barron, it dealt with the serious problem of illegal money-lending. Shot with great care and attention to detail over a period of several weeks, the programme sometimes used hidden cameras and microphones—techniques new to Irish television—to obtain evidence of illegal money-lending and the methods used by its perpetrators to entrap their victims. At a time of high unemployment and real poverty among the less well-off, illegal money-lending and its usurious rates of interest was a profound social malady. Many young mothers, in particular, were trapped in an unending stream of indebtedness to money-lenders, who held their children's allowance books and collected this social welfare payment to service the debts of their victims.

While '7 Days' was no stranger to political controversy and frequently came in for severe government criticism, this investigative programme, which also drew attention to the Garda authorities' indifference and cavalier disregard for the problem, caused a greater controversy than ever before. The Fianna Fáil government was furious, as were the Garda authorities, who accused the programme of dishonesty. In the Dáil, Brendan Corish, leader of the Labour party, called for a public inquiry into the problem of illegal money-lending. In response, Taoiseach Jack Lynch and his government decided to set up a Judicial Tribunal of Inquiry not into illegal money-lending but into the '7 Days' programme that had exposed the heinous criminality. Tribunals were a rarity in Ireland in the 1960s. In fact, this was only the third time in the history of the State that such a court of inquiry had been instituted.

As in all such tribunals, various interested parties were represented by legal counsel. RTÉ was regarded as the principal protagonist in the proceedings. However, as editor of '7 Days', Muiris MacConghail was determined that the programme itself and, in particular, those responsible for the money-lending programme should have separate representation. The new Director General, Tom Hardiman—the first internal staff appointment to the station's top job—agreed. The programme was represented by two of the most eminent senior counsel of the time, former Taoiseach, John A. Costello, and Ernest Wood, a formidable personality in any courtroom. Garret Cooney, then a junior council, and on my recommendation Martin E. Marren, a young solicitor from Co. Mayo, completed the legal team.

The Money Lending Tribunal started in January 1970 and ran over a two-month period. Up to that time, it was the longest running tribunal in the history of the State. In its report, issued in August 1970, the Tribunal was critical of the methods employed by the '7 Days' team in collecting its evidence and the manner in which the programme was presented.

I had little involvement in the actual programme or its consequences. However, I did approve the payment of £20, which was higher than normal, to two money-lenders, whom I regarded as specialists and therefore entitled to the special treatment they demanded. One was known as 'Golly' Green. During my brief appearance at the Tribunal the Chairman, Mr Justice Sean Butler, in accepting the integrity of my decision, remarked, 'They were professional people anyhow.' Media coverage of the Money Lending Tribunal frequently referred to the notorious illegal money-lender 'Golly' Green and the name captured the public's imagination. It was not long before a horse named *Golly Green* was running on Irish racecourses.

Muiris MacConghail and Bill O'Herlihy were the main RTÉ protagonists at the Tribunal. They each spent several days in the witness box. RTÉ management and the team of '7 Days' were disappointed with the findings of the Tribunal Report and the lack of condemnation of the social evil of illegal money-lending. Although the Report condemned its methods, '7 Days' was in fact ahead of its time. The hidden-camera techniques instigated by Paddy Barron for the programme are commonplace in modern investigative journalism.

Following the debacle of the Tribunal, morale in the '7 Days' team was low. The following year Muiris was appointed Head of Features and Current Affairs in RTÉ Radio. Later, he became an Assistant Secretary in the Department of the Taoiseach (Liam Cosgrave) and Head of the Government Information Service, which he totally revamped. Muiris was Head of Raidio na Gealtachta before returning to RTÉ as Assistant and ultimately Controller of Television Programmes. In a more favourable political climate, this accomplished broadcasting executive would have reached the top position in RTÉ instead of being, in the opinion of many, the best Director General RTÉ never had.

*   *   *

On Muiris' departure, I was invited to become Editor of '7 Days'. The Head of News and Current Affairs, Jim McGuinness, made it very clear that if I did not accept the offer, the new editor would be someone outside the programme. With some reluctance, I agreed. I was well aware that Jim McGuinness saw me as a conservative person, somebody who would be much easier to deal with and to influence than my predecessor. To counteract this, I persuaded Colm Ó Briain, the talented young radical, to become the programme's Senior Producer and my second-in-command. Apart from having great ideas, Colm was a skilful and stylish film director. Among others, his '7 Days' programme on Lissadell House, the home of the Gore-Booth family, which had been associated with W.B. Yeats and Countess Markievicz, had been widely acclaimed. When Colm left, Paul Gleeson joined the programme as Senior Producer. With his wide experience and logistical skills, Paul too made a significant contribution to the programme.

We no longer had Muiris at the helm, but '7 Days' continued with the same current affairs agenda as before. However, I never enjoyed the role of Editor as much as that of Senior Producer under Muiris MacConghail. The Northern Ireland Troubles provided a constant news story and, along with trade union disputes, was a prominent feature of our programmes. These events were not of great interest to me. (Jim McGuinness, the former IRA activist, was obsessed with Northern Ireland affairs. He told me that as a young man on his way to court in the prison van, his greatest concern was that he might receive a shorter sentence than his fellow defendants, indicating that he was an second-rate volunteer!) I enjoyed political programmes, but I had no sympathy for the IRA, then referred to euphemistically as an 'illegal organisation' or its 'political wing', Sinn Féin. After the events of Bloody Sunday in Derry, the IRA, in full view of the media, burned down the British Embassy in Dublin on 2 February 1972. That afternoon I drove by Merrion Square, where the embassy was located. I was outraged to see that the traffic in the immediate vicinity of the blazing building was being controlled by balaclava-clad members of the IRA. Shamefully, the government and Garda authorities did nothing to prevent or stop the outrage or control the mob, which was reported to have grown from 20,000 to 50,000 over the course of the afternoon.

Many are under the impression that politicians, and others on the political scene, are constantly endeavouring to change or influence RTÉ programmes in their favour. In my experience, this was not so. During my years as Editor of '7 Days', I was approached only three times in this manner. The first was on behalf of Charles Haughey in the period after his dismissal from the Cabinet. Before a live studio appearance, one of his aides wanted assurance that we 'would treat the boss fairly'. Following that programme, the same person complained about the lighting in the studio because 'it made Charlie's eyes look hooded'. I pointed out that Charlie's eyes *were* hooded.

In a phone call from Bundoran, where he worked as a schoolteacher, Daithi O'Connell, then one of the IRA's leaders, also pleaded for fair treatment. The third request came from Nuala Fennell, a women's affairs activist who was subsequently elected as a Fine Gael TD. In an unsuccessful attempt to impose herself on a discussion panel before a programme, she threatened to contact Director General Tom Hardiman, with whom she had been to college. It was hardly a move to endear oneself to a programme's producer!

After her accident, Sheila never flew as an air-hostess again. During her convalescence, she lived with me in Killiney. I was head over heels in love, but inwardly I felt that had it not been for her accident and my support during her long hospitalisation, it was unlikely that we would still have been together. After we moved to a new luxury apartment in Sandymount, Sheila worked in the Aer Lingus Hostess Training Centre at Dublin Airport. She later qualified as an interior designer and worked in the offices of architect, Gustav Sauter. Angela prevented me from seeing Teri during this period, so it would be some time before Sheila and Teri met. They now get on well together.

* * *

After the departure of David Thornley, Brian Farrell became my closest friend and confidant on the '7 Days' team. Brian was the principal presenter of the 1973 General Election Results programme. The main panellists were Ted Nealon and Basil Chubb, Professor of Political Science in TCD. Together, Ted and Basil made a redoubtable team of political analysts. English-born Basil were a kind and likeable man. He had been a rear-gunner in the RAF during and the Second World War and was one of the few who survived. A great fisherman, he sometimes bought freshly caught brown trout to Sheila and me when he lived near us in Ballsbridge.

Supplemented by outside broadcast units around the country, the Dublin studio was the main focus of attention during the election results. It was there, in the early hours of 2 March 1973, that Taoiseach Jack Lynch conceded the election. Fianna Fáil had been in power for exactly sixteen years. There was a poignant moment in the make-up department after the programme when Jack Lynch said to me, 'I'd better arrange Garda protection for Liam [Cosgrave] right away'. In the Fine Gael/Labour coalition that followed, Justin Keating was named Minister for Industry and Commerce. There was no way of knowing then that that General Election was to change the course of my own life forever!

*   *   *

In 1973 Sheila and I went to Cyprus and stayed in Kyrenia. We were utterly enraptured by the island and its people, and encouraged everyone we knew or met to visit Cyprus. Justin Keating and his wife Loretta took their children there in 1973, and there Loretta met Yannis Cleanthous, the man she later married after her divorce from Justin. Our circle of friends in Cyprus was widening. July 1974 saw us back in Kyrenia. Justin and Loretta Keating were due to arrive at the start of their children's school holidays.

The tranquility of our holiday that year came to an abrupt end with the *coup d'état* that deposed the Cypriot President, Archbishop Makarios. The *coup* was led by a right-wing militant group, 'Eoka B', the Cypriot equivalent of the provisional IRA, and was backed by the military junta that then ruled in Greece. The lawful president was replaced by Nicos Sampson, a former terrorist of notoriety and small-time gangster. A curfew was imposed; residents were allowed out of their homes for only a few hours each day. It struck me as amazing that people adapted so quickly to the situation. Every morning we would walk or drive the short distance from our rented apartment to the town centre. Despite sporadic gun-shots in the streets (the regular Cypriot army was still fighting the insurgents), people went about their normal business. We did our shopping, returning with wine and food for the day. In the afternoons we sat on our balcony or beside the pool, drank wine and listened to the gunfire, which increased dramatically during the curfew period.

Sheila was becoming nervous and decided to return home. My intention was to remain in the capital, Nicosia, which was now teeming with members of the international press corps, including Dominick Coyle, my old friend and colleague from the *Evening Press*, now a Senior Correspondent with the *Financial Times*. Dominick was an expert on the political situation in Cyprus. His father-in-law, Judge Barra O Briain, had drawn up the constitution adopted by the Republic of Cyprus in 1960. Maeve Binchy, then an *Irish Times* columnist, was also in Nicosia covering the emerging story.

I attended a press conference with the new president. He was young, small in stature and looked like a teddy-boy or a Dublin gurrier. The press conference was a bizarre affair. Nicos Sampson's elevation to the highest office in the land lasted only eight days, but the damage done to Cyprus and the delicate relationship between the two communities on the island was immense. A small cabal of gunmen, supported by the government of the country many Cypriots regarded as 'the Motherland', had created a situation that would inevitably bring about an invasion by the Turkish army. That invasion came sooner than expected. On the night of 19 July 1974, Sheila and I stayed in the Ledra Palace, Nicosia's top hotel. Sheila had a reservation on a flight to London the following morning. Most of the international journalists, including Maeve Binchy, Dominick Coyle and Brian Barron from BBC-TV, were also residents of the hotel that night. After an excellent dinner and a long night of talking and serious drinking, we all got to bed very late.

We were awakened by a commotion in the corridor outside our room and the noise of aircraft overhead. I opened the window shutters to be confronted by a sight I had thought I would only ever see in a movie: in the blinding early morning sunlight, soldiers carrying automatic weapons were dropping from the sky in great numbers. It was exactly four minutes past 6 a.m. on the morning of 20 July 1974 when the first Turkish paratroopers hit Cypriot soil. Our cherished island would be changed forevermore. Had the Greek-backed *coup* that deposed President Makarios not occurred, the Turkish invasion would never have taken place. Within a few days, more than 200,000 people were homeless and Cyprus was divided permanently.

Dressing hurriedly, we rushed downstairs to the hotel lobby. The scene was one of chaos and panic. The glass front doors had been shattered. Blood and broken glass covered the floor. The dining-room waiters, who a few short hours before were resplendent in their tailored red jackets, were now struggling into the ill-fitting tunics of army reserve soldiers. Along with some others we took shelter in the gents' toilet. A group photograph taken there, which included Sheila and me, appeared in the British newspapers two days later.

Maeve Binchy and I caught our breaths by sitting on the urinals, but we leapt up swiftly when the automatic flushing system went off. Two hours later we all moved into the hotel cellar. There we spent an anxious time, listening to the bombardment above. We were without food, water or toilets in the dimly lit vault. Our incarceration lasted for thirty-two hours; it felt like a week. My principal fear was not of dying immediately but of the hotel collapsing on top of us and causing prolonged agony before inevitable death. Eventually we were rescued by a young British Army major lugging a large Union Jack on his shoulder.

As the various nationalities were sorted, Maeve Binchy was astonished to discover that she was the only person carrying an Irish passport. Both Dominick Coyle and I also had British passports, which had come in useful before when travelling abroad. Sheila was a British citizen. Maeve was well able to look after herself, though. She and Dominick remained in Cyprus with the other journalists to cover the unfolding story and Maeve's graphic reports of the invasion and its aftermath appeared daily in *The Irish Times*. She went to Cyprus a newspaper columnist and returned home an experienced war correspondent.

The evacuees were loaded onto army trucks for transportation to Deklia, one of the three British Army bases in Cyprus. Two of our fellow evacuees on the back of our truck were Swedish. They had a bottle of Scotch whisky, the provenance of which was not admitted: it might well have come from the hotel bar before the remaining stock was looted by journalists the previous evening. They were easily convinced by me that all alcohol would be confiscated by the authorities at the British base, so that the only solution was to pass the bottle amongst us. I rarely drink whisky, but in the blistering hot sunshine of that Cyprus afternoon, it tasted like nectar, definitely the drink of the gods.

Exhausted, unshaven and unwashed, we joined the long lines of other displaced persons, many of whom were Cypriots, seeking refuge in the British base. After one night in the relative comfort of an army barracks, we returned to England on board an RAF Hercules aircraft. We landed at Lynham Air Force base, near London. That night we were welcomed and pampered in London's Tara Hotel by the general manager, Eoin Dillon, an old friend and former manager of the Shelbourne Hotel in Dublin.

*   *   *

After '7 Days' I began working on a new series, 'My Own Place'. This would take well-known people back to their place of birth or early upbringing. An eclectic group of subjects included: Joe Malone, then Bord Fáilte's top man in the United States; architect, Michael Scott; playwright, Hugh Leonard; writer, Edna O'Brien; and actress, Rosaleen Lenihan.

The short 'My Own Place' series was to be followed by a dream project: 'Even the Olives are Bleeding'. This programme featured Cathal O'Shannon as writer/presenter and examined the stories of the Irish men who fought on both sides in the Spanish Civil War. Many were still alive. It was a subject that had interested me since boyhood. Cathal and I were well advanced with research and making arrangements for extensive filming in Spain and Ireland for this one-hour documentary when the Minister for Industry and Commerce, Justin Keating, informed me that he intended to announce my appointment as Managing Director of Ardmore Studios within a few weeks. Until then, the matter was confidential. My predicament was that I had to withdraw from the Spanish project, but could not reveal the reason. Cathal and the Controller of Programmes, although surprised, were sympathetic towards my undisclosed personal reasons for giving up something for which I had shown such enthusiasm. For the third time in his RTÉ career, a talented young producer named John Kelleher stepped into my shoes. He had previously followed me into 'Newsbeat' and current affairs. John produced and directed the programme, which won a Jacob's National Television Award for Cathal O'Shannon. 'Even the Olives are Bleeding' triumphed at many international festivals and is regarded as one of the best documentaries ever made by RTÉ.

By the time the documentary was being fêted, I had hung up my RTÉ cap and was busy with the challenging task of trying to run a film studio on limited resources. Thus began another new phase in my life and career.

Chapter 11 ~

ARDMORE
STUDIOS

Ardmore Studios was founded in 1958 by Major General Emmett Dalton. A hero of the War of Independence and close friend and confidant of Michael Collins, in the 1950s. Dalton was a film producer based in London. His partner and joint managing director in the enterprise was Louis Elliman, the theatrical impresario and owner of Dublin's Theatre Royal. Financial assistance came from the State's Industrial Development Authority and the Industrial Credit Company. Once built, Ardmore was one of the most modern studios in Europe. Built on a 10 acre plot near Bray in Co. Wicklow, it had two large sound stages and one small one. It had construction and carpentry shops, a sound department and recording studios, electrical department, editing rooms, hair and make-up departments. There was an adjoining 'back lot' of some 27 acres, through which the River Dargle flowed. This was an attractive feature because it accommodated the building of extensive outdoor film sets.

Emmett Dalton's original idea was to bring the Abbey Theatre's plays to the international screen. And this, to a certain extent, is what he achieved. The first film made at the brand new studio was *Home is the Hero*, a screen adaptation of Walter Macken's stage play. It was followed by *Sally's Irish Rogue*, based on George Shiel's play, 'The New Gossoon', and then a screen version of Hugh Leonard's 'The Big Birthday'. Leonard's first play for the Abbey, it was staged at the Queen's Theatre, the new home of the Abbey after a fire destroyed its own premises. Distributed in the US as *Broth of a Boy*, it was Barry Fitzgerald's last film. The principal cast members in these productions were

Abbey players, many getting their first experience of acting for the big screen.

Over the following years more international films with Hollywood and British stars and well-known directors came to Ardmore, including: *Shake Hands with the Devil*, starring James Cagney and Dana Wynter; *A Terrible Beauty*, with Robert Mitchum, Anne Heywood and Dan O'Herlihy; *Term of Trial*, with Laurence Olivier; Carol Reed's *The Running Man*, with Laurence Harvey and Lee Remick; and *Of Human Bondage*, again with Laurence Harvey and Hollywood star Kim Novak.

In the 1960s Ardmore Studios experienced a number of industrial disputes, mostly brought about by the electrical trade unions. Electricians were a vital element of the technical crew of any film and they always instigated a disproportionate amount of industrial disputes on a film set. Ireland's first film studio suffered as a result. Such difficulties arose during the filming of *Of Human Bondage* and resulted in the film being over schedule and seriously over budget, which did not help. The withdrawal of subsidies paid under the British Eady Scheme to films made in Ardmore Studios also had a disastrous effect. For nearly a full year the studio lay idle. In November 1963, Dublin accountant William Sandys was appointed receiver and the studio was put on the market. The sale was advertised in the international film trade magazines, but no interest was forthcoming. Unable to find a buyer, William Sandys decided to promote rental of the Ardmore facility on the international market. He was remarkably successful and brought films such as *The Spy Who Came In From the Cold* and *The Blue Max* to Ireland. Other memorable films made in the studio at that time include *The Lion in Winter*, which earned Katharine Hepburn her third Oscar for her performance as Eleanor of Aquitaine. Peter O'Toole played Henry II.

Two more receivers, Alex Spain and Tom Kelly, took charge of Ardmore at different times. Holding the reins between their periods of stewardship was certainly the most flamboyant character the studio had ever seen, either on or off its stages. Lee Davis became head of the studio in 1967. A larger-than-life personality, Lee entertained royally in the studio restaurant, even opening it to the public as an exclusive dinner club at one stage. His office, which I later inherited, was an example of appallingly bad taste. The large desk had a cut-out semi-circle to accommodate his huge girth. There were wood-panelled walls, concealed lighting and a hidden safe. His large limousine had a crest, incorporating his initials and those of the studio, emblazoned on its doors.

When the government bought Ardmore Studios in 1974, it originally proposed selling off any surplus land that could be used for building development, thereby reducing the original cost. It arranged for RTÉ to look after the studio until further plans were devised. Dermot O'Sullivan, an RTÉ executive, was appointed to manage the run-down facility. This he did with great flair and enthusiasm. He encouraged producers of television commercials to use the facilities and was fortunate to attract some foreign feature films. The most important of these was Stanley Kubrick's *Barry Lyndon*, which made extensive use of the studio's shooting stages.

I was appointed Chief Executive of the new State-sponsored company that would take over Ardmore Studios from RTÉ. The selection of the company's board members was left to me. The appointment of Chairman I discussed with the Minister. We had both met and greatly admired the work of John Boorman. A few years earlier, John had settled in Co. Wicklow with his wife and young family. He was certainly an obvious candidate for the board, but we both felt he might not wish to devote his time to the more onerous task of Chairman. We agreed to offer the chairmanship to Lord Killanin, who had many powerful friends in the international film industry. He was a producer or executive producer on a number of US and British films made in Ireland and a close friend of the internationally acclaimed director John Ford. Lord Killanin declined the invitation, but promised his support. John Boorman, on the other hand, did agree to become Chairman of the board. Others I nominated to join the board were: my first RTÉ boss, Bill Harpur, Controller of Programme Acquisitions; lawyer Enda Marren; and cameraman and producer Vincent Corcoran. The Minister agreed with all of these and added Ruaidhri Roberts, General Secretary of the Irish Congress of Trade Unions. Ruaidhri had an impressive background in the arts and had been a member of the old Radio Éireann Players. Later appointments by the Minister were John Donovan, retiring

Assistant Secretary of the Department of Industry and Commerce, and trade unionist Michael McEvoy.

It was decided to re-name the studio National Film Studios of Ireland. This would distance the company from the old Ardmore Studios name, along with its history of receiverships and failure. The new name would also confirm government ownership, with its resulting stability. Over the difficult years, a lack of investment had seen the studio buildings fall into a state of disrepair. The grounds were overgrown and technical equipment and facilities obsolete. Our first task was to refurbish the structure and equip the studio to a basic level. Jimmy Quin, who had been Head of the Film Sound Department at RTÉ, was appointed Studio Manager. Kevin Moriarty, our accountant, also demonstrated his expertise in dealing with the perennial problem of negotiating with the many unions involved in film production. The design and rebuilding programme was handled by Kilkenny Design Workshops, another State-sponsored company under the aegis of the Department of Industry and Commerce. The Chief Executive, Jim King, with whom I had worked in the *Irish Press*, and his staff did a magnificent job in bringing the studio accommodation and facilities up to the highest international standards.

A tax-incentive scheme to encourage private investment in film production was devised by John Boorman's accountant, Gerry Wheeler. I travelled to Australia, Sweden and Denmark to learn about tax incentives for investment in film production and other government supports given to the industry in those countries. The proposals John and I submitted to the government in 1976 were the basis for the present tax-incentive schemes. It was an opportunity lost that the scheme was not implemented until Michael D. Higgins became the minister responsible and re-established the Irish Film Board almost twenty years later.

In November 1975 we invited Irish and international film-makers, politicians, media, theatre, film personalities and business leaders to the gala opening of National Film Studios of Ireland. The party was held on the studio's main sound stage and resulted in excellent publicity and editorial comment in the important international film trade magazines, such as *Variety* and *Screen International*. The Minister for Finance, Richie Ryan, promised financial support; Minister Keating informed the assembled gathering that the tax-incentive scheme we had proposed would soon become law. The remark prompted John Boorman to comment in his speech: 'Every country in Europe, with the exception of Ireland and Luxembourg, gives financial support to its film industry. Tonight, Luxembourg stands alone!'

Television commercials provided steady business for the studio. Feature films shooting on location in Ireland also used our facilities and staff. At this stage Bill O'Herlihy, who had started his own public relations business, came on board to look after publicity and public relations for the studio. George Hook was in charge of the restaurant. Our management team was strengthened over time by the appointments of Jackie Tyson as my personal assistant and James Barry as financial controller.

In December 1975 I made my first promotional trip to Hollywood. John Boorman was working there at the time, and we all stayed in a slightly ramshackle motel in Bel Air, an upmarket suburb close to Hollywood. Later we were joined by a mutual friend, the Hon. Garech Browne, whose luggage was lost in transit. As a result, Garech was obliged to spend two days wearing his heavy Irish tweeds in the hot Californian sunshine. I had contacted the major Hollywood studios or friends there to arrange meetings at top executive level. The various production executives I met expressed interest in Ireland and the possibility of reducing budgets with the expected Irish investment incentives, which we were sure would materialise.

Business at the studio was coming along nicely, but it was only a few months after the official opening that the world oil crisis occurred. The Minister for Finance had many things on his mind—enacting legislation to assist the film industry was not one of them. The government never provided capital for National Film Studios of Ireland. The subscribed capital was only £5; our entire building and refurbishment programme was financed by bank borrowing. Banks were more than happy to advance money because the government provided 'letters of comfort'. Now the economy was in trouble and the Exchequer was short of funds. While the company was making a trading profit, the level of borrowings and consequent burden of interest payments was a cause of concern. All the money available from the government went to service this debt. There was nothing left to develop the facilities or provide investment in feature-film production.

Unfortunately, the Minister's opening-night promise did not materialise as we had expected and our Chairman's gratitude proved premature. Luxembourg did not stand alone in Europe; Ireland still shared her lonesome position.

The Cannes Film Festival, held in May every year, is acknowledged as the most glamorous cinema event in the world. Beautiful weather and a fairy-tale setting provide the backdrop for the rich and famous, for international movie stars, all dripping with glitz and glamour, with limousines and expensive fast cars, photographers, film and television cameras tripping over one another for that Croisette exclusive. Over twenty films are entered in the main competition. The most important prize awarded is the Palme d'Or, the European equivalent of Hollywood's Oscar. The Cannes festival is the largest annual gathering of professionals and financiers involved in the international film industry in the world. Over a two-week period the representatives of the movie industry arrive to attend the festival, to market, promote and publicise their films and to make deals that will finance future productions. Hollywood studios have an important presence, with large offices in the luxury hotels lining the seafront. All the film-producing countries of the world have national stands in the main exhibition centre, each attempting to lure producers to their country with various government-backed incentive schemes. Cannes, then, was the obvious forum from which to launch National Film Studios of Ireland onto the international scene.

It was 1976 and I celebrated my fortieth birthday at the festival. Our team consisted of Bill O'Herlihy, his assistant, Isabelle Saint Ouen, Sheila and myself. Prior to our departure, a comprehensive studio brochure was produced. It detailed films made at the old Ardmore Studios and the availability of trained and highly skilled Irish technicians, many of whom were constantly working abroad. It highlighted the advantages of filming in a country where such films as *The Quiet Man*, *Ryan's Daughter*, *Barry Lyndon* and other successful movies had been made, utilising the studio's facilities and impressive natural locations.

The doyen of the Cannes Film Festival was Irvin Shapiro. I met Irvin on our very first day at the festival. He took the little Irish contingent under his wing and many doors were opened to us. Martin Scorsese, a young director whose first film, *Mean Streets*, had been supported by Irvin Shapiro, had his latest film, *Taxi Driver*, in the main competition that year. Scorsese was accompanied by two young actors who appeared in his film, Robert De Niro and Harvey Keitel. All three, along with their wives, actor/producer Michael Douglas and Alan Ladd Jnr (son of the movie star), who was then head of Twentieth Century Fox, came to lunch with us at the famous La Columbe D'or restaurant in the small town of St Paul de Vence, high in the mountains above Nice. Set in the garden of an old mansion, with mature trees and flower-bedecked terraces, it was seen in the film, *To Catch a Thief*, starring Cary Grant and Grace Kelly. The restaurant was *the* place to be seen. The subsequent publicity we received contributed to raising the profile of the Irish presence at the festival. Later that week, *Taxi Driver* won the top prize—the coveted Palme d'Or. Our luncheon guests were now the toast of the festival.

Before leaving for Cannes, I had been negotiating with Universal Studios in Hollywood to locate their upcoming film, *The Last Remake of Beau Geste*, in Ireland. This would be directed by Marty Feldman, a major star of British comedy television who had made the breakthrough to the big screen with such films as *Young Frankenstein* and *The Adventures of Sherlock Holmes' Younger Brother*. I arranged to travel on the same flight Marty was taking from Nice. He was seated a few rows behind me, in the first-class section of the plane. Shortly after take-off, I approached him. By any standards Marty was a most extraordinary-looking character, with a sharp nose and two large eyes that looked dramatically in opposite directions. It was one of the best-known faces in the world. When I introduced myself, Marty jumped up from his seat, threw his arms around me and said, 'Sheamus, tell me, how did you recognise me?' On the way from Dublin Airport to the hotel, I asked our driver to take us down O'Connell Street. I knew that Marty's most recent film, *Silent Movie*, in which he appeared with Mel Brooks and Anne Bancroft, was playing in the Savoy cinema. As we passed the long queue outside the cinema, Marty wedged the top half of his body through the open car window and to the astonishment of the surprised cinemagoers shouted, 'Don't go to see it. It's a terrible film!'

During the remainder of the Cannes Film Festival, we made many contacts and met people who were to become and remain firm friends to this day. Bill O'Herlihy's copious press releases were accepted and published in full by the trade magazines. Peter Noble, editor of *Screen International*, the most widely circulated magazine at the Festival, became a firm supporter. Each morning his magazine carried an item about our activities, or the benefits of filming in Ireland. All in all, our trip had been a success. I had achieved all my life's ambitions. I was head of Ireland's only film studio; I was in love; I was forty years of age; the Festival was twenty-nine years old: it was a very good year. The small boy from Ballaghaderreen who collected discarded bits of film from the projectionist in the local cinema had come a long way.

*   *   *

The Last Remake of Beau Geste was the first feature film made at National Film Studios of Ireland. Produced by William S. Gilmore Jnr for Universal Studios, it was a spoof comedy based on the original P.C. Wren story. This had first been filmed in 1926, when Ronald Colman was the star. Remakes appeared in 1939 and 1966, which explains the title of this version, written and directed by Marty Feldman.

The desert sequence was shot on location near the small village resort of Matalascanas, on the Gulf of Cadiz, near the Spanish/Portuguese border. It was there I first met Peter Ustinov, who would become a close friend. On the invitation of the film's associate producer, Bernard Williams, I went to Spain to meet the production crew and cast. On arrival in Seville, I was collected and taken to Matalascanas. When we arrived at the destination, it was late afternoon; I was exhausted. The seaside resort of Matalascanas was in the early stages of development. The hotel in which we stayed was far from finished. Everything seemed to be raw concrete. My room had an uncovered concrete floor and bare, unplastered walls. It was devoid of decoration, with only a wooden chair for furniture. The telephone rested on the floor beside the bed. After unpacking, I lay down for a rest and quickly fell asleep.

At the premiere of John Boorman's *Excalibur* in July 1981. John and his wife, Christel, with Garret FitzGerald and his wife, Joan. Garret had been elected Taoiseach three days earlier. This was his first official function. *Photo: Jack McManus*

Birthday Boys! Taking part in RTÉ's 'The Birthday Show' with host Shay Healy, Eurovision winner Johnny Logan and tenor Ronan Tynan in May 1994. *Photo: RTÉ*

On the set of *Un Taxi Mauve*. Jack Lynch, then leader of the opposition, with the movie's stars, Charlotte Rampling and Fred Astaire. When shooting finished I gave the sign bearing his name to Jack, who placed it over the door of his holiday home in West Cork. *Photo: Jack McManus*

With leading actress
Cherie Lunghi at the
premiere of *Excalibur*.
Photo: Jack McManus

March 1981. John Huston signs copies
of his autobiography, *An Open Book*,
in Dublin. *Photo: Liam Mulcahy*

Meeting Lee Marvin at Dublin Airport
when he came to make *The Big Red
One* at the studio in August 1978.
Photo: Jack McManus

On location in Dublin's Phoenix Park
with Her Serene Highness,
Princess Grace of Monaco.
Photo: Frank Fennell

On board her private aircraft with Indian Premier, Indira Gandhi. Less than twenty-four hours later she was assassinated by one of her Sikh bodyguards.
Photo: S.K. Chaudhri

In the Royal Palace in Amman with His Majesty King Hussein of Jordan.
Photo: Janusz Guttner

With Peter Ustinov and former British Prime Minister Ted Heath in his London home.
Photo: Sean Corcoran

In 1979 Terry O'Sullivan and I revived our partnership and filed a 'Dubliner's Diary' column from Cyprus. Terry is seen here with the famous pelicans at the harbour in Paphos, on the island's west coast.
Photo: Sheamus Smith

With Formula 1 Racing personality Eddie Jordan and golfer Tony Jacklin in Eddie's villa near Soto Grande golf course in southern Spain.
Photo: Bill O'Herlihy

Enjoying the wrap party after filming in Jordan with Polish stills photographer Janusz Guttner and my daughter, Teri.
Photo: Sean Corcoran

In October 1986 I succeeded Frank Hall as Ireland's eighth Official Film Censor. *Photo: Eric Luke,* The Irish Times

May 1994: At the opening of an office extension to facilitate video classification and enjoying one of predecessor Frank Hall's jokes with Justice Minister, Máire Geoghegan-Quinn. *Photo: Susan Kennedy*

Minister for Justice Nora Owen on an official visit to our office. *Photo: Susan Kennedy*

The politician responsible for creating Ireland's modern film industry, Arts Minister and friend, Michael D. Higgins.

The performer! On set, dressed
for my part as 'the doctor' in
The Old Curiosity Shop.
Photo: Jonathan Hession

With producer Greg Smith,
visitor Terry Wogan and
Peter Ustinov, who played
'the grandfather'.
Photo: Jonathan Hession

Riding in the stage coach with
British actor James Fox, who
played 'the single gentleman'.
Photo: Jean Skinner

At the Dublin premiere of *Mrs. Brown* with leading actress Judi Dench and director, John Madden. *Photo: Kevin McFeely*

With Pierce Brosnan at the premiere of his movie, *Evelyn*, which was based on the true story of nine-year-old Evelyn Doyle whom I photographed in 1955.

Meeting Meryl Streep for the third time at the premiere of *Dancing at Lughnasa*. *Photo: Robert Doyle*

After what seemed like a very short time, I was awakened by the loud, shrill call of the telephone. The person on the other end of the line identified himself as the hotel receptionist. In perfect English he informed me that Mr Peter Ustinov was waiting in the lobby to take me to dinner. I looked at my watch. It was 6 p.m.—far too early for dinner in Spain. I had never met Peter Ustinov, so I assumed this to be a hoax perpetrated by Bernie Williams. I replied that I never dined before 8 p.m. and that if Mr Ustinov wished to invite me to dinner, I would meet him in the lobby at that time. After some more rest and a shower, I went to the lobby expecting to meet some of the film crew. Imagine my surprise when the all-too-familiar figure of Peter Ustinov ambled over to me, put out his hand and said, 'Very nice to meet you. I got your message.' I was mortified.

The Last Remake of Beau Geste required extensive studio sets. The construction of these created full employment for the Irish workforce. When the location filming was complete, the unit moved to Dublin. Before leaving for Spain, I had arranged with my old friends Paddy Fitzpatrick and his son Paul that some of the crew and important stars would stay at his hotel in Killiney. Fitzpatrick's Castle was the only good hotel within a reasonable distance of the studio, so Peter Ustinov was booked in there. The Fitzpatricks provided a splendid suite, which Peter loved. It was the start of a relationship that brought him back to the hotel many times.

Before leaving Spain, Peter had asked my advice on good restaurants near his hotel in Ireland. Like all those who travel constantly, dining in a hotel on a regular basis, no matter how good the cuisine, becomes boring. Naturally, my first suggestion was Sean Kinsella's Mirabeau restaurant, regarded by many as the best dining experience in Ireland. Located on the seafront at Sandycove, just a short drive down the road from Fitzpatrick's Hotel, it was easily identified by the owner's distinctive black-and-white Bentley parked on the footpath outside.

In those days, communication was so different from now. The mobile telephone did not exist. Calling Sean from rural Spain to make a reservation or to alert him to Peter's arrival would probably have taken half a day. Anyway, I felt that Peter would not venture out of the hotel until a few nights after his arrival, thus he would have time to make a reservation. Once settled in Fitzpatrick's, however, Peter was anxious to experience the delights of the Mirabeau restaurant, which I had recommended so highly. He made his way to Sean Kinsella's door on the night he arrived in Ireland. As was customary, Sean Kinsella answered the door; this was not a restaurant into which one wandered without a reservation. Sean recognised Peter, of course, who quickly announced that the recommendation had come from me. Sean explained that the restaurant was completely booked out that evening. He added jokingly, 'The only place that I could put a table for you would be in the kitchen.' As he was alone, Peter thought this was a splendid idea. He would have something interesting to watch in the kitchen. To Sean's surprise, he quickly accepted the offer. So on this, the first of many visits to the Mirabeau, the famous star dined in the restaurant's kitchen.

*   *   *

Another place that benefited from such an introduction was the Kilkenny Design shop in Dublin's Nassau Street. I brought Peter there, and he became a devotee. On days when he was not filming, he loved to spend hours pottering about the shop. He replaced all the cutlery, glassware, tableware, cookware, bedroom linen and bathroom towels in his home in Switzerland with merchandise bought there. The Ustinov house was virtually a showcase for Kilkenny Design!

To express the company's gratitude for his exceptional patronage, Chief Executive Jim King gave a dinner party in Peter's honour. The venue was the shop, which did not then have a restaurant. Peter was delighted: 'I've dined in some great restaurants, in fine houses, on luxury liners and yachts, in palaces and castles, but never in a shop.' A table was set up near the large windows. Passers-by were amazed to see a group of people having dinner in the shop window. As ever, Peter entertained us with stories and impressions that years later would become the material for his one-man show, 'An Evening with Peter Ustinov'. I think Jim King's invitation to dine in a shop window surpassed Sean Kinsella's to have dinner surrounded by pot and pans in the kitchen of the Mirabeau restaurant!

*   *   *

Peter's dressing-room at the studio was next door to my temporary office accommodation. He usually rested in the dressing-room or studied his script when not required on set. In order not to disturb him, one morning I pushed a note under his door inviting him to dinner in the Mirabeau that evening. A short time afterwards his hand-written message of acceptance was delivered to my office in a similar manner. It was enclosed in an envelope, on which Peter had drawn two stamps depicting perfect likenesses of Sean O'Casey and W.B. Yeats. Overdrawn on these was the traditional post-office franking mark, showing a picture of an Irish coffee. It was surrounded by the slogan, DRINK IRISH COFFEE!

In response to a request for help, I once asked Peter to draw a self-portrait for a friend who was organising a charity auction. Always obliging, Peter quickly made a simple line sketch. It took him less than two minutes. The illustration was duly dispatched to my friend, who had it mounted and framed. Upon learning some weeks later that the drawing had been sold for almost £1,000, Peter remarked, 'My God, I should do more of those!'

Bill Gilmore, the producer of *The Last Remake of Beau Geste*, was accompanied by two executive producers, who were representing Universal Pictures and were constantly on set. Peter, a successful director himself, disapproved of this. He felt that three supervisors looking over his shoulder was something that first-time director Marty Feldman could do without! One morning, Peter pushed a small drawing under the door of my office. It depicted three vultures sitting on a fence staring down at their diminutive prey on the ground. The vultures had the faces of the Hollywood executives; the object of their attention was a tiny, birdlike Marty!

During filming Minister Justin Keating hosted a dinner for Marty Feldman with his wife, Lauretta, and members of the crew. The dinner was held in a private room in Sach's Hotel in Dublin and was also attended by some members of the studio board. One of my abiding memories of an enjoyable evening that turned into a very late night is of fellow director, Enda Marren, teaching Lauretta Feldman to make 'black velvet' as dawn broke over the redbricked terrace houses opposite the hotel. A few days later I received a telephone call from the Minister's private secretary. He told me that the bill for dinner had exceeded the Minister's budget and asked for our help in paying it!

The Last Remake of Beau Geste was not a box-office success. I attribute this to the fact that the American editor, although an Academy Award-winner and one of the industry's most distinguished, failed to understand or appreciate Marty Feldman's zany sense of humour. It was a terrible pity, as I liked it.

*　*　*

In the spring of 1976 we learned of a proposal to film *Equus*. The play by Peter Shaffer, with Bangor-born Colin Blakely in the lead, was having a successful run in London. It tells the story of a psychologically disturbed youth living in a small town in England who blinds six horses in the local riding school. Apart from the advantages our studio presented, Bray and its environs provided all the necessary locations for the film. Brennanstown Riding School, with its excellent stables and facilities, was five minutes from the studio. The studio itself had a fine yard with stables to one side. A big plus was that one of the town's cinemas had just closed down. A cinema was an important setting in the film. Michael Collins, a prominent member of Bray's business community and the owner of both cinemas in the town, made the now empty Panorama cinema available for use by the film crew. On top of all that, the local authorities were prepared to make the classical Town Hall building and the Public Library available as additional locations.

Arrangements to make *Equus* at Ardmore were at an advanced stage when, on 21 July, an event occurred that would have serious consequences for the studio and many other aspects of the Irish economy, including our tourist industry. As he left his official residence, Glencairn, in the foothills of the Dublin Mountains, the British Ambassador Christopher Ewart-Biggs was brutally murdered. The envoy, who had arrived in Ireland less than two weeks earlier, together with Northern Ireland Office private secretary, twenty-six-year-old Judith Cooke, was killed when a landmine detonated by the IRA blew up their armour-plated official car just outside the front gates. One immediate effect of this terrorist atrocity was the cancellation of the filming of *Equus* in Ireland. It was a disaster for our fledgling enterprise.

On the evening of the assassination, Jim King and his wife Maeve had arranged a dinner party. The guest list included Freddie Forsyth, his wife Carrie, the Australian Ambassador Brian Hill and his Dutch wife, Sam and Bernie Stephenson, Sheila and myself. As the enormity of the damage caused by the outrageous murders emerged, a few members of the diplomatic corps decided to show that they would not be intimidated by the IRA. They invited their colleagues, including our group, to meet very publicly in the Shelbourne Hotel. The gathering included every ambassador who was in Dublin that evening.

* * *

The escalation of terrorism led potential clients of the studio to change their minds about coming to Ireland to film. As far as the international film community was concerned, it was not a safe place. Insurance companies were reluctant to provide cover for high-profile personalities, such as movie stars or directors. We were still without the long-promised legislation that would provide incentives and investment finance for film production and were in danger of becoming a hostage to the lending institutions. The studio's future looked grim; instant action was necessary. I proposed to my fellow directors that we set up a group to be known as Friends of National Film Studios of Ireland. This would consist of well-known personalities in the international film community, none of whom were Irish, who had either worked in our studio or who were personal friends and supported our objectives. The plan was that any potential client of the studio who was reluctant to film in Ireland because of the political situation could independently contact a member of the group whose opinion they respected. The person contacted would then reassure them that the Republic of Ireland was a safe place to work and that the conflict in Northern Ireland would not impinge upon or threaten the success of their production in our studio.

This proposal was approved instantly. Everyone invited to join the special group accepted enthusiastically and pledged to do everything possible to encourage and reassure those who asked their advice about filming in Ireland. The Friends of National Film Studios of Ireland, established under the chairmanship of Peter Ustinov, were: Princess Grace of Monaco, John Huston, Sean Connery, Charlotte Rampling, Marty Feldman, Freddie Forsyth and Gerry Fisher, Director of Photography on *The Last Remake of Beau Geste*. It was our intention that this group would meet in one of the country's top hotels once a year. The idea was warmly welcomed by Joe Malone, then Director General of Bord Fáilte, who promised to sponsor the event. However, the busy work schedules of those involved prevented this happening. Nevertheless, the Friends of National Film Studios of Ireland became an important and valuable aspect of our marketing strategy. It all came too late for *Equus*, unfortunately. That film, starring Richard Burton, Peter Firth, Colin Blakely and Joan Plowright, was made in Canada. It received three Academy Award nominations and was an outstanding success at the box office.

* * *

The next large-scale film that came our way was *Un Taxi Mauve*. This was a co-production between the studio and a French production company. *Un Taxi Mauve* is a novel by the distinguished French author Michel Deon. Michel and his wife, Chantal, have been living in Co. Mayo for many years and Michel's romantic story is set in that part of Ireland. The film rights were owned by two sisters, Catherine Winter and Giselle Rebillion, who had a good record of film production in France. Their company was supported by Catherine's husband, Claude Winter, a wealthy French industrialist. Italian interests had also indicated a willingness to participate as a co-production partner.

Our man in London, Peter Rawley, was anxious to justify his position. Through the chairman, he had negotiated a contract with the studio board that paid him a salary three times greater than that of the chief executive. His commitment was to work two days a week! A potential producer with a number of projects in the development stage, Peter used our London office as his own. *Un Taxi Mauve* was at an advanced stage of development when Peter introduced it as suitable for the studio. In theory, it looked like a good proposition with positive advantages. A spin-off for the economy would be the obvious benefits to our tourism industry; everyone remembered the effect *Ryan's Daughter* had had on Irish tourism some years earlier. Everything seemed to be right. An Irish-based story, written by an author of international reputation, produced by successful European producers, the film would boast a top-class international cast. The director was Yves Boisset, whose previous movies were consistently successful at the French box office. The production would fully utilise the studio facilities and require extensive set construction. In addition to the regular staff, Irish freelance personnel would be used to augment the international crew. However, an investment from National Film Studios of Ireland would be required if the production were to get the 'green light'. The investment would include some studio facilities and staff, deferred rentals of stage accommodation and a cash contribution to the film's budget.

Un Taxi Mauve would be filmed in two languages, with the English version entitled *Purple Taxi*. On its completion, the French producers would own distribution rights in France and all French-speaking territories in the world. National Film Studios of Ireland would have distribution rights in the English-speaking territories of the world, with the exception of the USA, which would be shared equally. In terms of potential box-office receipts, the USA and the UK should amount to well over 50 per cent returns. Peter Rawley, who was acknowledged as the expert, having extensive international experience in such matters, convinced the studio's directors that this was as secure an investment as could be found in feature-film production.

The Department of Industry and Commerce arranged a further 'letter of comfort', providing one of our banks with the security required to raise additional funds for investment in the film. There were exhaustive negotiations and long meetings, one of which, between the company and the French producers, became acrimonious. It seemed to some of the National Film Studios of Ireland team, which included Enda Marren, who was also our lawyer, company secretary Jerry McCarthy and me, that Peter Rawley was more sympathetic to our partners' position than our own. Personally, I felt this was because of his certainty that the project would bring glory to all—not least to himself and his efforts on behalf of the studio. A lengthy contract was finally agreed.

What could only be described as a dream cast, together with a top-class director, was put in place. The acclaimed Tonino Delli Colli was named Director of Photography. He had previously displayed his great versatility behind the camera with subjects ranging from the urban realism of Italian director Pier Paolo Pasolini to the dazzling outdoor cinematography of Sergio Leone's spaghetti Westerns. The cast, headed by Fred Astaire, Charlotte Rampling and Peter Ustinov, also included award-winning French actor Philip Noiret and American actor Eddie Albert Jnr, whose father, the suave, grey-haired actor Eddie Albert, had played the lead in the successful television series 'Green Acres'.

On Monday 18 October 1976 *Un Taxi Mauve* started shooting at the studio. Outside locations included Ashford Castle in Co. Mayo, Renvyle House in Co. Galway and the surrounding countryside. Despite the season, the weather was perfect. The Irish landscapes looked stunning when photographed by Delli Colli. Charlotte Rampling had never looked better. Fine actress that she is, she played the complex and difficult part of the female lead with great style and conviction. Every scene that involved dialogue was shot in both English and French. Charlotte had lived in France for many years and was fluent in the language, as was Peter Ustinov and, of course, Philip Noiret. Fred Astaire and Eddie Albert experienced some difficulty, but this did not matter as their voices would be dubbed in the French version of the film. Fred, who was addressed as 'Mr Astaire' by everyone except Peter Ustinov, played the village doctor. His method of transport was the purple London taxi cab that gave the film its name.

I have always believed that the best time to become friendly with future government ministers is when they are members of the opposition. Jack Lynch was leader of the opposition when he accepted my invitation to have lunch at the studio with Peter Ustinov. Afterwards we visited the set of *Un Taxi Mauve*. The scene being filmed was set in Jack Lynch's bar. The studio set constructed for the purpose was a full-size replica of a country pub, with both the exterior and interior in perfect detail. The former Taoiseach took great delight in being photographed with Peter Ustinov, Fred Astaire and Charlotte Rampling outside 'Jack Lynch's Bar'.

We all went back to my office for a farewell drink with Charlotte, who was leaving that day. Prior to the visit, Jack had mentioned that there were three important meetings he was due to attend in Leinster House that afternoon. The first of these was at 4 p.m. As always, the conversation with Peter and Charlotte was entertaining. 'Mr Astaire' never turned up—he was a man of measured merriment and possibly disapproved of drinking alcohol early in the day. Jack was enjoying himself with his glass of Paddy. At 3.30 p.m. he asked my PA, Gemma Fallon, to call his office and cancel the first meeting. A little later he asked if Gemma would cancel his second meeting. As an afterthought he added, 'Tell her to cancel everything. I'm not going back today.' I can still remember looking at the scene from behind my desk: Jack Lynch seated comfortably in a large armchair, puffing his beloved pipe and holding his glass; Peter Ustinov sitting opposite in the other large armchair; Charlotte Rampling, happy and contented, sitting on the carpet and resting her back against Peter's legs.

The once and future Taoiseach was not the only one to pay a visit to the set. Various people were invited to the studio over the years, including bankers, ambassadors, politicians, movie stars and friends. The most extraordinary visit of all, however, was the day fellow-director Enda Marren and I had lunch with a convicted murderer. Arnljot Berg was a Norwegian film director and a close friend, whom I met through RTÉ. He called his only son, my godchild, Sheamus. After divorcing his third wife, Mie, Arnljot married a French lady and lived in Paris. During a domestic row, Arnljot killed his new wife. Charged and convicted, he received a relatively short sentence for his crime of passion. On his release from prison he came to visit Muiris MacConghail and me. Along with others, we had lobbied to secure his early release.

The day after Arnljot's arrival, Enda and I had arranged lunch with Eamonn Barnes, Ireland's first Director of Public Prosecutions, at the studio. I invited Arnljot to join us. We enjoyed a cordial meal together. Arnljot's conviction was never mentioned. Afterwards, Eamonn Barnes offered Arnljot a lift back to Dublin. As we waved goodbye to our guests, Enda mentioned the irony of the Director of Public

Prosecutions taking a convicted murderer back to his hotel in the State car. I never saw Arnljot Berg again. A short time afterwards he took his own life in a forest near his native city of Oslo.

* * *

An invitation to the Monte Carlo Television Film Festival was the reason for my second visit to Monaco, and it was on this occasion that I came to know Princess Grace. Prior to the Awards ceremony, the Prince and Princess hosted a small party for special friends in the Sporting Club of Monte Carlo. We were warmly received. A little later Princess Grace, standing in the centre of the room, beckoned me to join her. Stunningly beautiful, she wore an off-the-shoulder white and gold full-length ballgown. We spoke of Ireland, the movie industry, National Film Studios of Ireland, Monte Carlo, her family, life as a princess and much more, for about half an hour. Over her shoulder, I could see Bill Harpur and Sheila, with Tim Vignoles from Columbia Pictures Television, watching us. I tried my best to indicate that they should join me. No one got the message. Eventually, Prince Rainier joined us and suggested to his wife that it was time to leave for the banquet room. I stood back and went to accompany my friends to our table. I admonished them for not joining me with the Princess. Bill Harpur explained their reluctance saying, 'We were fascinated watching you. The Princess could not get away as you had your two feet firmly implanted on the front of her dress!'

The following year we were invited to the same party. On that occasion the Princess wore a black-and-white evening jacket over tight silk black trousers! With no opportunity to forcefully detain the lady, our conversation was shorter than in the previous year. This time the Princess had an opportunity to mingle with her other guests.

* * *

When we returned to Cannes in 1977, National Film Studios of Ireland was up and running, despite its myriad financial difficulties. *The Last Remake of Beau Geste* had been successfully completed, and *Un Taxi Mauve* was among the twenty-four official entries in the Festival. It was not the first time that Ireland had been associated with an entry in the Cannes Film Festival. In 1967 Joe Strick's *Ulysses*, which was made in Dublin, was a British entry. In 1968 Peter Lennon's *Rocky Road to Dublin* had been screened just before the Festival was aborted as a result of the student riots in France. *Leo the Last*, another British entry, won the Best Director prize for John Boorman in 1970. John had finished the post-production work on that film at Ardmore Studios. In 1972 Robert Altman's *Images*, filmed at Ardmore and on location in Wicklow, was an official Irish entry. The leading lady, Susanna York, was awarded the prize for Best Actress. Although *Un Taxi Mauve* was entered in the Festival as a French film, it was more Irish than any of its predecessors. It was the first time Ireland had a substantial financial investment in an international feature film.

The fact of having a film in competition provides exceptional publicity opportunities, especially with the presence of the producers, director and stars. It also requires a budget for advertising and for hosting a party for the media and others, such as distributors and cinema-owners. To do this in the traditional Cannes fashion, given the studio's limited resources, would have been impossible, so a plan was devised. Before taking off from the studio, we loaded up the car with a generous supply of smoked salmon and brown bread (such commodities were not readily available in the South of France in those days), and whiskey provided by our friends at Irish Distillers. Pierre Joannon, the Irish Consul General, offered us the use of his magnificent villa, Les Chênes Verts, situated at the fashionable Cap d'Antibes, which had previously been the home of writer Jules Verne. Pierre also arranged the purchase of the best champagne at a substantial discount.

The party was attended by the principal guests of the Festival and those associated with the film, international distributors and the press. It was held in the flower-filled gardens around the magnificent swimming pool of Pierre Joannon's villa. A number of supporters had come from Ireland, including one of the studio's bankers, Paddy McEvoy, Managing Director of the Irish Continental Bank in Dublin. The Irish Tourist Board sponsored my close friend and harpist Deirdre O'Callaghan's trip to entertain our guests. Peter Ustinov wore a white shirt with a green tie and delighted in raising the leg of his trousers to reveal his orange socks, which completed the colours of the Irish flag. It was very different from the usual parties of champagne and canapés in a hotel room. In fact, ours was considered to have been one of the outstanding events of that festival.

The official screening of *Un Taxi Mauve* a few days later was, in the best tradition of the film festival, chaotic. Formally dressed pedestrians, cars and limousines jammed the Croisette in front of the cinema and all side-streets were blocked. Many holding valid tickets were unable to gain admission to the theatre and wound up sitting on the steps outside. The film was received enthusiastically by the cinema audience and the press, and the crush to get in enhanced our reputation.

The English-language version of the film, *Purple Taxi*, had its first screening at the Cork Film Festival in June. Afterwards, Minister Justin Keating expressed his disappointment with the finished product in no uncertain terms. I was embarrassed when he publicly proclaimed it to be 'a bad film'. Irvin Shapiro, who was handling worldwide distribution, described the film as 'six characters in search of a story'.

The Gala World Premiere of *Purple Taxi* was held on Friday 26 January 1978 at the Metropole, now known as the Screen Cinema, in Dublin's College Street. A distinctive and very dramatic poster was designed by Philip Geraghty, who worked with Gustav Sauter, the studio's architect. With a predominantly purple background, it featured a landscape in silhouette, with hills in the distance. The silhouette was based on a picture of Charlotte Rampling's reclining naked body.

As invariably happens on such occasions, everything did not go smoothly. When he lowered himself into his cinema seat, Peter Ustinov felt the complete seam of one leg of his trousers bursting open. As he was due on stage for a brief introduction by Eamonn Andrews before the film started, immediate action was necessary. I mentioned the catastrophe to Sheila, who was seated on my other side. She had a ready solution. While I carefully extricated Peter from his seat and guided him to the manager's office through the throng now entering the cinema, Sheila somehow procured a needle and thread. In the privacy of the office, Peter removed his trousers and Sheila, an expert dressmaker, had the repair completed in minutes. On entering the office and being confronted with the sight of Peter's generous figure dressed in a beautifully tailored tuxedo, but without any trousers, Bill O'Herlihy exclaimed, 'Oh my God! Not a pretty sight.'

We returned to the cinema just as Eamonn Andrews was making his preliminary introduction. Dispensing with the usual interview, Peter took the microphone and proceeded to delight the audience with his amusing stories. He told of how his trousers had split while his feet were tapping to the sound of The Chieftains! The following day one newspaper report described Peter as having got the evening off to 'a ripping start'.

The after-party was held in Carroll's building, on the bank of the Grand Canal. This is now the head office of the Irish Nationwide Building Society. The magnificent buffet, which included Dublin Bay prawns, roast pheasant and suckling pig, was a credit to our hosts, as were the very fine French wines, brandies and liqueurs that followed. The festivities continued well into the early morning. The party was showing no sign of flagging when we left to take Peter Ustinov back to his hotel at 4.30 a.m.

As a result of the publicity generated by the premiere, *Purple Taxi* was reasonably successful during its limited run in Dublin. It failed to attract audiences in Cork, Galway and Limerick and was not distributed anywhere else in the country. This was the only distribution the English version of *Un Taxi Mauve* ever received. The title has never appeared in any work of film reference in the English language. The studio did not recover its investment; indeed, some of the debts incurred by the production company remain unpaid. On the positive side, however, *Un Taxi Mauve* opened to critical acclaim in France. This was followed by an outstanding performance at the box-office. French holidaymakers wanted to visit the West of Ireland locations that had been photographed so beautifully in the film. The Irish Tourist Board office in Paris was obliged to extend its opening hours for several weeks to cope with the demand for information. In an overall sense, therefore, our investment in *Un Taxi Mauve* was of substantial benefit to the national economy. From the studio's point of view, however, it was a minor disaster.

*   *   *

At the Cannes Film Festival in 1976 Bill O'Herlihy and I had a meeting with American International Pictures Chairman, the legendary Samuel Z. Arkoff. Sam was the archetypical Hollywood producer: a large, overweight man, flamboyantly dressed, he always sported a huge cigar and had a permanent chauffeur. He stayed at the Hotel du Cap, one of the most expensive hotels on the French Riviera, near Cannes. Like most of his fellow guests, Sam only ventured out of the hotel to attend one festival screening and have his photograph taken on the massive red carpet outside the Festival Palais. Otherwise, all of his meetings were held in his magnificent suite overlooking the ocean.

One of his upcoming films would be adapted from an original story, *The Great Train Robbery* by the successful novelist and screenwriter Michael Crichton. Set in 1855, it tells of an elegant but ruthless crook who sets out to rob the London–Folkestone express of gold bullion bound for the British troops in the Crimea. At our meeting, Bill and I told Sam of the great locations available in Ireland, the excellent facilities at our studio, the wealth of acting talent available, the highly skilled technicians and construction crews and the government support. The only support Sam cared about was financial. He wanted to know how much 'the Irish' would invest in his film, either from government or other sources. Sam was talking real money, not studio rental deferrals. The proposed budget for the film was $6,000,000— about average for the time. He emphasised that the lowest Irish investment that would secure the film for us was $500,000. I confirmed that this could be provided, even though I had no idea where the money would come from. As we left Sam said, 'I like you. When I'm going down the pike, I like to know who's going down with me!' I had never heard the expression before; Bill later explained it to me.

As we descended the magnificent winding staircase to the foyer of the hotel, Bill looked at me and said, 'Jaysus, you're some man! Where are *you* going to get half-a-million dollars?' I knew what he meant, but in time everything came right.

Bill O'Herlihy also accompanied me on my second visit to Hollywood in search of business. We stayed at the Sunset Marquis in West Hollywood. This upmarket motel is mostly frequented by out-of-town musicians. Shortly after our arrival, we were picked up by Bill

Gilmore, who had produced *The Last Remake of Beau Geste*. He invited us to a party in the home of the radio and television presenter Steve Allen, then an aging icon. The purpose of the party was to launch the West Coast Branch of The Ireland Fund, which Tony O'Reilly and some of his friends had founded in New York the previous year. Tony had been greatly impressed by the American United Jewish Appeal, which raised hundreds of millions of dollars for Israel every year. With 44 million Americans of Irish extraction as possible supporters, Tony was certain he could do the same for Ireland. He had spoken to me about the fund shortly beforehand. In contrast to Noraid, which was an IRA support fund contributed to by many non-thinking Irish-Americans, the Ireland Fund would concentrate on helping community-level projects throughout the whole island of Ireland.

Steve Allen's house was modest by Hollywood standards. Various speakers welcomed the establishment of this new branch of the Ireland Fund and those present promised their support. Tony O'Reilly was then, as he is now, one of the most sought-after and entertaining speakers in America; I was eagerly anticipating his speech. Bill O'Herlihy and I were relaxing and enjoying the wine when our host announced that before Tony addressed the gathering, there was another speaker. This person was of importance as, apart from Tony, he was, as far as our host knew, the only other Irish-born person in the room. In fact, this person had arrived in Los Angeles from Ireland just that afternoon. Bill and I scanned the faces surrounding us, wondering who this could be. We would expect to know someone who fitted that description. Steve Allen then announced, 'I would like to introduce you to Mr Sheamus Smith.'

I became weak at the knees. In that instant, the only thoughts that ran through my head were that I simply could not address such an august gathering and I had absolutely no idea what to say should I try to address them. Before I had time to dwell on the matter, a firm push on the back from my erstwhile friend, Bill O'Herlihy, propelled me into the centre of the room, where I found myself standing between Tony O'Reilly and the Governor of California. I spoke mostly about Tony, his achievements in the fields of sport and business and of how proud we all were of him in Ireland. It was some consolation to know that, as I would be followed by Tony, that orator extraordinaire, my performance would not only be overshadowed but completely forgotten! Twenty-four years later, in 2001, Sir Anthony O'Reilly finished a letter to me with the sentence: 'Do you remember that on that night in Steve Allen's home—Dorothy McGuire was there—because if you don't, I do!'

After the party Tony O'Reilly invited a group of us to Chasen's, then probably the most fashionable and expensive restaurant in Hollywood. We did not have a reservation, but the arrival of our host was sufficient to secure the two best tables in the house. These were occupied when we arrived, but the *maître d'*, accompanied by two waiters, almost frog-marched the unfortunate diners to alternative accommodation at the back of the room. To be fair, they received a complimentary meal for the inconvenience they suffered.

At a lunch in Warner Brothers' studio, we met Robert Shaw. At the age of fifty, he had suddenly emerged as a highly paid star in such films as *The Sting* and *Jaws*. After the tragic death of his wife, the actress Mary Ure, he had come with his children to live in Ireland. Robert was playing the lead opposite Jacqueline Bisset in *The Deep*. It was flattering that he came over to our table and introduced himself. He was interested in the developments in the Irish film industry and promised his full support to National Film Studios of Ireland. As we left the studio, Bill stopped by a small kiosk to buy cigarettes. In his Cork accent he asked the owner, an Italian-American with a marked broken accent, for 'A packet of Marlboro, please.' After repeating his request for the third time, the man looked at me and in his broken English said, 'Your friend, he can no speak English?' I translated and was more successful!

Before our arrival in Hollywood, Sam Arkoff had sold his interest in *The First Great Train Robbery* to Dino De Laurentiis, the Italian-born producer whose international career had been launched with the film *Bitter Rice* in 1948. De Laurentiis, whom I had not met before, was a small man behind a very large desk. He was accompanied by a lawyer called Sidewinder; it seemed an appropriate name for a Hollywood movie lawyer, being the name of the nocturnal rattlesnake found in America! Dino had just arrived from visiting a location in South America, where one of his films was shooting. He complained of acute deafness as a result of his flight. Afterwards, Bill O'Herlihy cynically suggested that this might have been a ploy that enabled the legendary dealmaker to hear only what he wanted to hear. My offer of an investment of $500,000 made to Sam Arkoff had travelled with the project. Dino was determined to avail of it. He had found his leading man, Sean Connery, plus the sidekick, Donald Sutherland, and now he wanted a good deal on the studio. I agreed to find the money to have the film made in Ireland. The producer was John Foreman, whose screen credits included *Butch Cassidy and the Sundance Kid*, winner of four Academy Awards in 1968, and the Academy Award-nominated *A Man for All Seasons*, starring Sean Connery and Michael Caine.

Our trip was a success. Subject to my finding $500,000, we had secured the making of *The First Great Train Robbery* for the studio and had raised awareness of National Film Studios of Ireland on the Hollywood scene.

* * *

The General Election in June 1977 saw the defeat of the Fine Gael/Labour coalition government. Fianna Fáil swept back into power with eighty-four seats and an unprecedented overall majority, and Jack Lynch was nominated Taoiseach by 82 votes to 61. Desmond O'Malley was the new Minister in the re-named Department of Industry, Commerce and Energy. I had met him when Editor of '7 Days', but did not know him well. John Boorman and I had our first meeting with our new Minister on 1 September. O'Malley, who had a rather abrasive manner, initially did not get on well with the Chairman. We pointed out the inadequate financial structure of the studio and the urgent need for enactment of the proposed Bill to provide funds for investment in film production. The new Minister was supportive. Slowly, the friction that had existed at first between himself and the Chairman evaporated. We both went away feeling the meeting had been a success.

Shortly after our meeting, Desmond O'Malley decided to seek independent advice on film financing in Ireland. His Department commissioned a report by Arthur D. Little Ltd, a firm of international consultants. *Finance for Film Making in Ireland*, although in itself not a very impressive document, confirmed the need for State assistance and financial investment in films made in Ireland. It was ultimately responsible for the establishment of Bord Scannán na hÉireann (The Irish Film Board). The Minister also filled the remaining vacancy on the board of the studio with the appointment of Dublin accountant, John Donnelly. A pragmatic man with a strong personality, John Donnelly was the first person appointed to the board who had no apparent interest in the film industry. Other board members were not impressed upon learning that, after his appointment, he contacted an official enquiring to whom in the Department he should report.

*   *   *

The budget for *The First Great Train Robbery* was, as I said, approximately $6,000,000. Negotiations with Dino De Laurentiis and John Foreman in Hollywood were reaching a crucial stage. A decision to commit our half-a-million dollars was now necessary. Time was running out. What the producers required was for National Film Studios of Ireland to approve the budget and ensure that building or other costs involved would not escalate. Our investment would represent a contingency fund, which would come into play only if the original budget were exceeded. For providing this fund, the company would receive 2.5 per cent of the film's worldwide profits. If any portion of the money were used, the profit participation would increase to 5 per cent. The budget had been examined carefully and would be policed by our new studio manager, Terry Clegg, a former associate producer on a number of major British and Hollywood movies and a person with wide experience in these matters.

By any standards this was an excellent deal, which should have shown a handsome return for the company. It would also ensure the full use of studio facilities, with extensive employment for freelance personnel. My fellow director, John Donovan, and I were in constant touch with the Department of Industry, Commerce and Energy in an effort to secure the money for our investment. That Department was trying to get the approval of the Department of Finance in order to proceed. The $500,000 I had originally promised to Sam Arkoff in the Hotel du Cap the previous May was now causing me sleepless nights; Bill O'Herlihy's remark had come back to haunt me.

Our deadline of 10 March 1978 was fast approaching. It was after 5 p.m. on that Friday afternoon that I received a telephone call from the Minister's office confirming that we could proceed. Des O'Malley had delivered. I had delivered. It was still early in the day in California when I called Dino Di Laurentiis in Hollywood to confirm that we would guarantee the contingency fund. He thanked me, then surprised me by saying he would not require the money. He said that, having undertaken to police the budget, he was happy that our studio would ensure it was not exceeded. He therefore saw no reason to give away any part of what he anticipated would be a considerable profit!

Ireland was the ideal location in which to shoot *The First Great Train Robbery*. Dublin's well-preserved Georgian buildings looked like London of the period in which the film is set. Heuston Station would be transformed into London Bridge Terminus, the South Eastern Railway's starting point for its routes to the coast. Kent Station in Cork would become Folkestone Railway Station on the south coast of England. The railway authorities were most co-operative. A section of seldom-used line in the Midlands was made available for the sequences that involved the moving train. Victorian railway carriages were built in the studio workshops. The first-class carriage used for interior shooting was finished luxuriously and furnished in the style of the period. Other carriages were left unfinished inside. Painted bright yellow, the carriages were transported through the streets to Bray Railway Station. There they were attached to a steam engine supplied by the Transport Museum. The train was a splendid sight when standing at the platform or puffing its way through the countryside.

Filming at busy Heuston Station took place on Sundays, when the station was relatively quiet. One main platform and a set of tracks were cordoned off and a period set erected, blocking it from the view of passengers using the other platforms. It looked for all the world like a London station in Victorian times. Men in frock coats wearing top hats, ladies in crinolines and bonnets, urchins with cloth caps selling newspapers, all the hustle and bustle of a busy railway terminal with lots of smoke and steam belching from the engine. Suddenly, into this Victorian bedlam stumbled a young man. He was wearing jeans and looked like a technician, so his entry to the set went unchallenged. A closer look revealed that he was obviously hung-over and recovering from the night before. Picture his shock when, while quietly attempting to get the Cork train home, he found himself in Victorian London!

In one scene Sean Connery was required to move along the top of the train as it sped through the countryside. This was filmed near Moate, in Co. Westmeath. Normally a job for a stuntman, Sean insisted on playing the sequence himself. A difficult and dangerous stunt, it included passing under a number of low bridges. Carrying a heavy coil of rope over his shoulder and moving along the roof, Sean would have to synchronise the speed of the moving train with the approaching bridge and then lie flat as the train passed underneath. A helicopter camera would record the scene. The engine driver was instructed to travel at 30 miles an hour. When shooting started, it was obvious that the train was travelling much faster than the agreed speed, but Sean carried on and played the scene magnificently. When he landed, the helicopter pilot confirmed that the train had been travelling at more than 50 miles an hour. When questioned, the train driver explained that the engine had no speedometer!

The First Great Train Robbery opened to critical acclaim and was a box-office success. It was regarded as a high point in Sean Connery's career and took him well away from his *James Bond* image. Lesley-Anne Down also received good notices for her performance. Beautifully photographed, it was a fitting tribute to a great cinematographer, Geoffrey Unsworth. It was his last film; he died shortly afterwards.

*   *   *

In 1979 I was reunited with my daughter, Teri, thanks to the intervention of P.V. Doyle, in whose Burlington Hotel Teri was hosting her twenty-first birthday party. I had not seen my daughter for ten years. She was now a fully-grown, self-assured young lady of whom I was very proud.

*   *   *

'Son of a bitch! It's Alec Guinness,' exclaimed the veteran Hollywood director Sam Fuller when I met him for the first time at Dublin Airport.

He was arriving with Lee Marvin to make *The Big Red One* at the studio after six weeks on location in Israel. John and Christel Boorman invited them home for dinner. I asked Christel, a superb cook, what she would serve as the main course. 'Pork, darling!' she replied. 'After six weeks in Israel, what else?'

One of my fondest memories of Lee Marvin is of a chance meeting in Los Angeles in 1979. After the eleven-hour flight from London, I was checking into the Beverly Wiltshire Hotel when a distinctive voice greeted me from behind. It was Lee. He was defending a lawsuit at the time, brought against him by Michelle Triola Marvin. The singer, who was represented by Marvin Mitchelson, afterwards one of California's best-known celebrity lawyers, was claiming half of Lee Marvin's fortune as palimony for a liaison she had had with the actor. Their relationship had ended when he married his school sweetheart, Pam Feeley. Lee was staying in the Beverly Wiltshire Hotel during the court case. Outside, the photographers, reporters and television cameras were assembled to waylay him. Lee greeted me like a long-lost friend and suggested that we go to the bar together as he needed a drink and someone he could trust to talk to. We spent the next few hours drinking heavily and discussing everything under the sun, except his court case, which was then the big news story not only in Los Angeles but around the world. Lee made a passing reference to the court action, saying that there were a lot of 'Marvins' involved!

My favourite cinematic memory of Lee Marvin is the scene he plays with the drunken horse in *Cat Ballou*, the 1965 film for which he won his first Academy Award. In his acceptance speech on Oscar night Lee said, 'There's a horse in a field somewhere out in the Valley which owns half of this!' He was a fine actor and a gracious man.

* * *

I met Princess Grace whenever she visited Ireland. One day she called me from Monte Carlo. Her old friend, Fr Patrick Peyton, who was widely known in America and throughout the world as the 'Rosary Priest', was coming to Ireland. He was making a film in Europe to support his crusade and required assistance. The film was to be screened the following Easter Sunday on American network television and would feature a galaxy of international stars, including Frank Sinatra, Italian tenor Luciano Pavarotti and The Chieftains; Princess Grace would present the television extravaganza. Fr Peyton's motto was, 'The family that prays together stays together'. He was always keen to point out that this slogan was aimed at all religions. In his heyday in Hollywood, he was helped equally by stars, film producers and television network chiefs of all religions. Many of his rallies featured Jewish and Protestant families, as well as Catholics, and on his Asian crusade he was also welcomed by Buddhists, Muslims and people of other Eastern faiths. Princess Grace advised Fr Peyton to come and see me. She had assured him that I would do everything possible to help with his production. She was now calling me to verify this.

Years earlier, on a visit back to my hometown of Ballaghaderreen, I had seen the Mayo-born Fr Peyton conducting a Rosary crusade meeting in the town square. I had photographed him. My mother, a staunch Catholic, was a great admirer of his. When Fr Peyton arrived in Dublin, we arranged to lunch in the Royal Hibernian Hotel. I invited my mother and Sheila. It was a great treat for my mother, who looked upon this man as a saint. During the course of the lunch, the gentle Fr Peyton repeatedly referred to Sheila as 'your beautiful bride'. I did not like to tell him that Sheila and I were not married. After the lunch Fr Peyton presented my mother with Rosary beads, which he blessed at the table. She treasured this gift all her life. When she died a quarter-of-a-century later, it was wound around her hands in her coffin and she took it with her to her grave.

Fr Peyton's film had been shot on locations in many European countries. We provided studio facilities and some other assistance. I persuaded Paddy Moloney to compose the music and got The Chieftains to appear in the film for nothing. Paddy later told me that he suspected everyone involved in the film had been paid, except The Chieftains. I think he may have been right. If there is a heaven, maybe our efforts on behalf of Fr Patrick Peyton will assist us in getting there!

At another of her parties in Monte Carlo, as we passed through the reception line with the other guests Princess Grace greeted me rather formally and without her usual warmth. When she came over to join us later, I teased her gently about her slightly frosty welcome. She just smiled her beautiful smile and said, 'Sheamus, at this stage you well know that without my glasses, I cannot see beyond the length of my arm. Until now I did not know you were here.' She always put her glasses on after the formal photographs had been taken.

During the Dublin Theatre Festival, a poetry reading entitled 'An Evening with Princess Grace' took place in Trinity College. Gay Byrne and Kathleen Watkins, Sheila and I were invited as guests of Gay's close friend, accountant Russell Murphy, who was Chairman of the Festival. We started the evening in Russell's office overlooking College Green, a short walk from the college. Russell served champagne before the short performance, and after it we dined in Mike Butt's popular restaurant, The Tandoori Room. Russell, accompanied by his friend, Bronwyn Conroy, was, as always, a perfect and overwhelmingly generous host. At one stage during the evening when he left the table, I suggested to Gay that the guests should order more champagne as a gesture of our gratitude. He agreed. After Russell's death, when the source of his generosity became apparent, I reminded Gay of that evening. A wry smile revealed that he was still smarting at the betrayal by his close friend. Some of Gay's money and that of Hugh Leonard had paid for our splendid evening with Princess Grace!

* * *

The greatest film made at Ardmore Studios during my stewardship was undoubtedly John Boorman's *Excalibur*. Since childhood, John had had an interest in the Arthurian legend. His ambition as a director was to make the definitive film of that story. In early movies he had included hidden references to the legend, such as naming a character in *Deliverance* 'Arthur King', or showing the arm of the corpse emerging from the water in the style of the sword rising from the lake. I was involved with John in his efforts to raise money from Irish sources towards *Excalibur*'s production budget of $11,000,000. This was before the establishment of the Irish Film Board or the creation of tax incentives by the government, so we had to try a different tack. Together we went to long and detailed meetings with the major Irish banks, but it all came to nothing. In the end, the money was provided by Hollywood's Orion Pictures.

The sets designed by Tony Pratt for *Excalibur* were majestic and enormous. We had to break through the walls of the studio's sound stages to accommodate them. The gleaming silver castle of Camelot filled the back-lot, while the studio's stables housed the knights' horses. There was a tremendous buzz about the place. The leading players were Nicol Williamson, the imposing Scottish actor, and Helen Mirren, even then a well-known and respected actress of stage and screen. *Excalibur* also introduced the talented and very beautiful Shakespearean actress Cherie Lunghi to the big screen, along with Irish actors Liam Neeson and Gabriel Byrne.

Shooting *Excalibur* was an exhilarating time for everyone in the studio. There was a magical atmosphere about the place. Watching John directing the actors as he wove the tale of loyalty, betrayal, love and battle was fascinating. His energy and vision were astonishing. We had many visitors to the studio during shooting and, despite his preoccupation with the job in hand and its attendant pressures, John Boorman would welcome them to his set. One such occasion was the return visit of the Minister for Industry and Commerce, Des O'Malley. He was enthusiastic about the level of activity and welcomed an opportunity to pose for photographs with members of the cast or with a live boa constrictor, which was appearing in the film, draped about his shoulders. The Fine Gael shadow minister for Industry and Commerce, Paddy O'Toole, also visited with Ted Nealon, director of the Fine Gael Press Office. During lunch, Ted constantly reminded me that the shadow minister was under pressure because he was due to participate in an important Dáil debate that afternoon, so their time on the *Excalibur* set would be limited. When we got there, John Boorman was shooting a nude scene with Helen Mirren. It was no surprise to me that Helen's attraction proved too great; the shadow minister's urgent desire to return to Leinster House quickly vanished!

Before shooting started John Boorman's film was simply called *Merlin*. When production started the title was changed to *Knights*, and the jackets and T-shirts worn by the crew were inscribed accordingly. One day Toddy O'Sullivan, then retired from the Gresham Hotel, and his wife Niamh were guests on the set. When she saw the magnificent silver sword, Niamh remarked, 'This film should be called *Excalibur*.' Someone else who later made a similar suggestion got the credit for the film's final title, but it was Niamh who said it first.

In 1981 *Excalibur* was the official Irish entry in the competition for the Palme d'Or in Cannes. John Boorman received a special award from the jury for the 'visual quality and technique' of his film.

* * *

One of the nicest people I met through the studio was Dana Wynter. Dana first came to Ireland in 1958 to star with James Cagney in *Shake Hands with the Devil*. As a student in London she had gone out with a young Irish artist named Louis le Brocquy. She had also met the architect, Michael Scott. Both encouraged her to visit Ireland. In her own words: 'The country immediately caught my heart and I knew I'd live there one day. And so I did—for thirty years. I grew to love Ireland, the Irish and their philosophy of life.' Within a short time of her arrival, Dana had a cottage built in one of my own special places, Glenmacnass, in the Wicklow hills. I have many recollections of times spent with Dana and sometimes her son, Mark, and other friends in that picturesque rose-and-clematis-covered thatched cottage.

Dana's lovely disposition and extraordinary kindness is legendary. Some years ago she arranged a lunch in Los Angeles, where I would meet one of her oldest friends, the great American film director, King Vidor. A small, well-dressed man in his eighties, this iconic figure of the cinema had left his home town of Galveston, Texas, and with his wife, Florence, set out for Hollywood in their Model-T Ford in 1915. Florence Vidor rapidly became a star of silent movies, but it was 1919 before King Vidor directed his first feature film, *The Turn of the Road*. Acclaimed as a first-class director of silent films, his career continued to blossom with the advent of the talkies. King Vidor completed nearly sixty feature films in all. Although nominated in the Best Director category five times, he never won an Academy Award. In 1979 he was awarded an honorary Oscar. King Vidor died at the age of eighty-eight, three years after our meeting.

* * *

In the 1981 General Election a Fine Gael/Labour government was returned to power, with Garret FitzGerald as Taoiseach. The financial situation of National Film Studios of Ireland remained parlous. The money promised by the government when the studio was established in 1976 had never materialised. By now frustrated by the lack of support from successive administrations, I had threatened to resign at the end of 1979, but was dissuaded from doing so by John Boorman. Ever the optimists, we carried on. The two accountant members of the Board of Directors were advocating drastic redundancies in the workforce. The Irish Film Board, established under legislation introduced originally by Minister Des O'Malley, had limited resources, which were quite insufficient to sustain or assist serious film production, even for a short period. Michael O'Leary was our new Minister in the Department of Industry and Energy. Young, bright, enthusiastic and an acquaintance from broadcasting days, I welcomed his appointment. Our company Chairman was becoming disillusioned, however. In a letter to the new Minister before our first meeting he stated:

> The Board should be disbanded and replaced by a new one which would have a positive attitude towards the film industry and a capacity to implement government policy. Unfortunately the present Board is not geared for development. In fact, on the contrary, a number of directors see their function as one of winding up the company. New membership on the Board should reflect new policy.
>
> A smaller business-orientated board should, I feel, be considered. While I will be pleased to step down as chairman, I would be prepared to serve as an ordinary member on a more congenial board.

An indication of a bright future for the film industry was the Minister's appointment of Muiris MacConghail as Chairman of the Film Board, which had been brought up to full strength. John was also a member of that board and he was impressed by Muiris, whom he regarded as being 'well-informed, clear-thinking, practical and purposeful'.

The *Sunday Tribune* published an article that was highly critical of John Boorman and, to a lesser extent, of me. The writer was Angela

Phelan, then a rookie journalist working under the supervision of Joe Carroll, one of the paper's senior staff. The source of the story was our fellow director, Vincent Corcoran, and most of the allegations contained in the article were untrue. John Boorman and I took legal action. Realising that their case was hopeless, the publishers of the *Sunday Tribune* agreed to settle out of court. Their offer of damages to John was 40 per cent higher than their offer to me. John felt that, as Chief Executive, I should receive at least an equal consideration. Before negotiations on this had concluded, however, the *Sunday Tribune* went into receivership and the case collapsed. No apology was ever published. John Boorman personally settled our legal fees.

Although John Boorman and I conducted several meetings with the new Minister, financial support for the studio was still not forthcoming. We were always received courteously, but in the end the Minister provided little more than 'tea and sympathy'. In a small gesture to vent our frustration, when writing to the Minister for Industry and Energy, John inserted an emphatic questionmark after the word 'Energy' in the Minister's title.

There was one silver lining, however, in that the proposal regarding the selection of a new board of directors was accepted. An approach was made and the chairmanship offered to Tony O'Reilly, but he declined. Letters of appointment for the new members were drawn up. Sadly, before these could be signed by the Minister, another general election was called. In February 1982 a Fianna Fáil government was elected, with Charles J. Haughey as Taoiseach. This would sound the death knell of National Film Studios of Ireland and bring our dreams crashing down.

* * *

In March 1982 the screening of Neil Jordan's *Angel* was boycotted by members of the Association of Independent Film Makers at the Celtic Film Festival in Wexford. There was criticism of John Boorman, who was a member of the Irish Film Board, and also the film's producer, although he had had no part in the board's decision to invest a small amount of money in the project.

One of the leaders of the campaign was Tiernan McBride, who, although well into middle age, considered himself one of the 'young' film-makers. He enjoyed a very successful and lucrative career making television commercials. Tiernan's larger-than-life personality attracted many followers. He had a heart of gold. But with a bellicose manner and booming voice, he tended to bully those with whom he disagreed. More than anyone else, Tiernan McBride was responsible for the creation of the Irish Film Centre in Dublin's Temple Bar.

Albert Reynolds was the current Minister for Industry and Energy. Another new minister, another new hope of support for our ailing studio. These hopes vanished quickly, however. We never officially met our new minister. Reynolds was elected for the constituency of Longford/Westmeath in 1977, three years after I left political broad-casting. At the Jacob's Television Awards presentation in the Burlington Hotel on the evening of Friday 2 April 1982, Sheila and I were enjoying the company of our table companions, Frank Hall, John McColgan and Twink. When I mentioned to Frank that I had never met Albert Reynolds, who was guest of honour and the evening's presenter of prizes, he offered to introduce me immediately. The meeting was brief. A curt greeting and perfunctory handshake and the Minister turned away. Very strange behaviour for a politician, I thought, as we went back to our table.

The next day, a telephone call from Philip Molloy, film corre-spondent of the *Irish Press*, explained the Minister's attitude. Philip had been informed by Reynolds that National Film Studios of Ireland would be closed and the company placed in voluntary liquidation. Neither the Chairman nor I, as Chief Executive, had been informed. Philip Molloy's telephone call asking for a comment was the first I had heard of the Minister's action. It was a shoddy and disgraceful way to wind up a State-sponsored enterprise.

I felt particularly aggrieved at the manner in which John Boorman was treated. It was a reprehensible way to treat somebody who had given so much of his time, energy, expertise and enthusiasm in endeav-ouring to create an Irish film industry. John took no remuneration or out-of-pocket expenses over his seven years as Chairman of National Film Studios of Ireland. When I informed John of the Minister's decision, he immediately came to our house. He telephoned Charlie Haughey at his Kinsealy home and left an angry message on the answering-machine. Then we had a drink.

Our hopes and plans for a new beginning under a different government had been dashed. In one stroke, Albert Reynolds had destroyed all the structures that had been built up and the international goodwill that had been achieved and single-handedly put the Irish film industry back years. Various efforts were made to rescind the government's decision. The disparate elements of the film industry, many of which had been critical of John Boorman and the studio management a few days before, now united in support. Meetings were held and petitions drawn up. We had been negotiating with the producers of *Never Say Never Again*, the film that saw the return of Sean Connery to play an aging James Bond, to have the film made in Ireland. They had given an undertaking to cover all studio costs up to and during the production of their film. This would have maintained staff and freelance employment and provided a handsome profit for the company. Lewis Gilbert, who was about to start filming *Educating Rita* with Michael Caine and Julie Walters, was obliged to shoot on location. I arranged the use of Trinity College, Dublin, for that production.

John Boorman, who had earlier resigned from the Irish Film Board, now resigned from the board of National Film Studios of Ireland. He presided over a meeting with film workers who were anxious to save the studio. An action committee of film workers was set up and telegrams of protest were sent to the Minister by the Friends of the Studios, including Peter Ustinov, Princess Grace, Charlotte Rampling and John Huston. Hollywood veterans King Vidor, Carroll O'Connor and Pat O'Brien also joined the fray, but it was all in vain. Rumours flourished; one was that the Minister had agreed to sell the studio to a businessman, Vincent Donohoe, the day before he announced his intention to close it down.

The receiver, Michael McNulty, a young accountant, a native of Longford and a friend and supporter of Albert Reynolds, arrived in the studio without delay. He was a sympathetic person and we got on well together as the various procedures of the liquidation went ahead. The exciting adventure of National Film Studios of Ireland, my 'One Spin On The Merry Go Round', was over. It had lasted just thirteen days short of seven years. I walked out of my office in Ardmore Studios for the last time on Thursday 17 June 1982.

Chapter 12 ∽

BETWEEN
ACTS

When the studio closed, I was downhearted but not desolate. Like Mr Micawber in *David Copperfield*—the first book I ever read—I am an optimist and always believe that something will turn up. While it's true that 1982 may not have been my favourite year, a movie of that name did bring some satisfaction and, more importantly, some badly needed money my way.

Hollywood director Richard Benjamin, who was finishing his film *My Favorite Year*, needed an extra line of dialogue from the star, Peter O'Toole, who was then living in Clifden, Co. Galway. I knew Peter and was asked to arrange this. Early on a summer morning, sound-recordist Pat Hayes, Sheila and I drove to Clifden. When we arrived in the afternoon Peter was still asleep. Burning candles from the previous night's party were visible through the windows. Finding an unlocked door, we entered the house and played snooker on the full-sized table in the games room. When Peter finally came around, I suggested that we record the required dialogue in my car in order to match the original scene filmed inside a car in New York. Peter thought this a stroke of genius, but insisted that we re-write and expand the script. Lying in his chosen position on the carpet, we both wrote new versions. My only concern was that the original line should remain intact so that all the other rubbish could subsequently be eliminated.

The film was about a legendary Hollywood star dedicated to wine and women, who in 1954 is invited to appear in a television series. It contained the unforgettable line from Peter: 'I can't go on LIVE—I'm a movie star not an actor!'

* * *

In 1982, on behalf of The Motion Picture Company of Ireland, Sheila and I took Neil Jordan's first film, *Angel*, to Cannes in the hope of finding some buyers. Irvin Shapiro arranged and paid for some screenings in local cinemas. Money was scarce; we could not afford to take Neil Jordan to Cannes, but John Boorman, who produced the film, was there in another capacity. As Neil Jordan was then an unknown, Irvin decided to highlight John Boorman's involvement when advertising the film. This ensured that it did not go unnoticed. Irvin was the kindest man I ever met. He suspected that I was short of money and, without being asked, he insisted on lending me $3,000 to cover my expenses in Cannes. He would never allow me to repay him, claiming that he could recover the money from another source. I know he never did. We spent many happy times together. He died aged eighty-three on New Year's Day in 1989. If there is a heaven, Irvin is surely there.

Pierre Joannon arranged a good rate for Sheila and me in the Martinez Hotel, where he knew the manager. We went to a local café each morning to save money. It was only when checking out that I discovered that breakfast had been included in the hotel rate!

The film, in six large tin cans, had to be transported between the cinemas for the various screenings. Sheila and I did this sometimes twice a day; she managed to carry two of the cans while I struggled with the remaining four. Such is the glamour of the Cannes Film Festival!

The screenings of *Angel* were an outstanding success. When the word got around, spread enthusiastically by the prominent British film critic Alexander Walker, that this was the movie to see, demand for tickets far exceeded our expectations. As all cinemas are booked well ahead of the Festival, our only option was to arrange a midnight screening. This is a time when buyers and critics are enjoying the social life in Cannes. Again to our surprise, every seat in the house was occupied. There were people standing at the sides and back of the cinema. Some who could not possibly fit in demanded that the doors be left open so that they could stand in the foyer and listen to the soundtrack. It surely was the hottest ticket in town. There is no doubt that the reviews of *Angel* written by Alexander Walker and Philip French launched the successful career of Neil Jordan.

Shortly before this, John Boorman and I had set up The Motion Picture Company of Ireland with the intention of producing and distributing Irish-made movies. The first such was *Angel*, which we distributed successfully in Ireland. The following year Neil Jordan attended the Cannes Film Festival for the first time. He was now acknowledged as a young director on the way up. Two years after that, in 1986, Neil was back with his film *Mona Lisa*, one of the British entries in the main competition. That year the Palme D'Or was awarded to another British film, *The Mission*, produced by David Putnam and directed by Roland Joffe. Bob Hoskins won the Best Actor award for his leading role in *Mona Lisa* and later won a BAFTA award for the same performance. After that remarkable film, for which he also wrote the screenplay, Neil Jordan was now up there with Hollywood's best. It was no surprise to anyone when, six years later, *The Crying Game* was nominated in the six main categories in the Academy Awards. It took the coveted Oscar for the Best Original Story and Screenplay.

*   *   *

During the summer of 1982, Sheila and I spent a month-long holiday in Cyprus. The Director General of the Cyprus Broadcasting Corporation, Charilaos Papadopolous, agreed to co-produce a three-hour television documentary on Cyprus with me. Charilaos and his wife, Freyni, a distinguished broadcaster, were friends from my RTÉ days. It was during this holiday that we learned of the tragic death of Princess Grace. Aged fifty-two and still one of the world's most beautiful and elegant women, she died in a fatal accident when her car plunged down a 45 foot embankment off a treacherous mountain road in Monaco. The circumstances of the accident remain a mystery. I was shattered by the dreadful news.

*   *   *

On our return from Cyprus there was a short period on the dole, which I found demoralising. The whiff of stale beer and cigarette smoke in the queue indicated that most of my fellow recipients had just come from the nearest pub. My old '7 Days' colleague, John Feeney, then writing the gossip column in the *Evening Herald*, was an imaginative champion of my cause. His daily column frequently predicted career prospects dreamt up in his imagination and great opportunities that were about to come my way, but never materialised. One day John noticed me cycling to the dole office. He stopped his car and invited me to lunch in Dobbins. As he now had a generous expense account, he suggested we should lunch together regularly. There were some job prospects during this time. Two potential buyers of Ardmore Studios asked me to return as Chief Executive if the purchase deals were successful. They both fell through. A tempting offer based in London ultimately did not interest me. I preferred living in Ireland.

We returned to Cyprus in September 1982 and began filming for our television series, 'Love's Island—The Story of Cyprus'. The camera crew was supplied by the Cyprus Broadcasting Corporation. Sheila worked as my production assistant and in due course got her first screen credit. The first phase of our filming ended in mid-October.

*   *   *

In November 1982 a General Election was called. I was approached by Bill O'Herlihy and Enda Marren, both of whom were dedicated members of Fine Gael and deeply involved in the party's election campaign. They asked me to direct the television party political broadcasts. It was well paid and work I enjoyed. Having an opportunity to observe the activities of the strategists behind the politicians was fascinating; these non-elected advisors were known as the 'national handlers'. The most impressive and pragmatic among them was Frank Flannery, a natural team leader. Chief Executive of the Rehab Group, Frank retired early to head up Fine Gael's strategy team as Director of Elections in the 2007 General Election. Apart from the Leader, Garret FitzGerald, and Deputy Leader, Peter Barry, the 'national handlers' seemed to have little respect for most of the candidates. Bill's clever and amusing scripts pointed out the disasters of previous Fianna Fáil administrations. However, one person we were instructed not to ridicule was a young politician named Bertie Ahern. He was then the acceptable face of Fianna Fáil.

When the film studio closed, opposition TDs had made platitudinous remarks, but when the Fine Gael/Labour government was elected in November 1982, nothing changed. Knowing politicians as I did, this came as no surprise. After the new government took office I asked to see John Bruton, the new Minister for Industry and Energy, to discuss my position regarding possible compensation for the loss of my job. He had previously been Justin Keating's junior minister and as I knew his father, I naïvely expected a sympathetic hearing. I was wrong. He refused to meet me, even when requested to do so by his old boss, Justin. I had no option but to seek legal advice, and subsequently decided to take legal action against the government. My case was based on the fact that I had been asked by the government to leave my permanent and pensionable job in RTÉ to run a State-sponsored enterprise. When that had failed through lack of government support and through no fault of mine, it seemed unfair that there was no compensation. Returning to RTÉ as a senior producer was not an option: during my seven-year absence, colleagues had progressed to levels such as Controller or Assistant Controller of Programmes, which would have been a reasonable expectation in my own case. The government's response to the threat of legal action was to retain Michael McDowell, one of the toughest lawyers in the country, to defend its position.

* * *

Fred Haines, the American screenwriter of Joe Strick's film *Ulysses*, had written a screenplay for a feature film based on Tom Barry's West Cork Flying Column. This was of great interest as I had met so many members of that heroic band when producing our memorable '7 Days' anniversary programme. Fred asked me to produce *The Boys from Kilmichael*. We received a small grant from the Irish Film Board and endeavoured to create interest in Britain and America. At the Cannes Film Festival in May 1983, Fred Haines and I toted the script around, but despite our best efforts, *The Boys from Kilmichael* never made it to the big screen.

* * *

After Ardmore closed, I kept in touch with those who had become friends through the studio. Liam Neeson and Helen Mirren had met when they starred in John Boorman's *Excalibur* and afterwards they lived together in London. Thanks to my daughter Teri, who worked for Aer Lingus, I was entitled to travel concessions with the airline. Greg Smith owned a large apartment in West Hampstead, where I stayed. It was easy to spend time in London. I frequently met Liam and Helen and Cherie Lunghi, whose friendship I cherished, and other London-based friends, including Peter Ustinov, who visited the city frequently. Gabriel Byrne and his partner, Aine O'Connor, who was briefly my production assistant in RTÉ, were also among my circle of friends during and after the making of *Excalibur*.

One day, when taking the lift up to Peter Ustinov's suite in the Berkeley Hotel, I met Alistair Cooke, the BBC journalist famous over many years for his weekly radio programme, 'A Letter from America'. Clad in an impeccably cut suit, his elegant appearance completely matched the perception one got from his eloquent radio voice and beautifully written scripts.

One hot Saturday in July I waited in the Berkeley Hotel to meet Peter, who was coming from Paris. He arrived, dripping with perspiration. After a shower and change of clothing we lunched together in the hotel restaurant. I was due to return to Dublin on an afternoon flight. When Peter learned this he expressed disappointment because he had two tickets for us to attend the women's tennis final in Wimbledon that afternoon. Naturally, I changed my airline reservation and joined Peter in the air-conditioned limousine that took us to the home of lawn tennis.

There we were, seated in the main stand, close to the Royal Box. The Duke and Duchess of Kent occupied the box, with others who we assumed were minor royals. As they waved to acknowledge Peter, who they knew well because of his lifelong commitment to tennis, he responded with a small wave and encouraged me to do likewise. Before the start of the ladies' final we visited a number of hospitality marquees to which Peter was invited. The principal sustenance offered was strawberries served in silver bowls, accompanied by vintage champagne. Peter's love of strawberries matched my passion for champagne, so we were both very happy. As we wandered back to our grandstand seats, we saw the German tennis ace Boris Becker quietly practising for his next appearance on the centre court. After the ladies' final, won by Martina Navratilova we adjourned to yet another hospitality marquee for late afternoon tea. There Isaac Stern, the world-famous violinist, and his wife joined our table; Peter had once lived next to them in New York. Meeting this great artist, who spoke warmly of his most recent visit to Dublin, where he performed in the National Concert Hall, was the highlight of my one and only visit to Wimbledon. No tennis star or minor royal could match the sheer enjoyment of being in the company of that great musician who, like Peter, was an outstanding raconteur.

*   *   *

Peter had a great interest in Irish politics. Politicians I introduced him to included Justin Keating and Garret FitzGerald, whom he admired greatly. In later years, when appearing on 'The Late, Late Show' he met Charlie Haughey. Peter displayed an uncharacteristic lack of warmth towards Mr Haughey and afterwards said to me, 'I wouldn't trust that man.' Peter disliked Margaret Thatcher. He was annoyed by her treatment of Taoiseach Garret FitzGerald during her 'Out! out! out!' speech. On the evening of that outburst, Peter was in Dublin with me. He wrote the following letter to the Taoiseach:

November 26th 1984

Dear Dr. Fitzgerald,
Please excuse both the informality and formality of my form of address. It is early morning, my wife is still asleep and I have no access to an Irish paper from which I can copy the word you are known by without risking a monstrous spelling mistake. I hope that by explaining my difficulty, I am displaying the merest shred of sensibility, a quality necessary in public affairs, and of which you seem to have been deprived in recent hours.
     This, then, is a hasty note to tell you that there is at least one Englishman (of Russian origin and Irish predilections), who is

appalled by the manner in which you have been treated by an administration which has announced its intention of leaving UNESCO at the very same moment. Not to allow you any room for manoeuvre may be frank, but it is also grossly insensitive towards another negotiator, and high-handedly dismissive of the temper of the Irish nation. Firm it may be, tough it may be, but it is also rude and fundamentally unintelligent, and I very much regret that you, of all people, should have been subjected to such abrasive short sightedness.

It seems that the present government in London is so intoxicated with monetarism that it gives as an excuse for walking out of UNESCO the fact that Britain is 'not getting its money's worth'. What 'money's worth' can any powerful nation expect to extract from an agency of the United Nations, for heaven's sake? Once again there is evidence of an insensitivity bordering on the sordid. Such sentiments could have been expressed by one of Dickens' most eloquent creations, so self-satisfied are they, and so mean.

I have served on several round-tables at UNESCO in recent years, and have even been chairman on at least three occasions. The fiscal structure of the organisation may well be open to criticism, as may the leadership of the director general, but I can honestly say that the only time I have come under pressure has been from a past Ambassador to the Human Rights Commission, a lawyer representing a great nation which finds itself frequently being the Leader of the Free World. I remember pointing out to this gentleman that if his part of the world is really free, it doesn't need a leader, it being a contradiction in terms. Finally let me tell you that I have asked an eminent member of the British cabinet, who happens to be a friend of mine, what it was like serving the present administration. He did not reply. Two minutes later he asked me if I knew the story of the Duke of Wellington's first day in office as prime minister. I said I did not. Apparently after the first cabinet meeting, he turned to his secretary and said 'I don't understand this new job. This morning I gave my orders—and they stayed to argue!' Here again a reputation for ironness did him scant service away from the battlefield. He, at least, had Waterloo, not merely the Falklands; Bussaco, not merely Belgrano.

Once we are destined to have successful conservative governments owing to the scandalous absence of proportional representation, it is extraordinary how Ted Heath can be regretted, more each succeeding day.

Be that as it may, know that your qualities of statesmanship and vision are deeply appreciated in many places, now more than ever. A person who finds it easier to talk than to listen possesses an Achilles' Heel and any amount of toughness for the sake of toughness will not prevent this from becoming more and more apparent with the passage of time.

Be of good cheer.

Yours ever, in admiration

Peter Ustinov

*   *   *

Early in 1984, Peter Ustinov and I met in London and I proposed making a series of television programmes called 'Peter Ustinov's People'. Peter was enthusiastic. Over lunch we came up with a list of names, which included the Indian Premier Indira Gandhi, King Hussein of Jordan, former British Prime Minister Edward Heath, Graham Greene, Fidel Castro, former German Chancellor Helmut Schmidt, Melina Mercouri, the actress and singer who had become Minister for Culture in the Greek Government, and Pope John Paul II. As I got into a taxi at the Berkeley Hotel to travel to Heathrow Airport, Peter shouted after me, 'When you phone me next week, I expect to hear you say, "The Pope is okay, but Castro won't do it!"'

I approached Indira Gandhi through Kiran Doshi, the Indian Ambassador to Ireland. Within a few days he confirmed that the Prime Minister would be delighted to participate in the programme. Three weeks later, having negotiated a deal with Controller of Programmes Muiris MacConghail that RTÉ would substantially finance the project, I acquired a German co-producer. We set out for New Delhi. I would produce the programme; Rory O'Farrell, my business partner at the time, would direct. Our German co-producer engaged a local Indian film crew. Before leaving home, I bought a professional Nikon camera to get some quality still photographs for publication and promotion.

I had met Mrs Gandhi before at the New Delhi Film Festival. She was then leader of the opposition. I was impressed by her. She was very attractive, although smaller than I had imagined. Then in her mid-sixties, dressed in a colourful sari she looked younger than her years. She was certainly a person who would make a charming and interesting dinner companion. She talked of Indian and world affairs. She told of a meeting with the Irish harpist, Grainne Yeats, and how she loved classical music. She mentioned that because of the presence of grandchildren in her home, the only music she ever heard there was that of Michael Jackson!

On this occasion she was in fine health and ebullient spirits as she prepared to seek a fifth term as prime minister of the world's most populous democracy. Mrs Gandhi invited us to travel with her on her pre-election visit to the state of Orissa, where she would hold a series of political meetings. These public meetings always followed the same pattern: the Prime Minister would emerge from her helicopter to orchestrated shouts of 'Zindabad Gandhi' (Long live Gandhi), she would stand in the front of a jeep and be driven slowly around the inner perimeter of the meeting ground, waving and being showered with flowers. Then she would mount a small concrete grandstand. She made her speeches in Hindi and spoke in a weak, unresonant voice, completely devoid of oratorical tricks. The average attendance at these rural meetings was 100,000.

Mrs Gandhi told us, with evident satisfaction, that these were small meetings compared to most. She seemed to be a microcosm of India, as capable of calmly making ruthless decisions—like the storming of the Sikh Temple at Amritsar—as of making engaging and even humorous banter. Five months earlier she had sent the army into Punjab and into the most sacred of all Sikh shrines, the Golden Temple, which Sikh extremists had turned into a sort of holy fortress. At least 600 people had been killed in the ensuing battle.

The main interview with Peter Ustinov was to take place in the garden of the Prime Minister's residence at 9.00 a.m. on the morning after our return from her political tour. This had included the laying of the foundation stone for a new ordnance factory in Saintala, a helicopter ride away from Bhubaneswar, the capital of Orissa, which was our base during the trip. I made the most of the many opportunities to take still pictures. On the return journey to New Delhi in the Prime Minister's private aircraft, Indira Gandhi told me about her son, Rajiv, a former airline pilot who had reluctantly given up his chosen career to become a politician and his mother's heir-apparent. After the death of her younger son Sanjay, four years earlier, she had been grooming Rajiv for leadership of the party. He was currently conducting similar campaign meetings in West Bengal and would not return to the capital until after our departure. However, as I proposed returning to India later in the year, she said that we would have an opportunity to meet then. Little did she or I know that within twenty-four hours of this conversation, Indira Gandhi would be dead and Rajiv would be sworn in as Prime Minister of India.

On the evening of our return to New Delhi, I received a telephone call from the Prime Minister herself to ask me what she should wear for her interview the next day. Over the previous few days we had seen a wide array of saris, so I suggested one that was predominantly orange-coloured. She agreed with this. We arrived at the official residence at 8.15 a.m. the following morning. Our camera was set up on the lawn in the extensive garden. This was no ordinary suburban garden, but rather a small park. At the appointed time, the Prime Minister's press secretary went to fetch her. I followed a little behind in order to meet her as she entered the garden from the living area. As I approached the high fence that divided the garden from the residence, three shots rang out. Behind me, in the interview area, the Indian cameraman explained the sounds to the other members of the crew. 'Fire-crackers,' he said. 'They are quite usual in these parts.' Then came an unmistakable burst from an automatic weapon: clearly not fireworks. I glimpsed briefly the figure dressed in the blood-stained orange sari lying on the pathway, surrounded by security guards.

Shocked, I slowly walked back to the film crew. Peter Ustinov later described me as 'looking white and shaken'. I told them that the Prime Minister had been shot. The whole situation seemed unreal. The early morning birdsong in the garden had ceased when the shooting started and it created an eerie silence. It made me think of film and television footage of public assassinations in other countries, with the attendant panic, shouting and general confusion. In India, it was different. Indiria Gandhi's assassination took place in her garden, in silence, as had been in the case many years earlier for her distinguished predecessor, Mahatma Gandhi, the father of modern India.

Indira Gandhi had been assassinated by two of her Sikh bodyguards, who then calmly dropped their guns and were seized by other security guards. A fight broke out and both of the assassins were shot dead. The day before her death, Indira Gandhi had told a large and enthusiastic crowd in Orissa's capital city, Bhubaneswar:

> I am not interested in a long life. I am not afraid of these things. I don't mind if my life goes in the service of this nation. If I die today, every drop of my blood will invigorate the nation.

These words are now displayed in a shrine erected in the garden of the Prime Minister's residence, along with other memorabilia, including her diary. The page open for the last day of her life includes two appointment entries—one for the early morning and one for the afternoon, with 'Sheamus Smith and Irish television crew'.

Shortly after returning to our hotel, when the news of the Prime Minister's assassination had broken and the international press corps was crowding into New Delhi, I was approached by *Time* magazine, which was seeking recent photographs of Mrs Gandhi. Her visit to the state of Orissa had been relatively low-key from a press point of view, so mine were the only pictures available. The publication of my photograph on a half-page over the leading article in the magazine was accompanied by a credit, which gave me enormous pleasure. Back in the days when we worked in the *Irish Press*, it was every photographer's dream to have a credit in *Time*. Colman Doyle, our leading photographer, was the first to achieve this and repeated it several times over many years; Basil King achieved it in Canda; and now, almost thirty years later, I had finally made it as a result of a tragic event that happened in the garden on that sunny October morning.

We remained in India to film the State funeral of Indira Gandhi, which was attended by Heads of State and dignitaries from around the world. Ireland was represented by the Taoiseach, Garret FitzGerald. The impressive and colourful ceremony culminated in the lighting of the funeral pyre by Mrs Gandhi's only remaining son, Rajiv.

Nine months later we returned to New Delhi to complete our filming and Peter interviewed the new Prime Minister. He was a charming, soft-spoken and determined young man, who demonstrated enthusiasm and optimism for the future of his country. I presented him with an Irish linen tablecloth originally intended for his mother. Some years later Rajiv Gandhi, while still Prime Minister, was assassinated. His Italian-born wife Sonia was eventually persuaded to follow her dead husband into politics, thereby preserving the Gandhi name in India's Parliament.

Widespread publicity in the Irish newspapers following the assassination of Indira Gandhi encouraged friends to joke about how unlucky it was to be associated with either Rory O'Farrell or me. Rory had previously directed a documentary on Mayor Richard J. Daly of Chicago, who had died in office during filming. Then there was our joint involvement with Erskine Childers, whose death occurred before our film was finished. Then there had been my own experience during the Turkish invasion of Cyprus, and now Indira Gandhi. We didn't exactly seem to have the Midas touch!

After Indira Gandhi, our next target for 'Peter Ustinov's People' was former British Prime Minister, Ted Heath. Peter Ustinov knew him well as they were both past pupils of St Paul's School, although they had not known each other while there. Before filming, Rory and I took Ted Heath to lunch in London. At first he was formal and aloof, but after the second bottle of wine he opened up considerably. By the time we finished the third bottle we were all relaxed and getting on famously. We shot the film at various London locations, including St Paul's School, The House of Commons and No. 10 Downing Street. The finale of the programme was a dinner party in Ted Heath's London home, which two years earlier had been damaged by an IRA bomb. Dinner guests were Gillian Whitticombe, the music critic who later married Jeremy Isaacs, former boss of Channel Four and The Royal Opera House, André Previn and his wife, and Peter with his wife, Hélène. Ted Heath spoke of his interests outside politics, his passion for music, travelling and most of all sailing. Born beside the sea, this had been a lifetime interest. He told of winning one of the world's toughest ocean races in 1969, the Sydney to Hobart, defeating seventy-eight other yachts, and of his experiences skippering his ocean racing yacht *Morning Cloud* in the Fastnet Race off Ireland's south-east coast. Despite the treatment he had received from the IRA, he liked Ireland and the Irish.

For what is known in the film business as 'differences in artistic interpretation', Rory O'Farrell and I parted company and went our separate ways. The next subject of 'Peter Ustinov's People' was King Hussein of Jordan. Peter had met him several times before. King Hussein was someone I had read a great deal about and was anxious to meet. The senior official at the London Embassy of the Hashemite Kingdom of Jordan, with whom I was dealing, told me about the King's private secretary, who was then visiting London with 'His Majesty'. Her name was Miss Moor. This I assumed to be an anglicisation of an Arab name. When I went to meet 'Miss Moor' at the Royal Garden Hotel early on a sunny July morning, I was therefore surprised to find not an Arabian lady but a typical English rose. Wearing a light floral summer dress, this lady, whose first name was Linda, made an instant impression.

Linda and I got on right away and spent much more time together than either of us had expected at our first meeting. I returned to Dublin later that day, but within a week was back in London to meet Linda Moor again. Over dinner in a small Kensington restaurant, I discovered that Linda, now in her thirties and hailing from the Border Counties, had been a hotel receptionist, schoolteacher, uniformed police officer and Special Branch detective before taking up her present position. She had previously been responsible for police 'protection' duties with Egyptian President Hosni Mubarak and his wife and with members of the Japanese Emperor's family before King Hussein, who was so impressed he invited her to work for him. I was intrigued that my charming, interesting and very feminine dinner companion obviously knew not only how to look after herself and others but could also handle firearms.

It was in April 1986 that I first went to Jordan's capital, Amman. King Hussein had immediately agreed to our proposal for the programme.

He was keen to meet again Peter Ustinov, on whom some years earlier he had bestowed the Order of Istiglal, one of the highest honours of The Hashemite Kingdom of Jordan. My visit was in order to finalise details and arrange the filming schedule with the Palace.

Amman is a beautiful city, a jewel among all the Arab capitals I have visited. Like their Arabian brethren, the people were kind, friendly and fascinating. The buildings and historical sites, including the Roman amphitheatre in Amman's city centre, were awesome. Large photographs of the king were displayed everywhere—on the street lamp-posts and in all the shop windows. Like their monarch, all the men wore a thin moustache. This was a much-loved king. One of those I encountered was the Crown Prince, Prince Hassan. He was very interested in children's hospitals and spoke warmly of his admiration for Lady Valerie Goulding, whom he had met several times. The palace took care of everything. They put a helicopter of the Royal Jordanian Air Force and a Mercedes limousine at my disposal. I was given priority access everywhere I went. The penthouse suite in the Jordan Hilton Hotel was my accommodation for a week. When I tried to pay for extras when leaving the hotel, the response was: 'The Palace has taken care of everything, Sir.'

* * *

The next day I was home in Ireland, far from sunny Jordan. As I cut two-thirds of an acre of the fastest-growing grass in Ireland around our home in Co. Wicklow, I reflected on the luxury of the previous week. Grass-cutting was not a pastime worth pursuing. I decided there and then to sell the house and move back to a more manageable situation near Dublin.

Sheila was now Banqueting and Conference Manager in the city-centre Westbury Hotel. I was spending a lot of time abroad, so a move to the city's suburbs suited both of us. I found a suitable new house in a small development overlooking the Dodder River near Rathgar. We have lived there ever since. Shortly after moving in, I went to the Cannes Film Festival. On my return I could not believe my eyes: the area behind the house, which I had left as a building site, had been transformed into a splendid garden by my very special friend, Suzanne Macdougald, with some help from gardening expert, Dermot O'Neill. The abundant foliage in the new conservatory was simply breathtaking.

*   *   *

A difficulty with 'Peter Ustinov's People' was co-ordinating times when both Peter and our subjects, all of whom had busy schedules, were available. It was the end of May 1987, more than a year later, that we returned to Jordan with Peter, my German co-producer Peter Köster and an Irish film crew. It was the holy month of Ramadan, which meant abstinence from food and drink during daylight hours—a great boon to someone like me, who disliked interrupting the work impetus for meal breaks. Although eating was permitted for non-Muslims, we did not wish to offend our hosts and survived in the intense heat on bottled water. The cameraman was Sean Corcoran, another old friend; our sound-recordist was Dermot Moynihan. Janusz Guttner, the Polish actor I had first met at the Cork Film Festival and who was now a photographer in London, came to take the still photographs. A Royal Jordanian Air Force helicopter was provided to transport us to distant locations, such as the ancient cities of Petra and Jerrash, both extraordinary places, and to the desert at Wadi Rum, the location of David Lean's film, *Lawrence of Arabia*. Flying across the desert, we could land at will beside the large Bedouin tents and interview the nomads living there.

King Hussein was a fascinating man. Small, nattily dressed and soft-spoken, he addressed all men as 'Sir'. It was slightly unnerving at first to have the king address one as 'Sir', but he quickly made everyone feel relaxed. When photographed beside His Majesty, the natural inclination was to bend one's knees to reduce one's height. As a result, we all look slightly uncomfortable in the pictures!

We enjoyed working with King Hussein, his Lebanese/American wife Queen Noor and their children. The king, who held a commercial pilot's licence, sometimes took over the controls of his personal jet airliner. He was also an enthusiastic radio 'ham' and spoke regularly to fellow 'hams' around the world from his well-equipped radio room.

During filming, he managed to get in touch with a contact he had spoken to before in Ireland. He spoke to me of his great admiration for Professor James Dooge, our former Minister for Foreign Affairs and eminent hydrologist, who had made a major contribution to solving Jordan's water problems.

As in all Muslim countries, when the Muezzin calls for prayer from the mosque, members of the faithful face Mecca, get down on their knees and pray. I was anxious to get a spontaneous shot of a driver stopping his car, placing a prayer-mat on the road beside it and praying. After a number of failed attempts, we finally had the camera ready as a man in Arab dress stopped his car, got out and placed the small mat behind the car. Sean Corcoran filmed as the gentleman solemnly knelt, but then, to our amazement, he did not take a prayer posture, but instead carefully examined the exhaust pipe!

When filming was over I remained in Jordan. Sheila and my daughter Teri joined me for a short holiday. Our wrap party to mark the completion of filming coincided with the ending of Ramadan. There was a great buzz about the hotel as Muslims celebrated the end of their month of prayer and fasting. For the party in my hotel suite, everyone wore their bed-sheets as Arab robes; it was literally a 'wrap' party. We all had genuine Arab headdress so we really looked the part. Earlier that evening a special messenger from the palace brought me a farewell gift. It was a Longines gold watch, discretely inscribed with the royal crest. Peter Ustinov was slightly jealous. Pointing to the lapel ribbon that indicated his Royal recognition he remarked, 'All I ever got was this.' When we checked out of the hotel, I requested the account for the additional guests. The response was, as before, 'The Palace has taken care of everything, Sir.' The programme about King Hussein of Jordan was the last in our series.

*   *   *

Liam Neeson returned to Dublin to take the lead in a stage production of 'The Informer' in the Olympia Theatre; he was accompanied by Helen Mirren, who invited me to lunch. The play was opening that evening. We went to Locks, a favourite restaurant on the Grand Canal. I was delighted to have the company of this wonderful lady all to myself. During the course of our conversation, I asked what motivated her to appear in the film *Caligula*, which contained some explicit sex scenes; it was banned in Ireland. '£20,000!' she replied. At the time she was offered the part, she wanted to buy a small apartment costing that amount in Paris. *Caligula* paid for what became a good property investment. On the way to the theatre we visited a wine bar and had champagne. We arrived at the theatre in good form for Liam's first night performance. Visiting his dressing-room after the play, Liam mildly rebuked his 'two best friends seated in the centre of the front row who slept throughout the entire performance'. He was more amused than offended.

* * *

I first met Graham Greene at a luncheon by the swimming pool in Pierre Joannon's house, Les Chênes Verts, in 1977. We had an immediate rapport. Graham liked the photographs I took of him. We got to know each other well and spent time together during the Cannes Film Festival every year until his death. We usually lunched in an old-fashioned restaurant, Felix au Port, near the ancient walls in Antibes. It was near to Graham's home and a regular haunt of his. Graham's conversation was always interesting—peppered with anecdotes of his vast experience of nearly seventy years of travel. There was little in life that he had not tried at some time: smoking opium as he lay on a bed in an opium den in Saigon, or spending an evening with film director Carol Reed in a brothel in Lisbon!

The first time I invited Graham to lunch, he enquired if he might bring along his lady friend, Yvonne Cloetta. Naturally I was pleased to invite Yvonne, a charming lady whom I had met previously with her husband in Graham's company. On that occasion, her husband had admired the tie I was wearing. At the end of the evening, I took it off and gave it to him. The annual lunch with Graham became a pattern over the next few years. I would meet Graham and Yvonne usually on a Wednesday and sometimes invite other guests to join us. One year I changed the day to Thursday. When I arrived at the restaurant, I

Another unrequited love! Sinéad Cusack, one of my favourite people since first meeting her as a very young actress.

On the set of *Michael Collins* with 'the big fella' himself, Liam Neeson.
Photo: John Hession

Visitors to the Film Censor's Office, Gabriel Byrne and his then wife, Ellen Barkin. *Photo: Rita Culkeen*

Making a point with Peter Ustinov.

In Dublin with Paul Hogan, whose first film, *Crocodile Dundee,* is one of my all-time favourites.

A couple I greatly admire, Bono and his wife, Ali Hewson. *Photo: Sarah Doyle*

At the premiere of *Agnes Browne* with director and star, Anjelica Huston.

On the set of *The Old Curiosity Shop* with Tom Courtenay and camera operator Seamus Corcoran, a friend from schooldays.

At the 1996 Cannes Film Festival with Director of Photography Seamus Deasy (right) and Technicolor Executive Simon Baxter.

Still going strong. At her eightieth birthday party, Maureen O'Hara and former Film Commissioner Roger Green. A formidable lady, Maureen remained enjoying the birthday celebrations until well after 3.00 a.m. When we met in Los Angeles a year later, she told me of plans for her next film. *Photo: Foynes Flying Boat Museum*

With Graham Greene near his home in Antibes. *Photo: Nice Matin*

One of the all-time greats, Harry Belafonte, now a UNICEF ambassador, at an early morning breakfast in Dublin. *Photo: Alma Carroll Ryan*

Farewell party for Vodafone Chief Executive Stephen Brewer, with former RTÉ colleagues Gay Byrne and Bill O'Herlihy. *Photo: Fennell Photography*

Presiding over the International Film Classifiers' Conference in Dublin Castle in 2001 with Deputy Film Censor, Ger Connolly.
Photo: Susan Kennedy

On a sleigh ride in Norway during my last international conference with the Director of Austria's Film Classification Board, Herbert Schwanda.
Photo: Jørgen Stenland

Enjoying retirement in Lisbon with Irish Ambassador Patrick O'Connor, his wife, Patricia, and Sheila.

With actress and former Miss Ireland Olivia Treacy at the Gala Dinner in Los Angeles in 2005 to raise funds for the Huston Film School at University College Galway.

My young friend Grainne Barron credits me for her very existence! I introduced her parents, Paddy Barron and Nuala Malone. *Photo: Fennell Photography*

Tea with the President! Peter Ustinov and I were entertained at Áras an Uachtaráin after Peter was conferred with an honorary degree from the National University of Ireland.
Photo: Colm Henry

At the reception in Áras an Uachtaráin to celebrate RTÉ's fortieth anniversary, a moment of hilarity with Cathal O'Shannon and incoming Film Censor, John Kelleher. *Photo: RTÉ*

My final cut! The specially made cake that dear friend Maxi presented to me after 'my last picture show' on the day of my departure. My favourite film, *Casablanca*, was screened for a small number of close friends. *Photo: Sir Ivor Roberts*

Brendan McCaul, Vice President Buena Vista International, looks on as Paddy Kelly, General Manager of Paramount Pictures, pours from one of the magnums of champagne commissioned with my own label for the farewell dinner given by friends in the cinema business in Dobbins Restaurant. *Photo: Sheila Hampson*

noticed that Graham was sitting alone at the table. I inquired where Yvonne was. Graham replied, 'You must know by now, Sheamus, that Yvonne always has lunch with her husband on Thursdays'! He was then in his eighties.

Shortly after Graham Greene graduated from Oxford University, he wrote to William T. Cosgrave, President of the Irish Free State, offering his services as a spy for the new state and suggesting that he could work in Northern Ireland. In reply he received a polite letter from Mr Cosgrave saying: 'Thank you for your kind offer, Mr. Green but we will not require your services. We have enough spies in Northern Ireland already!' Graham did in fact become a spy, working for the British secret service. His boss and close friend there was Kim Philby, who eventually defected and went to live in the Soviet Union. Graham often spoke of Philby; they stayed in touch and met whenever Graham was in Moscow. He once showed me a postcard he had just received from his friend. As befits a double agent, it was enclosed in an envelope!

During the 1989 Cannes Film Festival I met Graham for lunch as usual. He looked frail and much older than the previous year. When Graham did his annual signing for me, I noticed that his handwriting had deteriorated. Inside *The Captain and the Enemy* he wrote: 'For Sheamus, in hopes of another meeting and all good wishes. Graham.' In our hearts we knew it would not happen. We never met again. The following year Graham's failing health worsened. He moved to Switzerland to live near his daughter, Caroline. Yvonne went to look after him there. He never again returned to Antibes. Graham died in the Hôpital de la Providence in Vevey, Switzerland, on 3 April 1991. His beloved Yvonne passed away some years later. *The Captain and the Enemy* was Graham Greene's last novel.

*   *   *

In 1986 John Kelleher and David Collins launched their film *Eat the Peach* in Cannes. Their production company, Strongbow, mounted what was, by Irish standards, an elaborate advertising and promotional campaign. Stockton's Wing, the popular Irish band managed by Oliver Barry, came from Dublin and played a lunchtime concert in brilliant sunshine on the municipal bandstand in front of the Town Hall. *Eat the Peach* umbrellas, usually a vital accessory in Cannes' unsettled weather, were one of the promotional gifts offered. That year they were used as parasols! On the night of the principal screening, at the festivities in Jane's, the nightclub of the five-star Gray d'Albion Hotel, Stockton's Wing kept feet tapping until dawn! It was unanimously voted the best party of the festival. Looking somewhat the worse for wear, I arrived back to Pierre Joannon's house at 10 a.m. the next morning, dressed in a tuxedo.

Some weeks earlier, John Kelleher had asked me to arrange an *Eat the Peach* party for his guests at the swimming pool of Les Chênes Verts. By now, organising film parties was second nature to me. Pierre Joannon and his wife Annick were, as always, enthusiastic about the prospect and gave their full support. The day of the party was my fiftieth birthday. The weather was absolutely perfect. As usual, the Hotel du Cap provided the food, champagne and waiters for our party. The film's director, Peter Ormrod, was an enthusiastic pilot. With perfect timing he flew low over the gathering in his biplane emblazoned with the *Eat the Peach* logo on his way from Dublin. After landing at the local airport, he joined the party. The event was an outstanding success. As usual on these occasions, international journalists and other guests commented on the generosity and style of the Irish government, which provided such luxurious accommodation for its Honorary Consul General. It would have been churlish to let them know the truth or inform them of the modest compensation Pierre received from Ireland's Exchequer.

* * *

Apart from veteran Hollywood director Sam Fuller's remark when we first met—'Son of a bitch! It's Alec Guinness'—I had been told before that I looked like the star, although I could never see this myself. I met Sir Alec Guinness at the Cannes Film Festival in 1987. Greg Smith was in charge of the British film industry's promotional programme and two major events were scheduled. First, an unprecedented visit by the Prince and Princess of Wales. Second, a presentation to Sir Alec

Guinness in recognition of his lifelong contribution to British cinema. I asked Peter Ustinov to make the keynote speech and presentation. Peter agreed, although he disliked Cannes during the Festival because of the crowds and traffic jams. He also professed a family grievance with the town fathers of another generation because one of the small streets leading onto the main Croisette had originally been named Rue Ustinov in honour of his uncle, but had now been re-named Rue du Canada!

In the era before mobile phones, communication was a serious problem at the Festival. Limousines were invariably late or failed to arrive at all because of the constant traffic congestion. This happened to most of the cars that were to take Peter Ustinov, his wife Hélène and me to various functions. On the evening of the presentation to Sir Alec, we waited at our hotel for forty-five minutes. Greg, who was meant to collect us, failed to show. We finally decided to battle our way through the crowded streets to the Festival Palais. Seated behind us in the cinema was Robert Maxwell, to whom Peter introduced me. A tall, imposing figure with swept-back, jet-black hair, he was quite friendly. At the time Peter wrote a weekly column for *The European*, one of Maxwell's newspapers. He enjoyed doing this, but said that he neither liked nor trusted Robert Maxwell. He told of an experience he had had in the newspaper magnate's Fleet Street offices. After a meeting and early dinner one summer evening, Maxwell had invited him up to the roof, where his private helicopter was waiting. Before boarding the aircraft, Maxwell walked over to the edge of the flat roof and urinated over the parapet into the street below. He remarked to a disgusted Peter: 'The people down there will think it's raining!'

As the royal party entered the cinema to a fanfare of trumpets, we were surprised to see Greg Smith escorting Princess Diana at the head of the procession. Peter nudged me and with a twinkle in his eye remarked, 'There's our chauffeur.' At the last moment, Greg had been invited to meet the Prince and Princess of Wales aboard the royal yacht *Britannica*. He had been unable to contact us. After the Ustinovs returned to their Swiss home, Greg Smith sent a large floral bouquet. The accompanying card read: 'These flowers won't take you anywhere, but at least they arrived!'

The banquet that followed the screening was indeed a gala affair. Peter entertained the gathering with a humorous after-dinner speech. Sir Alec Guinness accepted his award and spoke briefly. Privately, he expressed dissatisfaction that the royal visit had coincided with his own big moment. He felt that the royal couple had upstaged him! He never bothered to thank those who had bestowed the honour upon him.

Later that night the Prince and Princess of Wales, accompanied by Greg Smith and the British Consul in Marseilles, left for Nice airport. A number of us, including our Irish Consul General, Pierre Joannon and the wife of the British Consul, a rather dowdy lady whose family name was Gladstone, repaired to one of the many bars along the Croisette to await the return of the royal escort. Mrs Gladstone was less than amused when the representative of the Irish government enquired how she felt about being named after a large leather holdall!

* * *

Valerie Heyward, a native of Co. Down who spent some years in Hollywood, now lives in Marbella. Sam Arkoff, whom I first encountered when negotiating the making of *The Last Great Train Robbery*, was the executive producer when Valerie's future husband, film producer Louis M. Heyward, was making *Murders in the Rue Morgue* with Herbert Lom and Lillie Palmer in Europe. Sam's generous wedding present was an expensive dinner service. It was some months after the wedding, when Sam had moved on to another production, that it came to light that his largesse was illusory. His wedding gift had been charged to the budget of *Murders in the Rue Morgue!*

At a small dinner party in the early 1990s, Valerie introduced me to the Romanian-born Hollywood director Jean Negulesco, then in his eighties. He lived in Marbella for the last twenty years of his life and died of heart failure in 1993, at the age of eighty-three. Meeting this iconic Hollywood figure was one of the most memorable experiences of my life. The first film of his I saw was *Johnny Belinda*, with Jane Wyman, in the newly opened Adelphi cinema in Dún Laoghaire in 1949. Afterwards I would see other examples of the work of this master director: *The Mudlark*, released in 1950, starring Irene Dunne and Alec Guinness, and *Phone Call from a Stranger*, with Bette Davis, Shelly

Winters and Keenan Wynn, which came to our screens in 1952. He also gave us the 1953 version of *Titanic*, starring Barbara Stanwyck along with Ireland's Brian Ahern and Audrey Dalton. Other Negulesco movies which have stood the test of time are *How to Marry a Millionaire* with Marilyn Monroe and *Three Coins in the Fountain*, a beautiful love story made in Rome and starring Dorothy McGuire (Tony O'Reilly's original screen goddess) and the stunningly handsome Rossano Brazzi.

As a young man, Jean Negulesco went to live in the south of France. There he was employed as a gigolo dancer in the world-famous Hotel Negresco in Nice, in 1923. His job, he told me, 'was to dance the tango with the daughters of rich Americans or on occasions their mothers.' When he returned to the French Riviera in 1960 as a successful Hollywood director to film *A Certain Smile* with Joan Fontaine and Rossano Brazzi, the Hollywood studio booked suites at the Negresco while the unit was filming in nearby Villefrance. Jean reminded the hotel's general manager that in 1923 he was engaged by the hotel as a gigolo dancer. He told how the manager had smiled that superior Gallic smile and with a twinkle in his eye replied, 'It is pleasant to see, Monsieur, that you have not changed. Twentieth-Century Fox is paying for your accommodation. Thirty-seven years later you are still a gigolo!'

Jean had a fund of stories of his early days in Hollywood. Many of them were about the legendary Sam Goldwyn, who changed his name from Sam Goldfish when he came to live in the movie capital. Sam was a genius at murdering the English language. A champion of using words improperly and incongruously, he gave to his well-known blunders a comic authority that became part of his fame. Referring to an actor with whom he had had a disagreement, Sam said: 'Never let that son of a bitch in my studio again—unless I need him.' Some of Sam's other malapropisms were 'include me out', 'Toujours Lautrec', 'tea and trumpets', 'I can only answer you in two words, Im possible', 'a verbal contract is not worth the paper it is written on' and 'this atomic bomb is dynamite'. Jean claimed that it was his wife who accompanied Sam Goldwyn on a walk in the garden of Jack Warner's house one Sunday before lunch when the classic Sam Goldwyn story was created. As they passed an old Roman sundial, Sam asked, 'What is this?' 'A sundial, Sam,' the lady replied. 'What is it for?' asked Sam. 'Well, as the sun moves across the sky, the shadow of the sundial moves around the numbers and tells the hour.' Sam thought for a moment, then shook his head and remarked, 'What will they think of next?'

Another Sam Goldwyn story is about Sam telephoning producer Sam Spiegel at 3 a.m. to discuss an actor. Irritated, Spiegel said, 'Look, Sam, can we talk about this in the morning? Do you know what time it is?' Goldwyn turned to his wife in bed and said, 'Frances, Sam Spiegel wants to know what time it is.'

*   *   *

In 1986 my legal action against the government was still unresolved. In the early part of that year I attended the Press Photographers' Association of Ireland Awards in Jury's Hotel. For the first five years of those awards I had been chairman of the panel of judges. John Boland, Minister for the Public Service, was also there. The first divorce referendum was imminent and the government was determined to win the support of the electorate and carry the constitutional amendment, despite the powerful opposition of the Catholic Church and the appalling attitude of Fianna Fáil, which claimed not to oppose the measure but in fact did so, vigorously. The Taoiseach was about to embark on a national tour of the electoral constituencies and it was felt that someone was needed to improve his style and image for that and for the campaign ahead. John Boland had been impressed by my handling of a difficult situation, involving himself, at the awards ceremony. He felt I was the person who should look after the Taoiseach on his extensive campaign trail; Bill O'Herlihy and Enda Marren supported the idea.

Thus the 'Gary and Joan Roadshow' got underway. My job was to visit the various constituencies, meet the relevant Fine Gael personnel, usually the local TD, set up the meetings and arrange hotel accommodation, interviews with local press and photo opportunities for the Taoiseach's visit. It was a splendid opportunity to work closely with Garret FitzGerald and his wife, Joan. On the day of the Taoiseach's visit to an area, I would travel ahead to the venue and marshall the local media to meet the Taoiseach on his arrival. When Garret started his speech I would move on to the next location and repeat the exercise.

There were some amusing incidents on the road, too. Each day's schedule provided time for Garret and Joan to rest in their hotel room after lunch. One afternoon I was relaxing in the hotel lounge when one of the Taoiseach's security men, who had been on duty near the bedroom, rushed in to tell me that the large bed in which Garret and Joan were sleeping had collapsed. The Taoiseach was annoyed and I was the only one who could help! I must admit that I found the sight of the collapsed bed very funny. The hotel manager immediately arranged alternative accommodation with more robust furnishings.

We navigated by constituency rather than by county. One of our trips took us from Mayo/East into Sligo/Leitrim. At the border we were met by Minister of State Ted Nealon, the Fine Gael TD for that constituency. One of Ted's supporters had arranged what he thought would be a great opportunity for a photograph. The previous evening he had caught a fine trout in the lake. The fish was kept alive in a bucket of water overnight. The idea was that Garret would don a pair of long, green waders and stride into the lake, where he would be handed the fishing-rod with the live trout hooked on the line. Knowing Garret's integrity, I knew this would not work. It didn't. Garret balked at the suggestion. It was just as well. When the fisherman went to retrieve his trout from the bucket, he found that the fish had died during its captivity!

In the end, the divorce referendum was defeated. The government was simply no match for the combined forces of the Catholic Church and Fianna Fáil.

It was all a far cry from champagne and the Croisette, but I relished this new opportunity and learned much from it. However, I was now more than ready for a more permanent challenge, and one found me very shortly thereafter.

Chapter 13 ❧

THE FINAL
CUT

In 1986 Ireland's official Film Censor, Frank Hall, was past retirement age. His successor was to be appointed by the government on the recommendation of the Minister for Justice. Noel Ryan, Deputy Head of Film in RTÉ, was interested in the post and asked me to mention this in the appropriate government circles. I spoke to Fine Gael trustee, Enda Marren and a few days later he confirmed that, as there were no other contenders, it was likely Noel would be appointed. He asked me Noel's age, but I didn't know for sure. Noel looked considerably younger than me, but I was unaware of his actual age. It transpired that Noel was over sixty at the time, which was considered too old for the post because the retirement age was sixty-five. Enda asked if I would be interested in the job. The thought had never crossed my mind, but I immediately said, 'Why not?'

I thought to myself that if I were appointed, I might try it for a few years. Enda suggested that I write a brief note to the Minister for Justice Alan Dukes, expressing an interest in the job. This I did. The government's last meeting before the summer break was held on 31 July 1986. That afternoon I was in the garden, engaged in the job I liked least—cutting the large area of what was still the fastest-growing grass in Ireland. Sheila called me to the telephone. It was the Taoiseach's office. Most of my normal dealings with the Taoiseach were through Fine Gael party headquarters, so my reaction to a direct call from his office was, 'Shit! What have I done now?' The Taoiseach came on the line: 'I just want to tell you, Sheamus, that in the last hour the government has approved your appointment as the new Film Censor.

Joan and I would like to wish you well in the job!' I was dumb-founded. I had not really considered myself a serious contender for the post and had forgotten about my application. Later, when we were in Cyprus together, the Taoiseach told me what actually happened at the Cabinet meeting. When he, as Chairman, came to the last item on the agenda, 'Appointment of new Film Censor', it was his intention to put my name forward. Before he could do so, Alan Dukes spoke up and said, 'I have someone in mind for that.' Garret was taken aback until the Minister continued, 'I would like to nominate Sheamus Smith for the job.'

The official announcement of my appointment was made on 23 September. Fran Quigley, the technician who organised the sound systems for the Taoiseach's constituency meetings, told me that while having his tea that day, he was paying little attention to the television until he heard the newsreader mention my name. When he saw my picture on the screen it was too late to hear the announcement, so he said to his wife, 'I know that man. He used to work with the Taoiseach. He must have died'!

* * *

The Film Censor's Office was established in 1923 by one of the first Acts of the Free State government. Since June 1945 it has been located in the grounds of Harcourt Terrace Garda Station. The first Film Censor, James Montgomery, was a former employee of the Dublin Gas Company and was selected after a public competition. All subsequent holders of the Office were appointed directly by the government. I was the eighth Film Censor. My predecessor, Frank Hall, often said that being the Irish Film Censor was like being the Pope or the Dali Lama—all three are jobs for which you cannot apply and for which there is no prior training.

Although he was past retirement age, Frank was none too pleased when my appointment was announced. He had hoped to continue as Film Censor indefinitely and blamed the Fine Gael/Labour coalition government for his demise. This was nonsense. Frank's paranoia could be attributed to his membership of the Fianna Fáil party and his belief that his party was the only one entitled to govern. In his television show, 'Hall's Pictorial Weekly', Frank had repeatedly lampooned an earlier government led by Liam Cosgrave. He invented characters such as 'The Minister for Hardship' and dubbed Finance Minister Richie Ryan, 'Richie Ruin'. While he grudgingly handed over the reins, Frank was nonetheless more tolerant of me as a replacement than he might have been of someone he did not know.

After the announcement of the appointment, I invited him to lunch. Frank was like Sean Connery: he was fond of his food and liked it even better when someone else was footing the bill. As with all meetings in Frank's spellbinding company, our lunch concluded only when the dinner guests arrived at the restaurant. Frank gave me plenty of advice, for which I was grateful. In the past I had been his guest at screenings in the Film Censor's Office. He now invited me along, as 'Censor-Designate', to view *Stand by Me*. A nostalgic tale of a 1950s' childhood, it was about a gang of boys who find the body of a missing teenager. It starred River Phoenix and Kiefer Sutherland and was not the sort of film I would go to see in a cinema. When I expressed surprise at the level of bad language used by the young boys and girls in the film, Frank's response was instant: 'Let me give you some advice, young man. Never mind the fucking language. If you cut that out, the films will only last twenty minutes!' Exaggeration, but I got his point.

Frank was far more concerned about sex and religion than I was. He had banned movies such as *Monty Python's The Life of Brian* and *Last Tango in Paris*. A short time before I took over he had cut a scene in *9½ Weeks*, the story of a passionate love affair between a Wall Street executive and an art gallery employee, played by Mickey Rourke and Kim Basinger. Frank also disapproved of fast car chases in which brand new expensive cars were ultimately destroyed or burnt out. Frank, who drove an aging yellow Volkswagen, found this distasteful to the frugality of his Northern Irish background.

During the first six months of my stewardship, Frank Hall, as was the tradition, remained on full salary as my advisor. He was helpful and generous with his time on the few occasions I sought his advice. Frank warned me about the press. As a journalist himself, I found his attitude to his former colleagues bizarre: he eschewed all contact and never trusted the media. He maintained that decisions made by the Film Censor were a private matter between the censor and the film's distributor and were not for public scrutiny or discussion. He was dismissive of efforts made by his predecessor, Dermot Breen, and by film journalist Ciaran Carty, a constant critic of the office, to enlighten the public on the operation of the Film Censor's Office by holding public debates around the country. Frank claimed that these spontaneous debates were 'scripted and pre-arranged'. His attitude to the public was also ambivalent. He told of ending a telephone conversation with an argumentative lady, whose call he deigned to accept, with the memorable words, 'And you, Madam, can fuck off!'

* * *

I was the first Film Censor for many years to look upon the job as a full-time occupation. My immediate predecessors all pursued other interests. Frank Hall had a regular commitment to RTÉ, Dermot Breen had successfully managed his own PR company while his forerunner, Liam O'Hora, the man I met when a child in Ballaghaderreen, was Manager of Dublin's Gaiety Theatre while also holding the office.

From the outset, I was determined to take a more liberal approach towards sex than my predecessors. My abiding philosophy was to make more films available to a wider audience, particularly young people under adult supervision. At my only meeting with Alan Dukes, Minister for Justice, he said, 'I don't believe in censorship. That's why I appointed you.' At that meeting I agreed with the Minister that in my new circumstances it would be invidious to continue my legal proceedings against the government in relation to the closure of National Film Studios of Ireland. I suppose I had been 'paid off', to some extent, despite the fact that my stipend did not equate in any way with a proper salary. That, of course, explained why my immediate predecessors had treated the job as a part-time one.

My first impression on taking over as Film Censor was that the office accommodation and facilities had been neglected. Frank Hall's involvement with administration was minimal. This was handled by the office secretary, Rita Culkeen, a civil servant provided by the Department of Justice. Rita, who was born in Ballyhaunis, just 12 miles from my hometown of Ballaghaderreen, was a paragon of efficiency. She handled all accounts, records and bookings and inscribed the film titles on the censor certificates in white ink. She also looked after the staff film projectionists, Kevin McCann and Des Dunne. Working conditions in the office were primitive. Frank Hall had a desk that he rarely used in the large room set aside for meetings of the Films Appeal Board. The telephone system was of 1940s vintage and consisted of two instruments; the one on the film censor's desk was activated by turning a handle to communicate with Rita in her office. Meanwhile, Rita's antiquated typewriter was manual. It was with a sense of *déjà vu* that I resolved to rectify these matters, having encountered a similar situation in Ardmore Studios eleven years earlier. Rita was sceptical, and well she might have been: for years the Film Censor's office had been neglected by the Department of Justice. This was slow to change. It took six months to inveigle the civil servants to provide us with an electric typewriter. When they eventually did, it was one that had seen previous long service in another office. The telephone system and office refurbishment took longer, but we did achieve it. The small cinema that forms the centrepiece of the operation also required revamping; the projectors and sound system were over forty years old and badly in need of an upgrade.

We were a happy little family in the Film Censor's office. The tea Rita brought into the cinema shortly after the film started was accompanied by biscuits supplied by the distributor. Each distributor had his favourite biscuits. Although they were never in the cinema at the same time, every distributor sat in a different seat. If other guests attended a screening, the identity of the distributor would determine which seat was to be reserved. The film censor sits behind a desk on a slightly elevated podium, with the distributors and other guests seated below; it is rather like a courtroom. Traditionally, at the discretion of the film censor, special guests may occupy one of the two seats on either side of his desk, in the same way that a judge sometimes invites a visiting judge to sit beside him on the bench. In bygone days distributors always addressed the film censor as 'Mr Censor'.

Hearing my introduction by some friends, who should know better, as 'The Film Censor, the man who looks at blue movies all day' was always irritating. Pornographic movies were never submitted to the office. In the first place, there was no cinema outlet for such product.

Secondly, no distributor would pay censorship fees for a picture that was certain to be rejected. Before my time, some distributors were reluctant to submit any film that had high sex content.

I found that meeting the film distributors and learning about their side of the business was a fascinating new experience. The distributor always attended the classification screening. Sometimes he would argue the case for a more generous certificate; a General certificate was seen as more profitable than a restricted one. The distributors, an all-male group, represented the major Hollywood studios, such as Paramount, MGM, Twentieth-Century Fox, Columbia Pictures, Warner Brothers and Disney. Most had entered the business straight from school and worked their way to the top. All had outgoing personalities, as befitted their profession as salesmen. The elders—such as Addie Ryan, who represented Rank and small independent distributors, Gerry Crofton of Columbia Pictures, Arthur McGuinness, an independent distributor, and Harry Band of United International Pictures, an Englishman who lived for many years in Dublin—were the most respectful of the Office and formal in their dealings with me. Mr Crofton always addressed me in the traditional manner as 'Mr Censor'. Once, when unhappy with my classification, he turned to my elevated position behind him with the words, 'Mr Censor, may I discuss your decision?' I was already late for a lunch arranged by another distributor, Brendan McCaul, with a visiting movie star and replied, 'You may Mr Crofton, with the Films Appeal Board!' A regular guy, Gerry smiled and accepted the verdict.

*   *   *

My first act was to immediately reduce the practice of cutting films. In the past, this had sometimes been done in collusion with the film's distributor to allow a more generous certificate and thereby increase audience potential. Looking back on previous records, I came across the film *Ashanti*. I had visited the location in Sicily as a guest of Peter Ustinov, who starred in it with Omar Sharif, Michael Caine and William Holden. In order to obtain a General certificate, the distributor, Harry Band, a veteran of the business, had accepted the thirty-eight cuts Frank Hall made in the film. My attitude has always been that a film is the work of a director and only the director should have the authority to alter that work. This rather high-minded ideal is not always followed by Hollywood studios, which frequently insist on having control over a movie's 'final cut'.

Since its establishment, the Film Censor's Office has been an independent entity under the aegis of the Department of Justice. The Film Censor is independent of the Minister in the exercise of his functions and the Minister does not have any power to alter his decisions. The Film Censor has the power to change the classification categories for cinema films. Video classifications are incorporated in legislation. From the outset, I regarded my task as one of classification rather than censorship. To reflect this, I tried, unsuccessfully, to have the name of the office changed from 'Film Censor's Office' to 'Office of Film and Video Classification'. The difficulty was that the original name is incorporated in legislation and therefore requires an act of the Oireachtas to change it. I altered the former restricted classifications and introduced new Over 12 and Parental Guidance certificates. The new certificates thus became: General, Parental Guidance, Over 12, Over 15 and Over 18. Two categories were later changed to 12PG and 15PG, allowing parents to accompany their children of any age to films they considered fit for viewing. These classifications are now 12A and 15A. This new system, by which parents, rather than the Film Censor, decide what their children can watch, was welcomed by parents, distributors and cinema-owners alike.

I often had cause to refer to the enlightened wording of the Censorship of Films Act 1923. Credit must go to the unknown civil servant who drafted this document. The only guideline given to the censor is that:

> … unless he is of opinion that such picture or part thereof is unfit for general exhibition in public by reason of its being indecent, obscene or blasphemous or because the exhibition thereof in public would tend to inculcate principles contrary to public morality or would be otherwise subversive to public morality.

This rather vague guideline stood the test of time and allowed successive censors to interpret the act in a progressively more liberal manner, if they so chose. After all, what was 'subversive to public morality' in 1923 was very different from what is considered subversive in the twenty-first century. It was fortunate that my tenure coincided with a time when Irish society was undergoing dramatic cultural and moral change, which made the liberalisation of film censorship not only acceptable but necessary.

*   *   *

My predecessors in office had never attended international conferences or had any communication with other film classifiers. They existed in isolation. Frank Hall had once been visited by the South African Film Censor when that country was seeking international support for its Apartheid regime, but that was the extent of international association heretofore. Shortly after my appointment, I attended a conference of world film classifiers in London organised by the British Board of Film Classification, whose director, James Ferman, had assumed the role of international convenor. James had the appearance and manner of a typical English public servant, but had in fact been born and educated in California. With the help of his personal assistant, Xandra Barry, James organised a splendid conference. It was there I met many colleagues of various backgrounds and nationalities who would become good friends over my term of office and beyond. My international colleagues were surprised that the Irish Film Censor worked alone. In other countries classification was carried out by groups of between two and ten people. Along with the Australian censor John Dickie, I was the only person at the conference with the title of Film Censor. This encouraged me all the more in my efforts to change the description of my office, just as James Ferman had done shortly before. He was now known as the Director of the British Board of Film Classification. Two years after our first meeting, the Australian government passed legislation changing John Dickie's title to Director of the Australian Board of Film and Video Classification. Sadly, my ambition to become 'The Last Film Censor' was not achieved.

Exchanging ideas and discussing recent classification decisions with international colleagues established that there was little difference between us. Surprisingly, Swedish classifiers were in some ways more conservative than the Irish censor. Most liberal of all were the French. I quickly became active among the group of European Film Classifiers and also attended conferences in Australia and the USA. One of the most significant was Show West, a general gathering of the disparate elements that make up the worldwide cinema trade. It is held each year in Las Vegas and is attended by over 3,000 delegates.

I met Vivian van Dijk, a young Dutch postgraduate student, at a European Film Classifiers' Conference in Berlin. She was conducting a research project on European film classification. We kept in touch. Some time later her parents, who are about my own age, invited me to their home. They owned a spa and health club nearby. After lunch, Vivian suggested we go for a swim and sauna; her parents would join us later.

The largest complex of its type in The Netherlands, the Elysium Centre for Well-being incorporated sixteen different types of sauna, an artificially constructed sandy beach, steam rooms, an indoor rain forest, huge indoor swimming pool, scented communal baths, various cafés, a luxury restaurant and extensive beauty salon offering all sorts of treatments and massages. We went inside and Vivian showed me to a luxurious dressing-room area while she went to attend to some family business. In this softly lit area individual lockers and fresh white towelling robes were available. I was still admiring the surroundings when two very beautiful blonde ladies walked in. They immediately started to undress. Gobsmacked, I must have looked embarrassed. As they continued to disrobe, my new companions explained that this was the communal dressing, or in this case undressing, room. As I rather sheepishly started to remove my clothes, a small group of people, all naked, came in from what I assumed to be the swimming-pool area. I finally got the message. *Everyone* was nude here. I was suitably stripped when Vivian returned. She undressed quickly. We had a swim before Vivian took me on a tour of the complex. Surrounded by naked bodies of all shapes, ages and sizes reminded me of Sunny Trails, the nudist colony in British Columbia so many years earlier, and also of the time when, while visiting Garret FitzGerald and Denis Corboy, we happened upon a beach near St Tropez peopled by similar folk *au naturel*.

When Vivian's parents joined us, we went to the bar. There we met a friend of theirs, an interesting but rather shapeless Dutchman. People become more difficult to describe without their clothes. This man was the Dutch publisher of Edna O'Brien and Peter Ustinov and knew both well. Peter was amused when he heard my story. Naked as the day we were born, we all sat around the table, nonchalantly drinking wine. A photograph of that scene would have been a scoop for an Irish tabloid newspaper!

In 1997 I reciprocated by inviting Vivian to a U2 concert in Rotterdam. The band's manager, Paul McGuinness, looked after us magnificently, inviting us to the VIP hospitality room before and after the concert. Unusually, there were only a few other guests there. Vivian could scarcely believe that we were talking to Bono, Larry Mullen, Adam Clayton and The Edge, all of whom treated me like a close friend. Eight years later I repeated that experience at U2's concert in Amsterdam with my daughter, Teri, who is a long-time U2 fan, and her partner, television director Peter O'Doherty. The show was spectacular. Apart from the music and lyrics, I am always astonished by the sheer force of energy that is Bono. Then in my late sixties, I was not the oldest swinger in the admiring U2 audience that hot August evening. Afterwards we were among the handful of privileged guests at a late-night supper with the band. It was intriguing to spend time with these world-famous Dubliners as they chilled out after their exhausting performance.

* * *

In 1994 Greg Smith produced a television film of *The Old Curiosity Shop* in Ireland for the Disney Channel. Heading the cast—which included Tom Courtenay as Quilp and our own Brian McGrath as the village schoolmaster—was Peter Ustinov, who played the uncle. Magnificent interior and exterior sets were built at Ardmore Studio. Shooting commenced on 7 June 1994 and continued until the end of

July. For me, it was like old times to be back in the busy studio for which I had made such efforts in the past, surrounded by friends. We filmed on location at Bunratty Folk Park, Dublin Castle and Kilmainham Gaol. I played the part of the doctor, a new experience and one I enjoyed. The director, Kevin Connor, wanted someone with 'a kind face', so Greg cast me! One of my short scenes was with the English actor, James Fox. A later scene included Peter Ustinov. Gloria Hunniford had a more substantial part as a street trader. *The Old Curiosity Shop* was made during the boom in the Irish film industry created by government support and the enlightened policy of Arts Minister Michael D. Higgins, who will be remembered as the father of the modern Irish film industry. *The Old Curiosity Shop* was a huge success. As a consequence, Greg produced *Kidnapped*, *David Copperfield* and *Animal Farm*, in which I also made cameo appearances.

The original star of *Kidnapped* was Christopher Reeve, famous for his large-screen portrayal of Superman. We met when Chris came here for costume fittings. A mutual friend, Sue Geggie, had taught his children when they lived in London. When we dined in Ernie's restaurant in Donnybrook, Chris was very impressed by the manager, Robert Cahill, and his encyclopaedic knowledge of movies. As well as chatting about US and world politics, movies and religion, Chris also spoke of his love of riding and horse-jumping, something he looked forward to doing during his stay in Ireland. When it was suggested that he might give this up until *Kidnapped* was completed, he scorned the idea. The next morning Chris called me to say how much he had enjoyed our evening, adding, 'I never thought I would find myself in a restaurant in Ireland with someone described as a censor while we both criticised the Pope!'

A few days later I took Chris to the premiere of *Rob Roy*. At the pre-show reception it was a pleasure to introduce Chris, a dedicated environmentalist, to Dublin's Lord Mayor, the young Green Party politician John Gormley. Chris was touched when, as we entered the cinema, the crowds outside shouted, '*Superman!*' Eleven days later, while participating in a jumping competition, Christopher Reeve was thrown from his horse, sustaining a near-fatal injury that rendered him paralysed from the neck down. His wife Dana, whom he adored, looked after Chris until his death seven years later at the age of fifty-two. As in so many great love stories, Dana herself died shortly afterwards.

*   *   *

The Film Censor's Office is self-financing. Fees charged to distributors for film classification were set arbitrarily by the Department of Justice, based on a film's length. The only exception to payment of a fee is if the censor deems a film to be of 'Educational' value. In that instance, the fee is waived. It was a tactic I resorted to much more frequently than my predecessors. They had used an Educational certificate only in terms of a General classification. For example, the distributor of Kenneth Brannagh's splendid *Hamlet*, which ran for over four hours, could not in 1996 justify paying censorship fees in excess of £3,000 for a film with a limited release. As a General certificate was inappropriate, *Hamlet* was classified in the higher PG category and still given an Educational certificate, thereby waiving the censorship fees. Other films would later benefit under this system.

I felt that the fee system as structured was outmoded. It discriminated against films that had a minority interest, or those in a foreign language. It did not make sense that a film that might have one or two prints in distribution should be charged the same censorship fees as a major American blockbuster. It also had an adverse influence on indigenous films. A young Irish film-maker could not afford to pay the same censorship fees as a Hollywood studio that distributed more than 120 prints, as did the *Harry Potter* films or *The Lord of the Rings*. It was a battle I fought unsuccessfully over fourteen years. Although promises were made and the active support of the Irish Film Board enlisted, successive ministers simply did not deliver on this. It did not require new legislation—a ministerial order was all that was needed. At a meeting in my office one senior civil servant promised to 'resolve the matter within thirty days'. Seven years later, nothing had been accomplished! Eleven months before my retirement Minister Michael McDowell promised to rectify the dilemma with the words, 'I will give you this as a going-away present'. He did not. Like that Minister's electoral promises that were delivered at all, it came late. My successor,

John Kelleher, was over a year in Office when the Minister announced that he was bringing into effect the initiative I had advocated more than fifteen years earlier.

*　　*　　*

When introducing me to the finer points of film censorship, as he saw it, Frank Hall had said, 'If you don't get the hang of this thing in three weeks, you never will.' He added, 'And if you are in any real difficulty about a decision, ask Mr Ryan.' Addie Ryan, the doyen of the business, was a quiet gentleman who represented Abbey Films, the Ward Anderson distribution company. He was the first distributor to whom Frank introduced me. Always respectfully known as 'Mr Ryan', Addie had spent a lifetime in the film distribution business. A formidable tennis player as a young man, Addie was over eighty years of age when he finally retired.

Another piece of Frank's advice was, 'Remember, it's your sole decision. Sometimes the certificate given depends on the state of the film censor's piles when he's watching a film!' A rather crude metaphor and not exactly scientific, but later I got the message when a film named *Bliss* was submitted for classification. An Australian black comedy, it included a scene in which a lady has sex on a restaurant table with her husband's best friend while the husband is undergoing heart by-pass surgery. The same day that I saw it, Bill O'Herlihy was having a similar operation in a Dublin hospital, where he was going under the knife of my old associate, heart surgeon Maurice Neligan. I found the film's treatment of a serious subject offensive, not to mention the misuse of the beautifully laid table in a fine restaurant. Removing that scene was the first time I cut a movie.

*　　*　　*

Except for a passing greeting, I did not get to know Michael York during the filming of *The Last Remake of Beau Geste* at Ardmore Studios. He had kept a low profile throughout and worked hard. Always perfectly groomed and courteous, Michael was accompanied by his wife, Pat, a professional photographer with a prestigious international reputation. Exhibitions of her work have been held in many world capitals. Michael is also an accomplished writer and lecturer. Their lack of enthusiasm for the excesses associated with a major Hollywood movie gave the impression that they were stand-offish. Some years later, when we met again, I realised that nothing could be further from the truth. Michael and Pat York are outstanding people and now staunch friends.

In 1994 Michael played the leading role in a television film, *September*, shot in Dublin. His co-stars were Jacqueline Bisset and Mariel Hemingway. It was through the American Ambassador, Jean Kennedy Smith, that I met the Yorks again. The filming schedule was somewhat erratic, leaving Michael with a good deal of free time. To the delight of the ladies in my office, he filled much of this by attending the daily screenings. Since then we have spent interesting times together in Dublin, Galway, London, Los Angeles and Washington. One of Pat's books, *Going Strong*, is a series of interviews and outstanding photographs of people aged seventy-five years or over who are still working full-time. It includes people of many nationalities. The variety of subjects count among them actors, writers, doctors, gardeners, producers and even President Ronald Reagan. Michael and Pat's own doctor, Michael McCready, then in his late seventies and living in Dublin, is also featured. A widely travelled exhibition of Pat's photographs shows men and women around the world engaged in their work. All are nude. A brilliant idea! A pity I was not invited to pose for that: a naked film censor might have been an amusing addition!

*   *   *

Over the course of my seventeen years as film censor I witnessed a dramatic change in the gender balance of distributors. The first female distributor to attend a screening with me was Jane Doolin, representing Clarence Pictures, a new Irish distribution agency that she ran with her partner, Niamh McCaul. For me, seeing a movie in female company beats watching it with a man any time. Jane was soon followed by a coterie of attractive, high-powered ladies who replaced their male predecessors. Sharon McGarry took over Twentieth-Century Fox, Barbara Murphy became boss of Columbia TriStar, Niamh McCaul later formed another distribution agency, Eclipse Pictures, and Catherine Hughes, a lady as charming as she was attractive, represented Polygram Filmed Entertainment. I can now admit that these ladies were usually more successful than their male counterparts in influencing my decisions in their favour. Business lunches with female distributors were also more fun than those with their male counterparts. One had a predilection for champagne; spending time in her delightful company was never a hardship.

*   *   *

The Censorship of Films Act states:

> Whenever the Official Censor is temporarily unable to attend to his duties, or his office is vacant, the Minister may appoint a fit person to perform the duties of the Official Censor under this Act.

For my first seven years in Office the 'fit person' who acted as deputy was a Kerryman, Jerome Hegarty. Jerome was a wonderful man with a background in the cinema business and a great sense of humour. He had a business card printed on which he was described as 'a fit person'! We were all saddened when he died in 1993 after a long illness.

*   *   *

Another aspect of the Film Censor's Office is the Appeal Board. It consists of nine people appointed by the Minister for a five-year term. The Board traditionally included a representative of the Catholic Church (usually nominated by the Archbishop of Dublin) and a Church of Ireland clergyman. In the period between 1964 and 1972, when Dr Christopher Macken, an extreme conservative, was Film Censor, the Board met frequently. Dr Macken rejected forty-two films in 1965, his first year in office.

In 1971 ninety films were viewed by the Appeal Board. The task of meeting several times a week encouraged the board's chairman, Judge

Conor Maguire, to arrange dinner in a restaurant for the unpaid members after each screening. Under the chairmanship of Judge Maguire, an enlightened, cinema-loving liberal who served two terms, the Board was responsible for allowing most films onto Irish screens. Other liberal members during this period included trade unionist John F. Carroll, who later became Chairman, and a young architect, the late Sam Stephenson, who replaced the Jesuit priest, Fr J.C. Kelly S.J. There were still two clergymen left, however, as the original board appointed by Charlie Haughey had two Catholic priests. Another member was Dermot Breen, Director of the Cork Film Festival. Dermot's enlightened attitude would begin to change film censorship in Ireland forever when he later took the Censor's chair.

John F. Carroll was Chairman of successive Appeal Boards from 1975 to 1997. This covered all of Frank Hall's term of office and the first ten years of mine. Frank had little respect for the Board and a definite dislike of its Chairman. When the tenure of the Board expired in March 1985, Frank was very pleased that the Minister for Justice failed to appoint a new one. This explains why, unusually, there is no record of any Appeal Board meeting during the last eighteen months of Frank Hall's term of office. The situation continued for my first seven months as Film Censor. In May 1987 a new board was appointed, again under the chairmanship of John F. Carroll. I knew John from my broadcasting days and we had always had a good relationship. A shrewd and tough trade unionist, he had a dry sense of humour, dressed smartly and was an accomplished clarinet player. His liberal attitude and personal commitment over many years had a positive effect on film censorship in Ireland.

My first encounter with the Appeal Board came eight months after my appointment. The decision to ban the British film *Personal Services*, starring Julie Walters, was appealed by the distributor. It was the story of Cynthia Payne, a former prostitute and London brothel-keeper known as 'Madam Cyn', whose clients included members of the clergy, parliament, the Bar and big business. She had been sentenced to eighteen months in Holloway Prison for 'keeping a disorderly house'. I found the scene in the film where she gives her son a present of a prostitute for his sixteenth birthday distasteful and the entire attitude to women reprehensible. It was the first questionable film I had come across and was a suitable vehicle with which to find out the Board's attitude to such films. My decision was overruled. By a majority decision, the film was granted an Over 18 classification.

The banning of *Personal Services* caused quite a stir in the media. During an interview on RTÉ Radio, Cynthia Payne invited me to one of her parties in London. The Chief Justice, the late Liam Hamilton, remarked to me in a pub, 'Nobody ever knows who the film censor is until he bans something.' *Personal Services* gave me an interesting insight into the Appeal Board's attitude. It was the only time during my seventeen years in office that the Board reversed my decision to ban a film. I did not cause the Board to meet again for over two years. On that occasion it was to hear an appeal for a change in a film's classification. Unlike the former Film Censor, Dr Christy Macken, who had instigated Board meetings ninety times in one year, the average number per year in my case was two.

I am frequently given the credit for removing the ban on *Monty Python's Life of Brian* in 1987. The film had been banned by Frank Hall in 1980 and his decision upheld by the Appeal Board. It was re-considered under the rule that allows a banned film to be re-submitted after seven years. In my absence it was the Deputy Film Censor, Jerome Hegarty, who classified the *Life of Brian* as Over 18. It had always been one of my favourite movies; in my opinion, an even lower classification could have been justified.

My only confrontation with the Catholic Church and other pressure groups came about over the classification of *The Last Temptation of Christ*. This Martin Scorsese film had stirred up controversy about blasphemy internationally before it reached Ireland. Vigorous campaigns against the film were mounted in America and Britain; Ireland would follow suit. Each day's mail brought a significant number of letters exhorting the prohibition of the film. This was a hitherto unknown experience. It was unusual for the Film Censor to receive any more than a handful of comments by letter or telephone over a full year. Now, letters containing prayer pamphlets, rosaries, holy medals and various publications on the lives of the saints poured through our letterbox. Rita Culkeen was swamped with the additional work and the filing cabinets became overloaded. Groups of people sang hymns outside the office gates and RTÉ camera crews frequently tried to doorstep me for a comment. Frank Hall, who used the office car park, was once accosted by an angry group of hymn singers. Throwing his hands in the air he shouted, 'I'm not the film censor anymore'. It was, I would say, the first time he was relieved not to have the job!

The great surprise to me was the people who joined the protest. At a social engagement I questioned former Fine Gael minister, Sean Barrett, on the wisdom of attaching his signature to a protest against a film he had not seen and could know little about. I was not prepared for the vicious verbal assault that followed. For that politician, there was no dichotomy. On another occasion, I received a phone call from a local councillor, a young lady of the Protestant persuasion, whom I greatly admired. She asked me to help a special friend of hers. Assuming that she was seeking employment or some favour for a constituent, I enquired as to her friend's name. 'Jesus,' she replied. She went on to say, 'You know, Sheamus, if you allow that film to be seen here, terrible things will happen to Ireland'!

In the middle of the furore, I was returning from London on an early morning flight when the Aer Lingus hostess, whom I knew, brought me copy of the *Irish Independent* and said, 'You'd better see this.' Emblazoned across the top of the page was the headline 'ARCHBISHOP WARNS CENSOR'. I was scarcely aware of the newly appointed Catholic Archbishop's name and certainly not impressed by Dr Desmond Connell's denunciation of a film neither he nor I had seen. It was the first time his Church had been confronted with an Irish film censor who was not of its denominaton.

The Last Temptation of Christ was passed uncut and classified Over 18. Under what Frank Hall often referred to as 'The Magical Powers of the Film Censor', cinemas showing the film were obliged to display a notice in the foyer pointing out that the film was based on the book *The Last Temptation* by Nikos Kazantzakis, and not on the Gospels. To prevent the later sex sequences being taken out of context, cinemagoers were not admitted after the film started. Personally, I felt the film was too long and could have been greatly improved by cutting some of the non-controversial scenes. But that is not the Film Censor's job. When asked his opinion after seeing *The Last Temptation of Christ* my deputy, Jerome Hegarty, remarked, 'Jaysus, I thought they'd never get him up on that bloody cross.'

Frank Hall frequently sent me comments from the provincial papers, which he perused in search of material for his RTÉ programme. Before classifying *The Last Temptation of Christ*, I received the following:

Dear Sheamus,

Nobody ever said it would be easy, but this is ridiculous. I'm sure that you have had opinions thrust upon you, and counter opinions, so I'll say no more than this: whatever you decide to do will be wrong, but in a year's time it will make no difference. Just keep your head down and don't allow yourself to get sucked into a controversy. The Archbishop should have consulted the Holy Spirit before opening his mouth. He may have rallied the faithful but they didn't need rallying; he may well have alienated considerable numbers of the uncommitted. Anyway, there will be many who won't give a damn; there are more urgent matters to worry about.

He later sent a newspaper report on the meeting of Longford Urban District Council. The councillors had unanimously called for the banning of *The Last Temptation of Christ* and the removal from Office of the Film Censor. None had seen the film! Frank commented:

The enclosed may give you a laugh. Isn't it encouraging to think that in spite of television, British newspapers, the European Community and so many other corrupting influences the country is still full of good, old-fashioned gobshites.

* * *

My relationships with Irish film distributors were always cordial. The older members of the group, Addie Ryan, Harry Band, Gerry Crofton and Arthur McGuinness, were truly old-fashioned gentlemen who, I know, disliked the trend in modern movies. They remembered when the great movie-makers entertained their audiences without resorting to explicit sex, foul language or obscene violence. To a great extent I was on their side, but of course had to cope with the reality of what was presented on the screen. In 1997 I delivered a paper at an international conference in Australia, run by my old friend John Dickie. I referred to the decay of language and the corruption of meaning that has been in progress ever since tongues started wagging. I went on:

> The vernacular has become the film words of dialogue. Key words in our culture have lost their significance and their awe. The very name of the founder of the Christian faith, once protected by the peril of blasphemy, is now used so frequently and without effect, that it has lost any role of significance and runs concurrently in English with words associated with obstetrics!

My closest friend among the distributors was a man of exceptional qualities. A northside Dubliner, Brendan McCaul had spent his whole life in film distribution, rising to the unprecedented level of Vice President of Buena Vista International, the distribution wing of Disney Studios. Our first encounter was with the film *Blue Velvet*, written and directed by David Lynch. A bizarre erotic mystery that contained scenes of obsessive kinky sex and deranged violence, it was both repulsive and fascinating. The beautiful female lead was played by Isabella Rossellini. I decided to screen the film a second time before making a decision. To Brendan McCaul, this was an ominous sign. He need not have worried. Isabella Rossellini is the daughter of my first screen love, Ingrid Bergman, so I could not be hard on her. I also met David Lynch when he was still a struggling young director in Hollywood. He invited me to lunch in the hopes of getting some financial support from Ireland. It was Friday, the one day of the week, he said, on which he fasted. I suspected this was to cover up the fact that his meagre resources did not run to the cost of two lunches. *Blue Velvet* was passed uncut. Frank Hall was right: the Film Censor is sometimes influenced by strange things! Film classification is not rocket science, just plain common sense.

When I banned Quentin Tarantino's gory, violent film *From Dusk til Dawn* in 1996, I assumed that Brendan McCaul would, like his colleagues, lodge an appeal. He did not. It was sometime later that Brendan told me that in his long career he had never met any member of the Appeal Board. In his words, he said he, 'Preferred to deal with professionals'—a compliment to me and my two predecessors, with whom he had worked.

Brendan was a showman of the old cinema tradition and entertained more movie stars when promoting films than his colleagues. In his company I met and dined with a plethora of notables, including Paul Hogan of *Crocodile Dundee* fame, Danny De Vito, an actor/director whom I admire, and Dame Judi Dench, who told me of her Irish parents and cousins in Sligo and Waterford. Brendan twice invited me to dinner with Anthony Minghella, whose splendid film *The English Patient* won nine Academy Awards in 1996, including Best Director. Anthony's parents once owned an ice-cream parlour in Dublin. We also had dinner with the lovely Andie McDowell. One of my all-time favourite lunches, however, was after my retirement as censor and before the release of *Tara Road*, when I was joined by Brendan, Maeve Binchy and her husband, Gordon Snell, on the open-air terrace of L'Ecrivain. We drank champagne and laughed until we cried.

The fee charged to the distributors for appealing the Film Censor's decision was a derisory £5, later converted to €6.35. This had been set in 1925 and despite my best efforts, the civil servants refused to have it changed. The cost of assembling the Appeal Board for a meeting could be in excess of €1,200. One distributor who spent a lot of time with the Appeal Board was Gerry Mulcahy who ran Columbia TriStar for some years. His appeals were usually instigated by his superiors in London, who were aware of his inexperience and frequently overruled his original acceptance of my decisions. Other distributors sometimes joked that because of Gerry's constant involvement, he would be invited to the Appeal Board's Christmas party. I understood Gerry's predicament and we remained good friends.

*   *   *

The Film Censor's Office changed with the passing of legislation to classify videos and DVDs. Additional civil servants were assigned by the

Department of Justice and our building in Harcourt Terrace was expanded to accommodate the increase in employee numbers. The new building was opened officially by the Minister for Justice, Máire Geoghegan-Quinn, on 12 May 1994. Apart from the official guests, I invited Frank Hall, Veda Breen and Kay O'Hora, the widows of two former Censors. I asked Frank what he thought of the improvements made to our accommodation since he left and he replied, 'I see plenty of changes, but I'm not sure about improvements'! The first new civil servant to join us was Ann Murray, an experienced officer who took overall charge of office administration and became my second-in-command. More civil servants followed. Two younger officials who made a valuable contribution to our changing systems were Yvonne Nolan and Elaine Roche. Later Thérèse Hogan was transferred from the department's Secretary General to job-share as secretary with Rita Culkeen. Together they were a formidable combination.

The Minister appointed seven Assistant Film Censors, whose task was to classify videos. Video shops and other outlets were now licensed by the Film Censor's Office. One of the new assistants was a full-time employee; the others worked part-time. All were political appointments and reflected the composition of the Fianna Fáil/Labour coalition government. As in any such arrangement, some showed a greater aptitude than others for the work involved. Outstanding among them was Ger Connolly, a friend of Charlie McCreevy. Peter Kelly, election agent for Albert Reynolds, was another who displayed uncanny skill in appraising a film on the cinema screen. Ger would become the first permanent Deputy Film Censor in the history of the State. Peter Kelly was elected to the Dáil seat vacated by Albert Reynolds in 2002.

With the introduction of video classification, the structure of the Film Censor's Office changed radically. My workload and responsibility increased enormously, although it would take some considerable time before this was reflected in a salary increase. It was on the recommendation of Tim Dalton, an outstanding Secretary General of the Department of Justice, that Ruairi Quinn, as Minister for Finance, agreed to review my salary. He immediately authorised 'a down-payment' in my favour. After the subsequent change in government, Charlie McCreevy became Minister for Finance. It was he who not only rectified the matter and instigated a proper salary structure for the job but also generously back-dated the arrangement to the time of my original discussions with his predecessor. His action allowed me to achieve a six-figure income before retirement.

*   *   *

The introduction of video classification substantially increased turnover in the Film Censor's Office. As a result, some in the Department of Justice were encouraging a form of 'privatisation'. Interminable meetings were held and a study proving the viability of such action was undertaken by a private firm of business consultants. If the Film Censor's Office proved to be a successful independent business within the Department of Justice, other money-making offices associated with the Department would follow suit. The exercise allowed some civil servants, and sometimes even members of my own staff, to engage in their favourite pastimes of blathering away at interminable, non-productive meetings while avoiding real work. Thankfully, this daft idea was jettisoned upon the return of one civil servant who really did make a contribution to the Film Censor's Office.

Steve Magner, Assistant Secretary of the Department, had been working on cross-border co-operation in Northern Ireland, but now he had returned to the Department of Justice. Previously he had some difficult dealings with the office before my appointment and was impressed by its present operation. Working on the axiom 'If it ain't broke, don't fix it', Steve ensured that the Film Censor's Office continued as before. His attitude was that an efficiently run office should be left alone, with minimal interference from the parent body. This had been the case since the establishment of the office in 1923. It had always been my attitude as well, but there were others who saw the Film Censor's Office as an integral part of the Department of Justice and would, if allowed, have brought the two closer together, thereby destroying the Office's independence. Thanks to Steve Magner, this did not happen.

*   *   *

Before I screened *Natural Born Killers*, the film was already controversial, with allegations of copy-cat killings in France and America. There was intense media coverage and calls for the film's banning in Britain. These were of no concern to me. My decision, just as with *The Last Temptation of Christ* or any other film, was always based on what I saw on the cinema screen. When I did see it, for me banning *Natural Born Killers* was a logical decision. The level of gratuitous violence in the film was excessive. In 1995 the island of Ireland was living with a gun culture; IRA murders and atrocities were daily occurrences. I also considered the effect the film had had on some who had seen it in other countries. There was substantial evidence to build a case that copy-cat killings in France and the USA had resulted from exposure to the film. My decision to ban the film was criticised by some film correspondents, notably Ciaran Carty in the *Sunday Tribune*. It was felt that I had missed, or did not understand, the whole point of the film. This was nonsense. That level of gratuitous violence was not, in my opinion, then acceptable.

I met Sheila Pratschke through a mutual friend prior to her appointment as Director of the Irish Film Centre. She often came to my private screenings. These were usually held on Friday afternoons and attended by people of all ages and backgrounds who were interested in cinema. Some time after the banning of *Natural Born Killers*, I suggested to Sheila that it might be an idea for the Irish Film Centre to screen the film. I anticipated a limited number of screenings, perhaps over a weekend, as was the standard practice. Shortly after Sheila proposed screening *Natural Born Killers* to her Board, I accidentally met board member Tiernan McBride in Ardmore Studios. He asked if I would have any objections to such a screening. I confirmed that I would not. The Censorship of Films Act makes no provision for cinema clubs or film festivals. Since the establishment of the Irish Film Institute in 1945 and the creation of the Cork Film Festival by Dermot Breen in the late 1950s, the practice of the Department of Justice and the Garda authorities has been to ignore these activities. Most clubs and festivals are well run and adhere to the rule that screenings be confined to *bona fide* members who join the club on an annual basis or for the duration of a film festival. The system, which could be described in the immortal words of Charles J. Haughey as 'An Irish solution for an Irish problem', has worked well. It allows for uncensored, or even banned, films to be seen by those with a genuine interest in cinema. Successive film censors since Liam O'Hora in the 1960s have acquiesced with this arrangement and in the case of Dermot Breen and myself, actually encouraged it.

However, Tiernan McBride's proposal to screen *Natural Born Killers* was totally different from normal practice. The film would be screened 400 times over a number of weeks. Membership of the IFC would be reduced to a fraction of the annual fee, thereby allowing anyone to join just to see this one film. It was anticipated that this action would swell the coffers of the under-funded IFC and get the organisation out of debt. It was a blatant attempt to exploit, for purely commercial reasons, a film that had been banned by the Film Censor. The London office of Warner Brothers, the distributors of *Natural Born Killers*, was delighted with the proposal, although their Irish manager, Terry Molloy, expressed reservations about the arrangement.

Following the announcement of the Irish Film Centre's intention to screen *Natural Born Killers* in this way, which would undermine the authority of the Film Censor's Office, I had no option but to inform the authorities. Department of Justice officials contacted the Irish Film Centre and made it clear that appropriate action would be taken if the screening went ahead. A public controversy ensued. Two hours before the film's proposed opening, the screening was cancelled. The negotiations were handled by Department of Justice officials, and the Film Censor's Office did not take any part in the ensuing debate. In radio and television interviews Sheila Pratschke, naturally, condemned the action. Our close friendship never suffered, however. Even before the crisis had abated, we could be seen lunching together in public. It would have made a good photograph had there been an enterprising press photographer around.

The *Natural Born Killers* debate reared its head again when, in a blaze of publicity, TV3 announced its planned transmission of the film. It did not mention that this would be the television version of the film, which was less violent than the original. Most popular films which include sex or violence have three versions: the original cinema version, an edited or altered version for television and a completely sanitised film for airline screening, which is a very good reason never to watch a serious movie when flying! After the Department of Justice conveyed its disapproval to TV3's management, the film was replaced in the schedule. *Natural Born Killers* was not re-submitted for reclassification as a film to the Film Censor's Office. A DVD version of the original was classified as Over 18 in May 2001, seven years after the original ban. The press release issued by the Film Censor's Office stated *inter alia*:

> The decision to grant an Over 18 certificate reflects the change in film and video classification criteria which has taken place in all age categories over the last seven years and which is under continuous review.
>
> Consideration was also given to the increased awareness among the viewing public of the nature of screen violence. Discussion on such issues as copy-cat killings has enabled audiences to make a more informed judgement on the possible effects of viewing violent material and on the potential for screen violence to be reflected in real life.
>
> In granting an Over 18 certificate the Film Censor advises parents and those with responsibility for young people that this video contains lengthy scenes of intense violence, strong language and explicit sexual material which is suitable only for an adult audience.

The saga of *Natural Born Killers* was finally over. Another film had been un-banned.

*   *   *

It was always accepted wisdom that film censorship in Ireland was stricter than in the UK. This is not so. I often gave lower classifications. For instance, Neil Jordan's *The End of the Affair* is rated Over 15 in Ireland, but had an Over 18 certificate in the UK. The Bond movie *The World is not Enough* was rated Parental Guidance here and Over 12 in the UK, while *Stigmata*, starring our own Gabriel Byrne, was Over 15 here and Over 18 in the UK. Director Alan Parker thanked me on 'The Late Late Show' for being more generous to his film, *The Road to*

Wellville, than my British counterpart. *In America*, the last film released with my classification was rated 12A. It was classified Over 15 in the UK. As it contains just one expletive, John Boorman's 1987 autobiographical film *Hope and Glory*, the adventures of a small boy and his family during the Second World War in London, was classified Over 15 in the UK. As he was well under that age, Sebastian Rice-Edwards, who plays the boy, was prevented from attending the film's London Premiere. I classified *Hope and Glory* as Under 12 Accompanied. Sebastian made a great impression on the Irish media and audience when, along with the other stars, Ian Bannen and Susan Wooldridge, he attended the Gala Premiere in Dublin.

The 1988 feature documentary film, *U2: Rattle and Hum*, was classified Over 15 in the UK and most other countries. In a powerful condemnation of the IRA during one of the band's concerts in America, Bono stopped singing to address the audience. Referring to Northern Ireland, he shouted, 'Fuck the revolution. There is no revolution. Fuck the IRA!' It was something I felt every child and adolescent in Ireland should hear from Bono's lips. Despite the language, *U2: Rattle and Hum* received a General certificate. There were no repercussions.

Of course, there were some who did not always agree with my decisions. A letter received from a lady in Kerry in 1999 berated me: 'There is no censorship. You're being paid to censor films but you don't do it. This film is full of nudity and gratuitous sex, but you are permitting 15 year old children to view it! You are possessed by Satan to offload that extreme obscene material on us!' The lady was writing about that charming film, *Shakespeare in Love*.

*   *   *

One groundbreaking decision I made as Film Censor was to classify Neil Jordan's film, *Michael Collins*. From my youth I had been an admirer of Collins and had read much about him, including an attempt to read his biography in French, written by my friend, Pierre Joannon. As a youth I was moved by a photograph of his body lying in state. I visited Liam Neeson on the set a number of times when *Michael Collins* was in production. There was considerable hype in the media before the film was released, due to the continuing IRA activity in Northern

Ireland and the attempt by some newspaper journalists, and others, to associate Michael Collins with the contemporary IRA. After my first viewing of the film, I was impressed and of the opinion that in Ireland *Michael Collins* should be seen by as wide an audience as possible. There was violence and bad language to contend with, however.

Before making a final decision, I invited a number of people to further screenings in order to observe their reactions to the movie. My guests included Minister for Justice Nora Owen, who is a grand-niece of Michael Collins, and her family, the Ombudsman Michael Mills, Brian Farrell, Gay Byrne and Kathleen Watkins, Justin Keating, Chief Justice Liam Hamilton, Maeve Binchy and Gordon Snell, Olive Braiden, Eithne Healy, Dana Wynter, Benedict Kiely, the Ambassadors of Mexico, France and the USA, along with politicians from most parties. Finally, I announced my decision to grant *Michael Collins* a PG certificate. A press statement was issued: a unique occurrence in the seventy-three-year history of the Film Censor's Office. An extract read:

It is unprecedented for the Office of the Film Censor to comment on the quality or content of any film. However, the release of *Michael Collins* in this year when Ireland celebrates a century of cinema is a major cinematic event. Written and directed by an internationally acclaimed Irish director and featuring some of Ireland's most accomplished actors, *Michael Collins* is in the opinion of the Film Censor a landmark in Irish cinema.

The Film Censor wishes to make the film available to the widest possible Irish cinema audience. Because of the historical significance of this film, many parents may wish to make their own decision as to whether or not their children should see it. For this reason, the Film Censor has decided to grant a Parental Guidance (PG) certificate to the film, *Michael Collins*.

The certificate is accompanied by a warning to parents and guardians that the film includes scenes depicting explicit cruelty and violence along with some crude language not usually associated with the Parental Guidance classification. The Film Censor advises that in all cases, children under the age of 12 should be accompanied by a parent or guardian.

Warner Brothers' Irish manager, Terry Molloy, had the film's poster reprinted incorporating this message. Possibly a valuable heirloom for my grandchildren, this unique poster now hangs in my home. As a going-away present, I gave a framed copy to US Ambassador Jean Kennedy Smith as a memento of her brief appearance in the film.

The controversy surrounding *Michael Collins* continued. In Dáil Éireann the Fianna Fáil deputy for Meath, Noel Dempsey, suggested that there was a political motive behind my decision and that the Parental Guidance classification was introduced specially for the film. He asked:

> Is there any connection between the fact that the Minister for Justice recently had a private viewing of the film about Michael Collins and its subsequent classification in a category which has never before been used by the Film Censor and not allowed for in legislation? In view of this does the Government intend to introduce legislation to amend the Censorship of Films Act?

I was outraged. Noel Dempsey's statement was utterly untrue. Either he or his advisors had not bothered to look at the official Act. After much personal research, I had introduced the Parental Guidance certificate more than two years earlier, on 5 July 1994, for David Putnam's *War of the Buttons*. I wrote to Deputy Dempsey, to Taoiseach John Bruton, to Cheann Comhairle Sean Treacy and to Leader of the Opposition Bertie Ahern to complain about this gross inaccuracy and 'misleading of the house', as telling a lie is euphemistically called in Dáil Éireann. The only acknowledgment I received was from the Taoiseach's office. A few days before the Dáil was dissolved, RTÉ Radio's 'What it says in the Papers' reported that Deputy Noel Dempsey had apologised to the Film Censor for 'erroneous remarks he had made earlier in the course of a Dáil debate'. I did not see the newspapers that day, but was satisfied with the report. It therefore came as a great surprise when two years later the actual contents of the 'apology' were brought to my notice. What Noel Dempsey actually said was:

With regard to a question I raised on the Order of Business on 22 October 1996, regarding the classification of the film *Michael Collins*, it has recently been brought to my attention that the question I asked might be construed as casting aspersions on the professional integrity of the Film Censor, Mr Sheamus Smith and his office. I did not intend to cast any such aspersion.

This was not a correction or a retraction of the original false statement. I now have little respect for a politician I once admired.

Michael Collins was an outstanding success at the Irish box-office. Its gross return of more than €5 million was a box-office record and it remains the highest grossing Irish film ever.

*   *   *

American director Joe Strick's film *Ulysses* was made in Dublin in 1966. Filmed in black-and-white, the script by Fred Haines was an excellent *précis* of Joyce's original work and was nominated for an Academy Award. The predominantly Irish cast included Milo O'Shea as Bloom and T.P. McKenna as Buck Mulligan, along with Maureen Toal and Anna Manahan. I took a great interest in the production because I knew so many associated with it and had briefly met the film's director. We got to know each other much better in the mid-1970s when we had adjoining offices in RTÉ. Joe Strick returned here to film another Joyce story, *Portrait of the Artist as a Young Man*. My favourite 'godson', Luke Johnston, played the schoolboy.

A request to use Joyce's original setting of Clongowes Wood College was turned down by the college authorities. Only the outside gates, filmed from the roadway, were seen. My first cousin, Fr Joe Dargan S.J., became Rector of Clongowes some years later; I like to think that he might have been more accommodating than his predecessor. When it was submitted to Film Censor Dermot Breen in 1967, *Ulysses* was banned. The decision was upheld by the Films Appeal Board. Seven years later the distributor re-submitted the film for classification. Once again it was rejected by the Film Censor and by the Appeal Board. It was only in 2000, thirty-one years after *Ulysses* had first been screened in the Film Censor's Office, that it was re-submitted for classification. It received an Over 15 certificate.

The decision created favourable publicity not only in Ireland but throughout the world. In the UK, Channel 4's main evening news included a substantial item, including interviews with Joe Strick and myself on the bizarre situation in which the film adaptation of what was acknowledged as one of the greatest works in English literature had remained banned in the author's native country for so long. I was pleased that, like *Monty Python's Life of Brian*, another film that in my opinion should never have been banned was now on Irish screens. The previous year Stanley Kubrick's controversial film *A Clockwork Orange*, originally banned in 1973 and not submitted for reconsideration until after the director's death, was passed with an Over 18 certificate. It had waited twenty-six years from its original rejection.

* * *

During my time as Film Censor, apart from meeting movie stars and directors who were promoting their films, I also kept in touch with the industry itself. Annual visits to the Cannes Film Festival, as well as my membership of BAFTA and regular visits to Hollywood and London, helped to maintain contacts made over many years.

I have been attending at Cannes for more than thirty years now, and have witnessed many changes over those decades. In the 1970s there were about 20,000 people at the Festival; now, there are in excess of 130,000 visitors, increasing the population of the town from 70,000 to 200,000 inhabitants. Huge pyramids advertising various movies rise 40 feet into the air from the beaches. There are 350 television teams and 4,000 journalists. French TV's Canal+ has a permanent studio on the beach, from which it broadcasts live throughout the day and covers the red-carpet activities in the evening. Giant portraits of movie stars painted on the gables of buildings—a practice started in 2005—has increased spectacularly.

It has been satisfying to experience the huge increase in the numbers of Irish attending. From our tiny group thirty-one years ago, which planted the seeds of Irish involvement, the Irish Film Board has been nurturing Irish talent since the early 1980s and now the Irish contingent numbers in the hundreds and the Irish Film Pavilion commands a prime site on the beach, next to the Palais du Festivals. The Minister for Arts, Culture and Tourism is an annual visitor. For this move, great credit is due to John O'Donoghue, whose contribution as Minister to developing the film industry in Ireland is on a par with that of Michael D. Higgins.

Over the years it has given me pleasure to be with many of the Irish on their first visit to the festival, including Morgan O'Sullivan, Michael Algar, first Chief Executive of the Irish Film Board, Tiernan McBride, whose short film *Christmas Morning* was an official Irish entry in 1978, Michael Dwyer, Noel Pearson, Sheila Pratschke, Seamus Deasy, John Kelleher and Hugh Leonard, who with accuracy and wit described his first impression of the Festival thus:

The port is jammed with yachts, some the size of the Holyhead ferry, and many are leased by hustlers, touting films that will never be made. One has to make a distinction between the real phoneys and the fake phoneys.

*   *   *

It had always been my ambition to retire on my sixty-fifth birthday. Apart from looking forward to retirement, I was anxious that my time as Film Censor should not exceed the time I had spent in RTÉ. When my grandchildren, Jessica and Richard, were growing up, they knew me only as the Film Censor. I regretted that they never saw a more exciting earlier life. I preferred to think of the major part of my career as being my involvement in the production, rather than the classification, of films.

As I approached retirement age, most of my plans and ambitions for the Film Censor's Office had either been achieved or were well on their way to fruition. My campaign to liberalise film censorship had brought improvements. Dermot Breen, the first Film Censor to espouse a liberal attitude had banned forty-six films and cut 818 over a six-year period. My own record of banning seven and cutting an equal number over fifteen years was, I believed, a move in the right direction. So I could

retire with peace of mind, but as the European Film Classifiers'
Conference would be held in Dublin in September 2001, it was
important that I remain in Office until then, and for a short period
afterwards, to look after the necessary documentation and wrap things
up. Our 2001 conference was held in Dublin Castle over three days of
idyllic autumn weather. Apart from the EU and Nordic countries,
delegates from Latvia, Cyprus, Canada and South Africa attended, as
did three of our Assistant Censors.

It had been known and accepted for some years that my successor
would be Assistant Censor Ger Connolly. At the Dublin conference I
had introduced him as such to my more intimate colleagues. Ger's
succession revolved around a deal that had apparently been struck
between two members of the Cabinet, John O'Donoghue and
Ger's close friend, Charlie McCreevy. In return for another favour, the
Minister for Finance's recommendation for the job of Film Censor
would be confirmed by the Minister for Justice. This was not an
unusual arrangement between ministers, and was certainly OK by me.
Of all my assistants, Ger was by far the most suitable for the job.

The office Christmas party took place on Tuesday 18 December 2001.
Afterwards a number of us went along to the Minister's Christmas
reception. As we entered the building, Ger Connolly mentioned that he
had never met John O'Donoghue. I immediately introduced him and
they exchanged pleasantries. Then the Minister took me aside and said,
'Why are you doing this to me, Sheamus?' Surprised, I enquired as to
what he meant. 'Leaving,' the Minister replied. 'What am I going to do?'
'Appoint the man I have just introduced to you,' was my answer. At that
point our conversation was interrupted by other guests wishing to
shake the Minister's hand.

It was later disclosed that another Fianna Fáil minister, one more
powerful than Charlie McCreevy, who was promoting a different
candidate from my office, had intervened and effectively scuppered Ger
Connolly's chances of becoming Ireland's ninth Film Censor in the
traditional manner. I learned of the impasse shortly after Christmas. A
year later, I would still be Film Censor.

In April 2002 advertisements inviting applications for the post of
Official Film Censor appeared in the national newspapers. The

traditional method of appointing the Censor had changed—this was the first time since 1923 that the new Film Censor would be appointed by public competition. The succession stakes were on. As expected, there was huge interest in the job. The large number of applications was reduced to less than thirty who would be called for interview. Long before my retirement was due, John Kelleher, who regularly attended my private screenings, had asked about the possibility of succeeding me. He sent me a copy of his CV to use as necessary. He now confirmed his interest. We met two days before the closing date for applications. John expressed a reluctance to go through the interview process 'at my age'. But I pointed out the obvious: if you're not in, you can't win.

After the General Election in May, Michael McDowell became Minister for Justice. The shortlist of five applicants was submitted to the new Minister for consideration. His decision was finally announced on 8 November 2002. The new Film Censor would be John Kelleher. My loyalties were divided: I was pleased for John, whom I knew would do a good job, but disappointed for Ger Connolly, who had been a loyal and enlightened colleague and, when called upon, a reliable deputy. John was producing a film when the appointment was announced and was unable to take over until April 2003. I was obliged to remain in Office until then. That meant I would be in that job longer than any other in my life. I would wind up alongside James Montgomery, the first Film Censor, who also served over a seventeen-year period, as the longest serving Film Censor in the history of the State.

At exactly midnight on Sunday 6 April 2003, the moment when he officially became Ireland's ninth Film Censor, I sent a text message to John Kelleher wishing him well. He now had the 'magical powers'! I left to attend the Cannes Film Festival for the twentieth-eighth time on 13 May, my sixty-seventh birthday. I was free at last. My long term as Film Censor was over. There were no good wishes for the future from Minister Michael McDowell on my departure, nor had he delivered the 'going-away present' of a ministerial order to make screenings of low budget and foreign language films available to Irish cinemagoers. The last film distributed with a certificate carrying my signature was *In America*. It was an outstanding box-office success in Ireland, but failed internationally!

The matter of John Kelleher's appointment ahead of Ger Connolly was resolved quickly. Due to changed circumstances, the new Film Censor was able to appoint Ger Connolly as permanent Deputy Censor, something I would like to have accomplished years earlier. As in the three previous instances when he followed me into a job, John Kelleher adapted swiftly to the challenge and proved himself to be more innovative and dynamic than his predecessor. Our proposed website was soon up and running and within a year office procedures had improved, tired staff had been replaced with new young faces and, miracle of miracles, John Kelleher finally succeeded in getting the Minister, Michael McDowell, to deliver on a promise he had failed to fulfil on my watch. A sliding scale of charges was approved to assist minority interest and low budget films and to encourage the distribution of foreign language films in Ireland. The efforts of fifteen years were, at last, vindicated.

EPILOGUE

Most of my mother's family had a strong tendency towards alcoholism. They managed to cope with the problem and all lived to a good age. My mother avoided alcoholic drink for the last fifty years of her life. In November 1997, my mother, who was showing signs of dementia, finally agreed to move to a nursing home. My father had died in 1971 and she had lived alone since then. While she would have lucid moments from then on, I knew that it was the end of our real relationship as mother and son. She survived in the nursing home for fifteen months. Several times when I visited her, she expressed a wish to die. She asked me to bring Dr Paddy Leahy, whom she had met and liked, to see her. She had read Paddy's newspaper articles and heard him speak about death with dignity. Mother said, 'Paddy Leahy will know what to do.' I did not have the heart to tell her that Paddy had died shortly before. On 3 March 1999 I had just finished recording a long interview with Gloria Hunniford for her radio programme, 'VIP Suite', when I heard that my mother was in her final moments. I rushed to her bedside. Sadly she had just slipped away before I arrived. She was in her ninety-eighth year.

At her funeral my mother, who loved flowers, accomplished something I wish she could have seen: wreaths were sent by all the major Hollywood studios. She would have enjoyed reading the names. We later buried her ashes in her parents' grave in Ballaghaderreen. It was the final resting place she had chosen. On the way to the graveyard, I noticed a boy of Arabic origin wearing the customary dress of his ancestors adjusting the satellite dish fixed to his home. There are now fourteen different nationalities living in my home town. The late-night fast-food restaurant is thriving. At weekends the pulsating sound of the discothèque disturbs the quiet of the town square well into the early hours of the morning. Nearby, the Baptist church illustrates how things have changed since my youth. The business premises owned by one of my cousins boast two fine bars, along with an excellent restaurant and some comfortable guest rooms. So Ballagh has indeed come a long way since my time, when many houses did not enjoy electricity or running water and the water-pump on the main street opposite our shop was in constant use.

The Roxy Cinema, where all our dreams were born, has long since closed its doors. Before retiring as Film Censor, I arranged for the mobile cinema based in Galway to visit the town. While it was there, parked within 30 yards of the house in which I was born and beside the field in which my mother saw the first 'talkie' film years before my birth, an official classification screening was held. Distributor Brendan McCaul provided the film *In the Bedroom*. I invited some old school-friends and other townspeople. Former RTÉ colleague Lelia Doolin, who lectures on film, brought along a group from University College Galway. After the show, we had a lively discussion on film classification.

I met President Bill Clinton during his official visit to Dublin. Our second meeting, at a dinner hosted by Sir Anthony O'Reilly in Trinity College, Dublin, was more relaxed. I suggested that as the American Film Censor, Jack Valenti—an eloquent, high-level power-broker who had reigned as Head of the Motion Picture Association of America for almost four decades and was responsible for the institution of the US movie ratings system—was about to retire, the former President might take the job? He maintained that his passion for movies would make it impossible for him to be objective, thus he would be unsuitable.

As with the American Film Censor, so with the Irish Censor and I must say, retirement has been even better than I expected. There is more time to play golf, garden, meet old friends, make some new ones and journey to exotic places with my favourite cruise line, Silversea. I have also achieved a lifetime ambition and taken flying lessons. In 1949 I learned to swim the old fashioned breast-stroke in Dún Laoghaire Baths. My consummate swimming coach, Magdeleine McKeon now optimistically endeavours to teach me the front crawl. There is time for cooking in my new kitchen, and to see my daughter Teri, her partner Peter, and my grandchildren, of whom I am very proud. Nineteen-year-old Jessie is studying at University College Dublin; Richy will be eighteen when he completes his second-level education at my old school, Monkstown Park, in the summer of 2009.

My interest in cinema and the film industry remains strong. The annual visits to see friends in Hollywood continue, and I am still an active member of the British Academy of Film and Television Arts. The Cannes Film Festival is also an item on the annual agenda. One of the joys of my retirement was attending the ceremony in Los Angeles to confer honorary degrees on screenwriter Ray Bradbury (who with John Huston won an Oscar for the screenplay of *Moby Dick*), Anjelica Huston and celebrated TV talk show host Merv Griffin, by the Chancellor of the National University of Ireland, Dr Garret FitzGerald in May 2005. It was the first time such a ceremony had taken place outside Ireland. The gala dinner at the Beverly Hilton Hotel which followed raised $1.2 million for the Huston School of Film and Digital Media at University College Galway.

I have been a panel member of juries at international festivals, notably the Monte Carlo Television Film Festival in 2003. Working there with jury members from Italy, Japan, the UK, Canada and the US was a stimulating experience. There was also an opportunity to spend time with Dame Helen Mirren, who had just received her honour from the Queen of England, and to meet her husband, Academy Award winning film director Taylor Hackford, who directed *Ray*, the Oscar-winning film based on the life of Ray Charles. Prince Albert, whom I had only met briefly on a number of previous visits, hosted a small private dinner party for jury members in the royal palace. It was on this trip to Monaco that I finally had the courage to visit the scene of the dreadful accident in which Princess Grace lost her life in the summer of 1982. Later, I visited her tomb in the cathedral near the palace for the first time. Standing on the spot where her remains lie, I wept as memories of times spent in her company came flooding back.

I sat on the jury of the Dubrovnik Film Festival in 2005. While there it was good to renew my acquaintance with and present a special award to Peter Medak (who had directed *David Copperfield* in which I made a brief cameo appearance) and to meet again British actor Charles Dance. Emily Watson, another talented actress whose work I admire, was a guest of the festival too. She proved to be a delightful person and exceptional company.

I sometimes attend screenings in the Film Censor's Office. Film distribution in Ireland continues to change dramatically. What was once an exclusively male preserve is now predominantly under female control. When Brendan McCaul retired as boss of Buena Vista Distribution in March 2007, his place was taken by his former deputy, Trish Long, a lady who has already made her mark on the cinema business.

Over the years I have tried to help many young people who were ambitious to work in the film industry. The most successful of these was undoubtedly Claire Simpson, who went on to a prominent career winning an Oscar for editing Oliver Stone's *Platoon*.

Sheila and I have lived together for over thirty-eight years; we never married. She too is retired and leads an active life with weekly painting, ballet, French conversation, swimming and ballroom dancing sessions.

Most of all, retirement allows time for reflection. Perhaps I should have done some things differently, but now it's too late to change anything. I have few regrets. A broken marriage brings sadness, but, like so many others that took place under similar circumstances, its failure was perhaps inevitable.

Shortly before she died, in her ninety-eight year, my mother told me that she had one great regret in life: that her son never had a proper job! She was right. Everything I did over a long career was great fun. It never felt like real work! For that I am thankful.

Sam Goldwyn once said: 'No one should write their autobiography until they are dead.' Perhaps he too was right! Most things about my life are in this book. I have tried to write about people and events as they affected me and to present a montage of large and small pictures for readers to see and interpret as they will. If there are omissions, it is simply because one cannot fit everything into a memoir such as this.

The passing years have done little to alter my opinion of organised religion or to create an understanding of why so many innocent people die as a result of wars and persecution. Man's inhumanity to man is still incomprehensible. I remain a committed atheist.

My intention is to continue enjoying life as it gallops by and to take pleasure in the moments of happiness, which may never return.

On his seventieth birthday, I heard the singer Liam Clancy say that having reached such an age there is *one* thing which a person cannot do: *die young*! Now, there's a thought on which to end my story.

INDEX